FREEDOM
TRAILS

T0333462

FREEDOM TRAILS

GREAT ESCAPES
FROM WORLD WAR I
TO THE KOREAN WAR

TERRY TREADWELL

The
History
Press

For my grandchildren,
Rex and Bebe Treadwell

First published in 2008 as *Great Escapes*
This edition published in 2018

The History Press
The Mill, Brimscombe Port
Stroud, Gloucestershire, GL5 2QG
www.thehistorypress.co.uk

© Terry Treadwell, 2018

The right of Terry Treadwell to be identified as the Author
of this work has been asserted in accordance with the
Copyright, Designs and Patents Act 1988.

British Library Cataloguing in Publication Data.
A catalogue record for this book is available from the British Library.

ISBN 978 0 7509 8798 1

Typesetting and origination by The History Press
Printed and bound in Great Britain by TJ International Ltd

CONTENTS

ACKNOWLEDGEMENTS

I WOULD LIKE to thank my wife Wendy for proofreading and editing the manuscript. Also the late Group Captain W.S.O. Randle, who told me the story of his evasion and about the people who helped him.

INTRODUCTION

TWENTY YEARS AFTER the 'war to end all wars' ended, the Second World War erupted and once again Germany was the instigator. This time the war was to encompass and involve almost the entire Western world and spread to countries in the Middle East and Far East. Commonwealth countries 'rallied to the flag', and the United States' entry into war after the attack on Pearl Harbor was to be one of the major turning points, but also added to the cost of human lives, which was to be incalculable.

With the German military's Blitzkrieg in Europe, and the sudden collapse of Allied armies, came the inevitable prisoners of war. These were, in the main, young men who had been thrust into battle and had fought with the zest that young men do, only to find themselves incarcerated behind barbed wire, under the gaze of searchlights and machine guns, manned by trigger-happy guards. These prisoners of war were taken to camps called *offizierenlager* (*oflags*) for officers and *stammlagers* (*stalags*) for other ranks, where food was short and clothing, when worn out, could not be easily replaced. It was this environment that was to spawn some of the most ingenious and audacious escapes ever devised or imagined. It also encouraged men to discover talents and bravery that they never knew they had. However, the majority of those who either evaded or escaped did so with the help of hundreds of nameless and faceless civilians, who daily risked their lives to help them.

Within days of the tragedy of Dunkirk, groups of civilians were helping soldiers to escape detection. Within months, escape organisations were beginning to be set up. The role of the Resistance fighter was highlighted by sabotage and assassinations, and was an extremely dangerous position; whereas the role of a member of the escape organisation was so low profile as to appear non-existent – but in fact was equally as important, and just as dangerous.

The men and women, and indeed children, who helped run the escape lines came from all walks of life – doctors, lawyers, housewives, shop assistants, farmers and labourers, covering all classes and age ranges. So efficient were these escape lines that the Gestapo (Geheime Staatspolizei) – the secret state police – often used fluent English-speaking agents to pose as downed Allied airmen in an effort to infiltrate them. The infiltrators were often successful, as was demonstrated when the Comète Line was betrayed. The Germans arrested two-thirds of its members, over half of whom were executed. The Germans even helped some Allied airmen to escape so as to penetrate and gain information about the escape lines and the helpers. But what makes a person in an occupied country, controlled by ruthless Nazis, put their life on the line on an almost daily basis in order to help someone from another country that they don't even know? When asked, most just shrugged their shoulders and said, 'Because we had to do something!'

Such was the need for absolute secrecy that some of the escape lines operated independently from the others, although they did help each other on the odd occasion. The Pat O'Leary Line was an example of this.

In France, more than 29,000 people were executed by the Germans for being members of the Resistance, and that figure is not included in the 40,000 that died in prison for various other reasons. In Denmark, reprisals were carried out on its citizens by shooting five of them for every German said to have been killed by the Resistance. The Danish Resistance itself saw more than 3,000 of its members killed. The proud boast of the Danish Resistance was that, of all the Allied airmen placed in their care, not one was ever captured by the Germans.

The total number of Resistance and escape organisation members killed throughout Europe will never be known, as it was impossible to keep records and such was the necessary secrecy behind these organisations that very few people knew who was a member and who was not.

Such was the fear of the Resistance that Field Marshal Keitel issued the infamous Nach und Nebel Erlass (Night and Fog Decree), which decreed that anyone suspected of opposing Nazi rule would be arrested in the dead of night and simply vanish from the face of the earth. In a rider to the decree, Keitel wrote, as an explanatory note:

> If these offences are punished by imprisonment, even with hard labour for life, this will be looked upon as a sign of weakness. Efficient intimidation can only be achieved either by capital punishment or by measures by which the relatives of the criminals and the population do not know of his or her fate.

Some of the escapees and evaders joined up with local Resistance fighters and fought alongside them. One such man was Sergeant Cyril Rolfe, RAF, who, after being shot down twice, had escaped on both occasions from German prisoner-of-war camps. After his second capture he was being taken to Germany when he escaped and headed towards Russia. Making his way through the German lines, he joined up with Russian Cossacks and for the following ten weeks was involved in a number of cavalry charges before being repatriated to England.

First Lieutenant John Read, USAAF, a B-24 pilot, was shot down during a raid and was picked up by a French Maquis group. Because of the situation at the time, he found it impossible to get back, so instead he fought alongside them and eventually took over the leadership of the group after its leader was killed in a gun battle with German forces.

Some of the atrocities suffered by captured airmen were brought before the Nuremberg trials. One particular incident concerned forty-seven British, American and Dutch aircrew. Imprisoned at Mathausen, the airmen, all barefoot, were taken into a deep stone quarry and made to carry large rocks, weighing about 60lb each, to the top of the quarry. SD (Sicherheitsdienst) troopers lined the route and beat the men with whips and clubs. On their second trip, the load was increased and those who fell were whipped or kicked to their feet. By the end of the day twenty-one of the men were dead; the remaining twenty-six were killed the following day.

Fifty escapees from Stalag Luft (Luftwaffe-Stammlager) III were murdered after they made a mass escape from the prison camp. This was in retaliation for causing the authorities huge embarrassment after the Germans had declared that the camp, full of habitual escapees, was escape-proof. Most of those involved in both atrocities were later hunted down and brought to account at Nuremberg. They were either hanged or sentenced to life imprisonment.

Even when the news of these atrocities filtered through to the other prisoner-of-war camps, it was not enough to stop escaping or evading airmen risking their lives in an effort to get back to England and join the fighting again. The moment they discarded their uniforms and carried forged identity and travel documents, it made them liable to be shot as spies if caught. Not one of these young men was necessarily equipped for escape and evasion, but they all felt it was their duty to get back to England.

At the end of the war it was estimated that, of the Royal Air Force, forty-six officers and sixty-three other ranks had escaped from prison camps, and 401 officers and 946 other ranks had successfully evaded capture. Of the army, 106 officers and 711 other ranks had escaped from prison camps, thirty-six officers and 344 other ranks had successfully evaded capture. Of the navy, ten officers and thirteen other ranks had escaped from prison camps, six officers and eight other ranks had successfully evaded capture. This, compared with just *one* German officer, Leutnant Franz von Werra, who successfully escaped from a prison camp in Canada, was a truly remarkable achievement, due to a great extent to the courage and fortitude of the citizens of the occupied countries of Europe. The reason for the small number of naval personnel becoming escapees is because there were very few ever captured, as most either went down with their ships or were picked up at sea by rescue vessels.

The Americans also set up their own section of the OSS (Office of Strategic Services) called MI.S-X. Unfortunately, after the war virtually all the records of this section were destroyed on the orders of Major General George V. Strong, the Deputy Chief of Staff for G-2 (Intelligence).

1. THE RUMBLINGS OF WAR

FOR SOME YEARS Britain and the rest of Europe had watched the rise of Nazism in Germany, under the leadership of Adolf Hitler. Hitler had fought in the First World War as a corporal in the army and had returned to a defeated, destitute Germany. The rise of socialism in Germany gave Hitler the platform upon which to build a ruthless regime. After taking over as President and Chancellor from Otto von Hindenburg, Hitler set about rebuilding Germany's military strength under the guise of rebuilding the country.

One or two minor acts of aggression by Hitler towards neighbouring countries were enough to make Britain and France take note of Germany's intentions. Hitler had sent some of his troops into the Rhineland. This was in breach of the Treaty of Versailles and when France objected and asked Britain for support, Britain refused to get involved. Seeing that Hitler's act had been unopposed, the Italian dictator Benito Mussolini saw his opportunity to make an alliance with Germany and form an 'Axis' around which Europe could revolve. This act of aggression caused rumblings of war to filter through Europe, and the British government started to make plans in case they became involved.

At the beginning of 1934, Hitler encouraged Alfred Fraunenfeld, the self-exiled Austrian Nazi Party leader, to broadcast anti-Dolfuss propaganda against the Austrian Chancellor. During this period Austrian Nazis carried out terrorist raids on essential facilities, with weapons and explosives supplied by Germany. There was also an Austrian Legion, consisting of several thousand men, camped along the border ready to move at a moment's notice.

Then on 25 July 1934, seven Austrian members of the Nazi Party dressed as Austrian Army soldiers burst into the Austrian Federal Chancellery and murdered the Austrian Chancellor Englebert Dolfuss. The attempt to seize the Chancellery failed, and Dr Kurt Schuschnigg, with the backing of the government, regained control. Efforts were made by the Nazis to give the assassins safe conduct to Germany, but they were arrested and hanged.

Under the Treaty of Versailles, Germany was forbidden to have a union with Austria, even though the majority of the people there spoke German as their native language. When Adolf Hitler became Chancellor of Germany he had written in his book, *Mein Kampf* (*My Struggle*), 'The reunion of Germany and Austria was a task to be furthered with every means.' In short it meant that the expansion of Germany would include Austria.

All the time Hitler was building his armed forces and by the end of 1934 had increased the military personnel from 100,000 to 300,000. He also declared that he would repudiate the Treaty of Versailles and introduce conscription in Germany. The shipbuilding programme was increased, including the development of the U-boat and the building of two battlecruisers, later to be known as the *Scharnhorst* and *Gneisenau*.

All of this, of course, was in direct contravention of the treaty, but such was the apathy of the surrounding countries to get involved that only mutterings within the diplomatic corps were heard. It soon became obvious that the Treaty of Versailles was now meaningless and toothless, as Germany began to openly rearm. It was only then that Britain and France made strong representations to the German government. Germany then stated that it would show 'unconditional respect' to the non-military clauses in the Versailles treaty, which included the territorial provisions. As for disarmament, Hitler stated that he would agree to limitations on both weapons and ships, but for Germany this would be final and abiding.

In 1936 Austria and Germany signed the Austro-German agreement in which Germany agreed to respect Austria's independence and not to interfere in the political affairs of the country. Two years later Hitler was to renege on this agreement when, after rigged elections, a union (Anschluss) between the two countries was announced, with an Austrian Nazi, Arthur Seyss-Inquart, as Chancellor.

Mussolini, on seeing Hitler flex his muscles and the rest of Europe back down, decided that the time was right for him to take over Abyssinia. On 3 October 1935, Italy invaded and on 2 May 1936 entered the capital Addis Ababa, taking complete control of the country. The League of Nations, which had voted for sanctions against Italy, that had only been partially implemented, capitulated. Encouraged by this, Mussolini then invaded Ethiopia and took control of the country.

Two weeks later Hitler, who was at the Wagner festival in Bayreuth, was given an urgent letter from General Franco, who had staged a coup in Spain, requesting aircraft and weapons. Hitler immediately dispatched an air force unit that was to become known as the Condor Legion, together with tanks and other weapons. Italy also sent some 60,000 troops as well as weapons to help Franco in the Spanish Civil War, which raged from 1936 to 1939. The success of the war and the alliance with Spain gave Hitler another border to France and another country that owed its allegiance to Germany.

It was while this was going on that Hitler took the military gamble that was to be the catalyst that would plunge Europe, and ultimately the rest of the world, into war – the reoccupation of the Rhineland. After the First World War the Rhineland had been classified as a demilitarised area and the Treaty of Locarno guaranteed this. Two of the signatories to the treaty – Britain and France – were becoming increasingly concerned with the situation in Abyssinia. Taking advantage of this, Hitler moved his troops into the Rhineland and occupied the area, and had Britain and France retaliated there is no doubt that the Germans would have had to withdraw. As it happened, no retaliation occurred, and Hitler's confidence in his ability to do whatever he felt like doing received a massive boost.

This was further endorsed when an Anti-Communist Pact with Japan was signed. This pact was specifically directed against Russia, and both countries agreed to have no political dealings with the Communists. In the event of one of them being attacked by Russia, both countries would take measures to protect the agreement.

On 12 February 1938, Hitler summoned the Austrian Chancellor, Kurt von Schuschnigg, to Berchtesgaden, and asked him to appoint Austrian Nazis to his government. Realising that there was an underlying threat to take over his country if he acceded to the request, von Schuschnigg returned to Austria and ordered a vote to see if the people wanted a union with Germany.

Hitler then issued an ultimatum: either he agreed to the 'request', or the soldiers massing on the German–Austrian border would be unleashed. The reason for this ultimatum was that Hitler feared a vote would go against the Nazis, and so decided to use the threat of violence to 'persuade' the electorate that his was the best option. In the early hours of 11 March, von Schuschnigg was awakened by a telephone call from the Austrian Chief of Police, saying that rail traffic between Austria and Germany had been stopped, the border at Salzburg had been closed and German soldiers were massed along the border. Von Schuschnigg had no choice but to resign and hand over the Chancellor's position to the Austrian Nazi Dr Arthur Seyss-Inquart.

The writing was on the wall as far as the British military were concerned, but still the politicians held out for a peaceful solution to the ever-growing problem.

It soon became obvious that Hitler was now switching his sights to Czechoslovakia, and British Prime Minister Neville Chamberlain sent

Lord Runciman to the country in an effort to persuade the government there to form some sort of agreement with Hitler. This was a pointless exercise because Hitler was determined to destroy Czechoslovakia. The country was made up of several provinces, Slovak and Czech, together with Bohemia, Moravia, Hungary, Ruthenia and Sudetenland, all of whom wanted a measure of autonomy. The Republic had been formed in 1918 just after Germany had been defeated but since its formation it had suffered domestic problems concerning its minority nationalities. The sudden rise to power of Hitler and the expansion of Germany gave the Sudeten Germans in Czechoslovakia the encouragement they needed to push for autonomy.

In Britain, Prime Minister Chamberlain became increasingly concerned that Hitler's continuing demands on the countries bordering Germany would bring about a war in Europe. He flew to Germany for talks with Hitler, who demanded that the Sudetenland province of Czechoslovakia be returned to Germany. If this were to be granted he would make no more territorial demands. Chamberlain managed to persuade the French that this was the best way to prevent a confrontation. They in turn told the Czechoslovakian government that unless they agreed to surrender the Sudetenland, they would withdraw their support. Reluctantly the Czech government agreed and all parties signed an agreement to that effect. Chamberlain returned to England, confident that he had averted a war, waving the famous piece of white paper and declaring 'peace in our time'.

President Hácha of Czechoslovakia was invited to Berlin for talks with Hitler. Under extreme pressure, both political and military, from the Germans, he agreed to place his country under the protection of Germany. Immediately the Germans annexed Bohemia, Sudetenland and Moravia, whilst Ruthenia was placed under the protection of Hungary and Slovakia was made a protectorate.

While Germany was in the process of fragmenting Czechoslovakia, it cast its eye over the territory that bordered East Prussia, and which Poland had acquired as a result of the Treaty of Versailles. In the centre was the city of Danzig that Germany insisted should revert back to its control. If Poland agreed to this it would be invited to join the Anti-Comintern Pact, Germany would guarantee its frontiers and would extend the existing Polish–German treaty from ten to twenty years. Poland refused and warned Germany about trying to take Danzig by force.

Germany wanted to build a road and a double-track railway between Czechoslovakia and East Prussia. This meant going through a strip of land now held by Poland, with Danzig at the centre. On 19 November 1938, the Polish Foreign Minister, Colonel Józef Beck, told his German counterpart Count Ribbentrop that his country gave an emphatic refusal to this proposal. Hitler's response was to order the mobilisation of his military.

On 5 January 1939, Hitler invited the Polish Foreign Minister to Berchtesgaden for talks, at which he informed Beck that Danzig was German, always had been and always would be. He was also sure that the two countries could reach an agreement over this 'little' problem. The city was under the control of the local Nazis and, in the event of an attempted takeover, it would be simple for them to create a quasi-revolutionary situation there.

Within days the situation regarding Poland deteriorated and in Britain Prime Minister Chamberlain now announced his country's support of Poland. This created a new dilemma for Hitler, as up to now his occupation of surrounding countries had gone unopposed. In a top-secret directive code-named Fall Weiss (Case White), Hitler spelt out his plans to his armed forces. These plans were for the invasion of Poland and the crushing of the Polish military, making the Free State of Danzig part of Third Reich territory. The occupation of Danzig was to be effected from East Prussia with the help of the German Navy.

Well aware that Poland also shared its borders with Russia, Ribbentrop set about cementing German–Russian relations, the Anti-Comintern Pact conveniently forgotten. Using the pretence that the deterioration of Polish–German relations was the fault of British policy, Ribbentrop went to Moscow with a letter for Stalin in which Hitler described the tension between Germany and Poland as having become intolerable. Because of the possible intervention of Britain and France, he suggested that it would be in both their interests if they signed a non-aggression pact. Stalin agreed and on 21 August 1939 the two countries signed the Nazi–Soviet Pact. Four days later Britain signed the Anglo-Polish Pact.

On 1 September 1939, German SS soldiers dressed as Polish soldiers, under the command of Sturmbannführer (Major) Alfred Naujocks, attacked and took over the German radio station at Gleiwitz. Claiming that Polish soldiers had attacked the radio station, Hitler stated that the German people had no other choice but to retaliate. He ordered his troops to cross the borders and his bombers to attack Warsaw.

Chamberlain gave Hitler another opportunity to withdraw but, on hearing nothing from the German government, announced in a memorable broadcast to the British people on 3 September 1939:

This morning the British Ambassador in Berlin handed the German government a final note stating that unless we heard from them by 11 o'clock that they were prepared at once to withdraw their troops from Poland a state of war would exist between us. I have to tell you that no such undertaking has been received, and that consequently this country is at war with Germany.

Within days Britain had started to mobilise its armed forces.

2. THE INITIAL YEARS

WITHIN A YEAR of the Second World War starting the British Army found itself on the back foot and retreating in an effort to escape the oncoming German Army. In the hasty retreat, a number of soldiers and airmen found themselves stranded behind enemy lines. Initially the majority of men who found themselves in this position, or had been captured, belonged to the British Expeditionary Force (BEF). In later years this number was increased by Allied airmen who had been shot down while on raids on targets over occupied Europe, and a small number of Royal Naval personnel. It was from these beginnings that the various occupied countries formed their resistance organisations and escape lines.

The first British servicemen to be captured were Sergeant George Booth and Aircraftsman Larry Slattery, who were flying a Blenheim bomber of No. 107 Squadron when they were shot down during an attack on Wilhelmshaven, the day after war was declared. The first officers to be captured were Squadron Leader Murray and Pilot Officer Thompson. They were shot down while attacking warships in the Wilhelmshaven area just four days later. The German sailors who picked them up from the sea had no idea what they were going to do with them. Initially they treated them like civilians and put them in the local prison, but later transferred them to an old fortress in the middle of Germany – Spangenberg. The British government asked the Red Cross to keep an eye on them and look after their welfare.

Later, other prisoners of war found themselves taken to various prison camps where, in the main, they were treated reasonably well. There were, of course, a number of prison camps in which the inmates suffered harsh and barbaric treatment at the hands of their guards. The Germans opened up special camps for airmen, soldiers and naval personnel, and even separated the officers in some cases. Special camps, known as *Sonderlagers*, for persistent escapees were also set up, such as Offizierenlager (Oflag) IVC (Colditz Castle) in Saxony and Stammlager Luftwaffe (Stalag Luft) III near Sagan.

One of the most famous of all the POW camps was Colditz Castle. Originally built in 1014 as a hunting lodge for Saxon kings, Colditz became a castle over the following years because it occupied a stronghold position on top of a hill. It was destroyed in the fifteenth century but rebuilt in 1583. Over the next 200 years it changed hands through various wars, and then in 1800 was converted into a prison. Thirty years later it became a mental hospital and remained such until the outbreak of the Second World War, when it was turned into a POW camp for Polish officers after the fall of Poland. In November 1940, a small number of RAF officers arrived to join the Polish officers, followed by six British Army officers and then some French officers. During the next few years the camp became truly international with the addition of Belgians, Dutch, Canadians, South Africans, Indians and a number of other nationalities.

Situated nearly 200 miles from the nearest border of a neutral country, the camp was filled with notorious and persistent escapees. Almost all of the inmates had made three or more attempts to escape from other camps and were considered a dangerous nuisance by the Germans. The boast by the Germans that the camp was escape-proof only gave the inmates more of an incentive to prove them wrong. At one point the camp was visited by Leutnant Franz von Werra, the only German to successfully escape from an Allied POW camp, who then advised on security.

With the debacle of Dunkirk well under way, troops were attempting to make their way back after finding themselves behind enemy lines. Some of these were RAF pilots who had been shot down and then joined the thousands on the beaches waiting to be rescued. Others, finding the roads jammed with fleeing troops and civilians, decided to head across country and find other ways of getting back to England.

Aircrew who were shot down over Germany found themselves being hunted not only by the military but also by the local people who would, on some occasions, capture and then lynch them. Heinrich Himmler actually issued a directive to the local police, saying that they were not to interfere with justice being carried out on the *terrorfliegers* by local people. On the Eastern Front the SS units took no prisoners and anyone captured was immediately shot.

From the beginning of the war, Allied soldiers, sailors and airmen were told that it was their duty to try to escape. In the event of their being captured, it was incumbent upon them to put the enemy to great inconvenience, both in time and manpower, in keeping them incarcerated. The POW camps themselves were not the most pleasant of places and some of the guards were chosen for their harsh attitudes. In Italy and Japan the vast majority of the guards were just brutal thugs selected for the task. In Germany, however, the majority of German guards were relatively reasonable and the majority of Kommandants were elderly officers who had been recalled to service to release younger men to fight.

It became the responsibility of the International Red Cross to look after the welfare of prisoners of war, irrespective of nationality. The beginnings of the organisation began as a result of strong representation by Florence Nightingale and others after the Crimean War. She had complained loudly about the inhumane treatment suffered by the sick and wounded. Her cause was helped by the publication of a book by Jean Henri Dunant in Switzerland called *Un Souvenir de Solférino,* which gave an account of the victims of the war. Dunant had witnessed the sight of thousands of wounded men lying helpless and abandoned after the Battle of Solferino and decided to try to do something about it. In 1863 he invited twelve European countries to send representatives to Switzerland to attend a diplomatic conference. This resulted in the first Red Cross convention in Geneva, where the twelve European countries decided to lay down the rules of war concerning the treatment of the wounded. In 1864 the Geneva Convention, as it became known, came into being. In 1906 the rules were revised to include the treatment of prisoners of war and, in 1946, further revised to include the civilian population, which included members of organised resistance groups.

There were four Geneva Conventions at the time; they covered the sick and wounded, armed forces on land and sea, prisoners of war and civilians. With regard to the rights of prisoners of war under the rules of the Geneva Convention, they were as follows:

Prisoners should be:

Treated humanely with respect for their persons and honour.
Allowed to inform their next of kin and the Red Cross.
Allowed to correspond with relatives and receive relief parcels.
Allowed to keep their clothes and personal effects.
Given adequate food and clothing.
Provided with quarters not inferior to those of their captors.
Given medical care as and when their state of health requires.
Paid for any work they do for their captors.
Repatriated if their medical condition is such that they would no longer be able to resume active service.
To be released the moment hostilities cease or as soon as possible.

Prisoners must not:

Be compelled to give any other information other than their name, age, rank and service number.
Be deprived of any monies or valuables without a receipt.
Given any special privileges except for reasons of health, sex, age, military rank or professional qualifications.
Held in close confinement except for breaches of the law or security reasons.
Forced to carry out military work, work that is dangerous, degrading or unhealthy.

The Geneva Convention was put in place to try to prevent brutality and inhumane treatment of prisoners, and was usually monitored by the Swiss, who were neutral. Unfortunately the Japanese and some Italian guards had never read (or in some cases, even heard of) the Geneva Convention, or just simply chose to ignore it. Under the rules of the convention it was perfectly legal for prisoners of war to try to escape, but although the Germans had signed up to the convention, they had a different interpretation of the escaping clause. They held that if the enemy had spared your life and accepted your surrender you had no right to attempt to fight again. If you were placed in a hospital because of injuries you had received, and had been treated humanely by your enemy, it compounded the offence if you tried to escape.

One of the methods put forward for getting escape kits to prisoners was to place them in Red Cross parcels. Norman Crockatt, Head of MI9, fought against this very successfully, arguing that if the Germans found the escape kits they would confiscate not only them, but also the Red Cross parcels. The fact that food and medicines were in desperately short supply placed the health of the prisoners at great risk. This was highlighted when a number of Russian prisoners died from malnutrition when their Red Cross parcel supply was cut off.

Time behind the wire could be used beneficially by learning new skills and languages, but in some camps, with the exception of officers and senior NCOs, prisoners were sent to work in factories and on farms, which left little time for study. Among the most popular languages to learn were French and German – for obvious reasons. Another use of time was seen in the development of theatres, which enabled the prisoners to put on shows. This also gave the prisoners access to materials for props and costumes, which were also utilised in the making of civilian clothes and in some cases German uniforms.

In all prisoner-of-war camps escape committees were formed, using all the civilian skills that the soldiers, sailors and airmen brought with them.

Being on the run in the spring or summer was preferable to the winter as raw vegetables and fruit were plentiful to forage, and moving around in the countryside was considerably easier. It also has to be remembered that not all the local people were friendly toward the Allies. The fear instilled in them by the Germans if they aided any escapee or evader was enough to deter all but the bravest. These people faced torture and death if discovered, but the real number of the many unknown and faceless people in the occupied countries, who daily put their lives on the line, will never be known.

3. ESCAPE LINES

MI9

In December 1941, MI6 had created a special section called MI9. It was staffed by some former escapees and evaders with the aim of aiding the escape organisations in occupied Europe and the escapees. The department was in two sections, MI9a and MI9b: 'a' was concerned with helping Allied escapees and evaders, while 'b' dealt with captured enemy agents and servicemen.

Placed under overall command of Major (later Colonel) Norman Crockatt, MI9's headquarters was at a secret location in Beaconsfield, Buckinghamshire, but it also had offices in the War Office that were just known as 'Room 900 War Office'. Crockatt was the ideal person to head the organisation – he had fought at the front line in a number of major offensives and had been wounded several times. He was also a good judge of men, an effective organiser and, more importantly, he had no respect for red tape, as many department heads were to find out.

Colonel Crockatt concerned himself with department 'a' and placed a Major A.R. Rawlinson in charge of department 'b'. The whole of MI9 came under the umbrella of military intelligence, but Crockatt saw his role as helping to facilitate the escape of British prisoners of war and aiding their return to the United Kingdom. By doing this he would not only bring back men ready to fight again, but would also secure vital information about the enemy. This would have the additional benefit of helping raise the morale of the troops held in prison camps when they heard of successful 'home runs'.

MI9 helped to fund the escape lines that were operating in Europe and developed a large range of aids that could be concealed in everyday objects and sent to men in prison camps by means of the international postal service. Items included compasses hidden in the tops of fountain pens and playing cards that when soaked in water displayed a map of Germany and its surrounding borders.

A school was set up in Highgate, London, where intelligence officers (IO) from the army, navy and air force could go to learn about escape and evasion techniques from men who had actually escaped or evaded and had managed to make their way home. Armed with this information the IOs would return to their respective services and pass on what they had learned to their men.

Major Airey Neave had been recruited by MI9 and was the ideal person to give lectures on escape and evasion as he had escaped from Colditz Castle, the so-called escape-proof POW camp. It was important to learn that the every-day habits of escapees and evaders might betray them. For example, smoking English or American cigarettes, or eating chocolate in public places, was some-thing very few people had even seen in wartime Europe. Even placing a knife and fork together in the English way when finishing a meal was likely to get an escapee or evader caught. If travelling by bicycle it was essential to remember to cycle on the right-hand side of the road. Escape packs, which contained foreign money, silk maps of Europe, hacksaws, bottles of water, compasses, chocolate and even a fishing line, were developed by MI9 and issued to airmen and commandos.

Interrogation methods used by the Germans when questioning escapees or evaders were an aspect of this school's curriculum. The planting of English-speaking Germans among prisoners was one ploy used by the Gestapo on a regular basis, so the need to be wary of your companions until you knew them better was highlighted. Questioning under the threat of violence, sleep depri-vation, solitary confinement in windowless and airless cells and torture were among the many subjects examined.

As more and more escapees and evaders managed to return, so more and more important information filtered through to MI9. Crockatt gradually increased his staff, using experienced servicemen, all of whom had seen action at first hand, to interview the escapees and evaders when they returned.

Throughout the war, and indeed for some time afterwards, MI9 looked after the needs of the returning airmen to the best of its ability and was responsible for saving many lives. It also lent financial, physical and moral support to those faceless people who ran the escape lines throughout Europe.

After the war, Major Neave was appointed Chief Commissioner for Criminal Organisations. Together with MI9, he and his team were instrumental in bring-ing many members of the Gestapo, Abwehr, SS (Schutzstaffel) – Protection Squad – and SD (Sicherheitsdienst) – Security Service, as well as traitors, to the attention of the authorities for their mistreatment, torture and murder of Allied servicemen and members of the various escape organisations.

THE COMÈTE LINE

The Comète Line was an escape network that was set up in Belgium during the war to aid escaping Allied soldiers and airmen by helping them return to England. At the outbreak of war, the German Army quickly overran Belgium, France and the Netherlands. In Belgium, the King surrendered his army even though the consensus was to continue to fight. With their armed forces disarmed and imprisoned, some of the civilian population took it upon themselves to create a resistance organisation.

Although it was known as an organisation, the Comète Line was in fact more like a structure of many parts, because the majority of the people concerned in its make-up never knew each other. Such was the secrecy required that it was necessary that no one person would ever know the full extent of the structure. Initially the escape line formed part of the humanitarian section of the Resistance, when Belgians visited the hospitals where hundreds of Allied soldiers were being treated after becoming injured during the fighting. The retreating Allied army had left these troops behind for a variety of reasons, the main one being that they didn't have the facilities to take them with them. When the captured troops had recovered, they were taken to POW camps in an area east of the German Reich. Hundreds of captured soldiers were also being transported to these camps, and because they were lightly guarded a number managed to slip away from their captors.

Hidden and helped by local townspeople and farmers, those who escaped found themselves with a restricted type of freedom but with no opportunity of getting home to England. It soon became obvious that those troops that were hidden by local people could not be concealed indefinitely. The penalty for those found harbouring or helping Allied troops was torture or death, and in some cases both. The decision was made to make arrangements to start moving the evaders, and in Brussels Baron Jacques Donny began to organise safe houses to where Allied troops could be moved prior to be taken through Belgium. In addition to finding safe houses, forged travel and identity documents had to be obtained. The plans were to take the evaders by train to France and from there over the Pyrenees and into Spain.

From the start of the war, the Allied troops in France were almost entirely soldiers. However, by August 1941, the RAF was beginning its bombing campaign on the industrial area of north-west Germany and the first of the aircrews who had either baled out or crash-landed after being shot down were being picked up by the resistance. The number of Allied troops requiring help was increasing. In addition to this, German Intelligence was becoming increasingly active and was beginning to penetrate the organisations. The GFP (Geheime Feldpolizei), the plain-clothes section of the military police, concentrated a large part of its efforts in this quarter.

Then in December 1941, when the United States was thrust into the war, the number of bombing raids by B-17 bombers increased dramatically and so did the number of airmen shot down. The number of airmen requiring help was growing daily. It was during this period that a 25-year-old Belgian nurse by the name of Andrée de Jongh, code-named Dédée, one of the main founders and leaders of the Comète Line, came to the attention of the Allies. Together with some of her friends, she took to hiding Allied airmen and arranging help for them through the Belgian Resistance.

One of her first triumphs was when she and her friend, Arnold Deppe, took a British soldier, Private Jim Cromer, through France and over the Pyrenees, the natural border with Spain. Deppe had already carried out a dummy run travelling by train through Paris and Bayonne, and then walking and climbing over the Pyrenees into Spain.

Together with two other Belgians, who wanted to join the organisation as couriers, Dédée and Deppe, led by the Basque guide Florentino Goikoetxea, guided Cromer over the Pyrenean Mountains to the British Consul in Bilbao. The Consul, amazed at seeing the slight figure of Dédée, asked how the organisation was being funded and she informed him that it was through the generosity of a few rich Belgians. He told her he would contact the British embassy in Madrid and attempt to secure additional funding for her. This would be based on 6,000 Belgian francs per person and 1,200 pesetas for the mountain guides. This was to be the first of many such trips and lead to the rescue of dozens of Allied airmen and soldiers.

Together with her father, Frédéric de Jongh, Dédée set up a chain of safe houses along the route. Among these was one owned by Madame Elvire de Greef (code-named Tante Go) who had left Brussels when the Germans invaded and moved to the town of Anglet, close to the border of Spain. It was with Tante Go that servicemen were rested before starting on the last leg of the journey.

Back in London there was a certain amount of scepticism about the young girl running the Comète escape line. A number of people thought she might have been a 'plant' by the Germans in order to infiltrate the Resistance organisations that they knew were being developed. But when three of the men she guided through Belgium, Vichy France and over the Pyrenean Mountains into Spain were questioned on their return to England, they could not speak highly enough of her incomparable firmness, resolution and courage. With that kind of endorsement MI9 felt it had no other option than to fund the escape line – which it did.

On her return to the Consul's office in Bilbao, Dédée met Michael Cresswell, an MI9 officer from the British embassy in Madrid, and was told of the decision. She was delighted, but emphasised that although London was funding the Line, the overall control would be hers and that London was not to interfere. Cresswell agreed and told her that every time she crossed over into Spain and reported to the Consul in Bilbao he would give her what money she required and any other items she may have requested.

Over the next two years Dédée often travelled along the escape line, taking scores of Allied airmen with her. Together with Basque guides they escorted the weary, frightened and sometimes injured men over the mountains into the relative safety of Spain. Dédée then returned to Brussels to start all over again.

On one trip, Dédée returned to Brussels to discover Deppe had been arrested while boarding a train in the Belgian capital with a party of Allied airmen. It appeared that a Belgian officer who had been arrested some months earlier attempting to escape using the Comète line had been tortured and persuaded to talk. In addition to giving up Deppe, he had also given the Geheime Feldpolizei (GFP) an accurate description of Dédée. The Gestapo had also questioned Dédée's father, but he had managed to persuade them that he had no idea of his daughter's whereabouts or her activities; he was just a simple schoolteacher. Fortunately they never searched his schoolroom, otherwise they would have found a hoard of forged identity cards and ration books in one of the desks.

It was quite obvious that Dédée could no longer operate in Brussels, so she moved to Paris. In Brussels the Germans were making arrest after arrest as the city's section of the Comète Line crumbled. In one incident, Tante Go, with Dédée in Paris, returned to Brussels to collect two British soldiers. The journey through Belgium was uneventful, but at the border crossing with Vichy France, one of the British soldiers presented his forged papers to the French official together with his British Army identity card. Without batting an eyelid, the official glanced at all the documents and handed them back without a word. It is not known whether or not the official saw the identity card or simply chose to ignore it.

In Valenciennes, Dédée joined the group and they crossed over the Somme River in a boat owned by a woman known only by the name Nenette. The river was the unofficial crossing point for the Zone Interdite (Forbidden Zone) and once across the group boarded the train for Paris. There the group changed trains, went on to Bayonne and from there continued to the town of Anglet, where the Basque guide Florentino Goikoetxea was waiting.

Goikoetxea was Dédée's first choice of guide. Although he only spoke Euskera, the Basque language, Goikoetxea's knowledge of the mountains was second to none. His strength and stamina was another of his many assets and although he had a fondness for alcohol, as many an Allied escapee discovered when he provided refreshments for them halfway across the Pyrenees, he proved to be the most reliable.

The escape line's priority was to help Allied airmen escape and it was becoming so successful that Herman Göring ordered Luftwaffe Intelligence to destroy it. All the German Intelligence sections were now exerting pressure and a large number of arrests were made.

In Brussels, the role that Dédée had vacated was taken over by a Belgian aristocrat by the name of Jean Greindl. Code-named Nemo, Greindl ran a Red Cross section that looked after destitute children and set up the headquarters for the escape line on the premises. From that moment on, all escapees were referred to as Les Enfants.

In order to continue the line, Greindl also set up 'clearing houses' in various areas such as Ghent, Liege, Namur and Hasselt, where Allied airmen could be brought before being put into the escape line. While in these houses they could be interrogated by the Resistance to make sure they were not Gestapo infiltrators.

With the pressure being intensified to discover who was running the escape lines, Airey Neave, who had escaped from Colditz Castle and was now working in MI9, tried to persuade Dédée and her father to leave Paris and come to London, but they refused.

Among those who worked with Dédée in Paris was Kattalin Aguirre, also known as Kattalin Lamothe. She worked as a cleaner in a hotel that billeted German officers and it was here that she picked up snippets of information that proved helpful to the Resistance. Gaining the trust and respect of the Germans, she used this to her advantage and smuggled parts of radio equipment while working for Resistance groups in the area. She was also a key figure at the Paris end of the Comète Line.

The journey from Paris to the Pyrenees was becoming more and more hazardous as the Germans and Spanish border guards increased their patrols and vigilance. On three separate occasions Dédée and Goikoetxea came under fire from both the German and Spanish guards. It was only Goikoetxea's expert knowledge of the mountains and the smuggler trails that helped them get away.

Such was the spirit that Dédée inspired in others that when Jean Greindl approached her to say that more than 100 people in Brussels had been arrested in two days and felt it was too dangerous to go on, she managed to persuade him that he was necessary and vital to the escape line, and so he continued.

Then disaster struck. Dédée was about to take three airmen over the Pyrenees when the weather closed in, making it too dangerous for even Goikoetxea to cross over. It was decided to shelter in a farmhouse close to the foothills where a lady known as Frantxia, who owned the farmhouse, sheltered and helped to prepare the escapees for the arduous journey over the mountains.

It was while waiting in the farmhouse that gendarmes, accompanied by German soldiers, raided the house and arrested them all after a tip-off by a renegade Basque guide by the name of Donato who had once worked for Frantxia. They demanded to know where the other one was, obviously referring to Goikoetxea, and as Donato was the only person who could have known who was in the house, they all knew it had been him who had betrayed them. Goikoetxea had left just hours before and so was able to escape. Imprisoned first at the French-administered Château-Neuf prison in Bayonne, Dédée was questioned by the French. She told them that she was a French girl local to the area, showing them her forged papers. Despite her excellent French, it soon became obvious that she was lying and the Germans insisted that she be transferred to the notorious Fresnes prison just outside Paris. At first she denied everything, then admitted just to being a courier for the Resistance, but when she realised that they had information that would eventually lead to her father she decided to admit everything.

Dédée was handed over to the Gestapo but after some hours of interrogation, in which she told them a mixture of truth and lies, they refused to believe that such a young girl was capable of organising and running the Comète Line. She was interrogated alternately by the Gestapo and Luftwaffe Intelligence. Luck then played a part when Luftwaffe Intelligence, who had always been at odds with the Gestapo, insisted on moving her to Germany for further interrogation. Over the next few weeks she was moved between prisons in Essen, Zweibrücken and Westphalia before being placed in a concentration camp. Somehow she got lost within the concentration camp system, whether by design or by accident, but she survived the war at Ravensbrück and was able to give evidence against collaborators.

Dédée's father, Frédéric, was arrested when a Belgian by the name of Jacques Desoubris, a Gestapo double agent who also called himself Jean Masson and Pierre Boulain, infiltrated the Comète Line and set a trap using escaping airmen. After his interrogation by the Gestapo, Frédéric was taken to Mont Valérien prison and executed by firing squad.

A man by the name of Camille Spiquel, a member of the Belgian Resistance, had introduced Masson to Frédéric. He had taken the word of others but no one checked his background. Had they done this they would have discovered that the Belgian police wanted him for a variety of offences. Masson managed to destroy the organisation run by Spiquel soon after joining the Comète Line.

The arrests of Dédée and Frédéric de Jongh seemed to open the floodgates for arrests. Among those detained was Jean Greindl, who was interrogated by the Gestapo, and then condemned to death when they were unable to make him talk. Sent to one of the Gestapo's barracks to await execution, he was killed during an air raid when Allied bombers decimated the barracks, also killing a large number of Gestapo officers.

With the Comète Line seemingly in tatters, Madame Elvire de Greef (Tante Go), took over its running until Baron Jean-François Nothcomb (Franco), a Belgian Army officer who had been operating in Paris, took control. Elvire's husband, Fernand, worked as an interpreter in the German Kommandant's office in Anglet and so was able to obtain copies of identity cards and travel documents. A number of attempts were made to try to get Dédée out of prison but none were successful.

Madame de Greef was also arrested at the same time as Greindl, but she 'persuaded' the German authorities that arresting her would only reveal their extensive dealing with the local black marketers, and that was an offence that meant either a court martial or a posting to the Eastern Front. She was released.

With Dédée in prison, another young Belgian woman stepped into her shoes: Micheline Dumon (Michou). Michou had joined the Resistance after leaving nursing school just after the beginning of the war. Within months of joining, her parent and elder sister, Nadine, had been arrested by the Gestapo and imprisoned in the St-Gilles prison in Belgium. Michou was a petite, dark-haired young girl who looked about 12 years old, but was in fact 22 and a fully trained nurse. She had contacted Dédée and offered her services to the Comète Line, and was soon in charge of organising safe houses, arranging for forged identity cards to be made and escorting airmen to the French border.

Her training as a nurse became extremely useful when Allied airmen who had been wounded or were ill were delivered into her care. Her position became extremely risky and after one incident, when she escaped from the Germans by a matter of minutes, it was decided to give her a new identity as a 16-year-old student.

One American pilot by the name of Bob Grimes has reason to be thankful for her attention. He had been shot down in a B-17 while on a bombing raid and had suffered a serious leg wound. It was thanks to Michou's nursing skills that he didn't lose the leg. When he recovered, she was instrumental in helping him to escape through France and into Spain.

Then during one trip over the Pyrenees, when Goikoetxea was returning from Spain after delivering some important documents, he was ambushed by German soldiers, badly wounded and taken away for interrogation. Questioned by the Gestapo, he said nothing; fortunately they thought that he was just a Basque smuggler and handed him over to the Spanish Guardia. So bad were his injuries that he was sent to a civilian hospital in Bayonne. Tante Go, on hearing of his capture and subsequent hospitalisation, took the opportunity to rescue him and he was spirited away and hidden for the remainder of the war.

As the war neared its end MI9 became more and more concerned with the number of Comète Line operatives being betrayed and summarily executed. It knew of the existence of a traitor among the members of the Line but found it increasingly difficult to pinpoint who it was. Then information came with a name – Jacques Desoubris, also known as Jean Masson.

Michou had been working with a Parisian dentist by the name of Martine Noel and had met Masson at a meeting in a restaurant with her. The meeting was about the moving of a number of Allied airmen, who had been secreted at various addresses in Paris, including Martine's apartment. Some days later, Michou tried to contact Martine by telephone but it was answered by a woman who called Michou by her real name, Micheline, saying that Martine was not there but would be there soon and could Micheline come over. Very wary of what was going on, as no one in Paris knew her real name, she decided to go to Martine's surgery. On arriving, she was warned by the concierge that the Gestapo had been there and everyone had been arrested. Word then spread around that a series of raids had been carried out on addresses in Paris and a number of Allied airmen and their helpers arrested.

Michou heard that Martine had been taken to the French prison and decided to pay her a visit. On her arrival at the prison, so shocked were the guards to see a visitor that they locked her up. Michou protested that she had come to see her friend. Locked in a cell, Michou called out for Martine. The prison had been built in a circular design, much like a spoked wheel, with all the cells around the perimeter. Calling out for Martine, Michou heard her friend reply. She asked who had betrayed her and the others; the reply came back, 'C'est Pierre, Pierre Boulain.'

Then fortune smiled upon Michou when the governor of the prison, who was French, interviewed her and then released her, saying that he would not be responsible for sending such a young girl into prison. Her appearance once again belied her age.

At first it was difficult to believe that Boulain was the traitor as he had come highly recommended, and had been instrumental in transferring airmen to Paris and then down the Line to the Pyrenees. There were, however, a couple of things that always concerned fellow members: the ease with which he could obtain fool-proof forged identification cards and passes at short notice, and his ability to be able to cross borders undetected. Masson continued to work with the Comète Line, unaware that he was being watched. At one meeting he was asked to take 500,000 francs to Belgium to pay for the setting of refuges for Allied airmen. Information came their way confirming his dealings with the Gestapo, and the organisation knew that Masson had no intention of taking the money to Belgium but intended to pocket it and betray the courier. In the meantime, the Line had contacted the French Resistance, informing them that they had a traitor in their organisation and that they wanted him dealt with. The following evening, after another meeting with a member of the Line, a member of the Resistance's assassination squad placed Masson under observation. Then, as he was walking near his home, a car pulled alongside and a single shot was fired. Masson crumpled to the ground dead and rolled into the gutter – many in the Resistance would have said it was a fitting end.

The Gestapo reacted immediately and started a massive hunt for the killer. It was this reaction by the Germans that confirmed beyond all doubt that the Comète Line suspicions were correct, as it was obvious that Masson was working for the Gestapo and that they regarded him as being a very important part of their infiltration plan into the escape lines.

However, British Intelligence was not convinced that it was Masson that had been killed, as more and more members of the Comète Line were being captured, along with evading airmen. The US counter-intelligence officers were made aware of an SD agent who was working within the escape line. He was delivering airmen and their handlers to a hotel in Paris, where the Gestapo arrested them. His description was circulated and matched that of a man who lived on the Rue de Douai, but who moved out some months earlier. This was the street where Masson had been said to be living some *weeks* earlier.

The intelligence officers finally got a photograph of the man, and the one person who could identify him was Michou, as she had seen him at close quarters. An American intelligence officer sent for her and she immediately recognised him as the traitor Masson. It appeared that as the US Army approached Paris to liberate it, Masson had approached the Americans offering to work for them as an agent. With Michou's positive identification, Masson was immediately arrested and imprisoned. He was later taken to Lille, tried before a French court and executed.

Who the man the French Resistance executed was no one knows, but one theory was that it was a colleague of Masson's, a man by the name of Prosper Desitter, who was also a known collaborator.

Many of the other unknown, faceless members of the escape lines just returned to their normal jobs after the war, happy with the fact that they were able to do something to help towards the defeat of Germany.

The Comète Line rescued a significant number of Allied airmen and a smaller number of soldiers. Without the bravery and resourcefulness of a large number of people, the chances are that almost none of these men would have ever escaped. Of those that helped to run the Line, twenty-three were executed, 133 died in concentration camps and an undisclosed number survived imprisonment or just simply disappeared. The debt that is owed to these people can never be repaid.

Postscript

At the end of the war Kattalin Aguirre was made a Chevalier of the Legion of Honour and held the Medaille Militaire, both the French and the Belgian Croix de Guerre, the French and Belgium Medailles de la Resistance and King George VI's Medal for Freedom. She died in 1992. Andrée de Jongh (Dédée) was awarded the George Medal by the British and the United States Medal of Freedom by the Americans, among numerous other awards for bravery from other countries. She was made a countess by King Baudouin of Belgium in 1985. After the war she worked in leper hospitals in Africa and died in October 2007.

THE PAT O'LEARY LINE

Unlike the Comète Line, the Pat O'Leary Line was more of an organisation than a structure. The majority of its members knew and trusted each other, which made it easier for the Germans to penetrate. This was because each member was known to every other member, so in the event of one of them being captured and made to talk they could identify and name the others. The Comète Line, on the other hand, was fragmented and each person's identity was only revealed on a need-to-know basis.

The name Pat O'Leary was given to a Belgian doctor whose real title was Médecin-Capitane Albert-Marie Edmond Guérisse. He had served with a cavalry regiment during the eighteen days that Belgium fought before it capitulated. Disgusted with the Belgian government, he joined the crew of a converted French merchantman, HMS *Fidelity*, which was operating clandestine missions in the Mediterranean. He joined the ship under the *nom de plume* of a Canadian friend, Patrick Albert O'Leary, and was commissioned as a lieutenant commander. The all-French crew were given Royal Navy ranks and assumed names, because of their undercover work.

After a number of successful undercover missions, O'Leary was assigned to take two Special Operations Executive (SOE) agents ashore at Collioure near the Etang de Canet. After depositing the men on the beach, O'Leary was starting to return when a sudden squall overturned his small boat. He managed to swim ashore, but was arrested later by French coastguards and sent to St-Hippolyte-du-Fort near Nîmes. He heard later that HMS *Fidelity* had been torpedoed and all hands had been lost.

After spending some weeks in the prison, he escaped with the help of Ian Garrow, a captain in the Seaforth Highlanders. Garrow was running an escape line from Marseille for escaping and evading soldiers and airmen.

Marseille had been a magnet for any Allied soldier or airman on the run, and it was here that Garrow, with the help of some of the residents, set up an escape route over the Pyrenees into Spain. One of the helpers was the Reverend Donald Caskie, who ran the Seaman's Mission in Marseille.

Garrow had already made his way through France after Dunkirk and had established a chain of contacts that would pass Allied servicemen down the Line. Establishing safe houses in Marseille itself was one of the main priorities and some of the most ideal places were the numerous brothels that inhabited the waterfront and dock areas. There were other ordinary hiding places for the men, among them the apartments of a local doctor, Georges Rodocanachi, and his wife Fanny, and a wealthy businessman, Louis Nouveau, and his wife Renée.

When an evader or escapee arrived in Marseille, he was taken to a local waterfront bar, La Petit Poucet, where he was interrogated thoroughly and his credentials checked before moving him on to a safe house. This was necessary to make sure that the serviceman was who he said he was, as it was becoming common practice for Luftwaffe Intelligence to try to infiltrate the Resistance groups with English-speaking agents in the guise of escaping airmen. The penalty for being discovered as an infiltrator was just as ruthless as that of the Gestapo – death.

O'Leary wanted to join Garrow, but permission had to be obtained from London for this to happen. When this had been obtained the two men set to work establishing a network. Firstly they had to set up a communication system. The group had been communicating with Donald Darling, an MI6 agent stationed in Lisbon, but he had since moved to Gibraltar and the only way to contact him was by using Basque guides with messages secreted in toothpaste tubes.

Another problem of some concern was the behaviour of a Sergeant Harold Cole. According to Cole, he had been at Dunkirk but had been left behind.

He had then joined up with the Resistance and was working with them as a courier taking escapees down the Line. Garrow thought very highly of Cole, but O'Leary had an instinct for people and mistrusted him.

Then O'Leary found out that Cole had been having a wild party in Marseille when he should have been in Lille. He suspected that Cole was using the Line's funds for his own gratification, although when questioned about it Cole casually dismissed it as 'a one-off party'. O'Leary went to Lille to visit agent François Dupré, to whom Cole was supposed to have handed over some money for the Line, but Dupré had received nothing. More disturbing news came in from some contacts on the Line, saying that Cole had been passing himself off as a Captain Colson of British Intelligence.

O'Leary returned to Marseille to find that Garrow had been arrested by the French Vichy police. Cole was picked up and questioned by members of the Resistance. At first he denied doing anything wrong, but when confronted by Dupré he confessed to having used the Line's money to fund his lifestyle. He was locked in a bathroom while it was discussed what to do with him. The Resistance wanted to shoot him there and then, but it was decided to send him back to Britain to face charges of embezzlement. In the meantime, Cole had escaped and word was sent down the line that he was not to be trusted. Two weeks later the Line heard that the Abwehr (German Military Intelligence) had 'arrested' Cole and it was discovered later he had been working for the organisation as a double agent. This came to light when a letter, written by the jailed abbot of a monastery, was smuggled out of prison. In the letter he stated that Cole had betrayed him when he had turned up with five escapees – two Belgian pilots, one English soldier, one RAD officer and a Polish pilot. Although the others spoke some French, the Polish pilot spoke neither French nor German. It turned out later, after they had been arrested, that the Polish pilot was in fact the head of the Lille branch of the Geheime Feldpolizei.

With Garrow under arrest, O'Leary took over control of the escape line. Back in England, James Langley, who himself had travelled down Garrow's escape line and who was now working with MI9, was struggling to find O'Leary a wireless operator. A volunteer was found and Langley decided to take him with him when he went to meet O'Leary in Gibraltar to discuss the Line and the traitor Cole.

Just as he was to leave for Gibraltar, Langley was contacted by Scotland Yard regarding Cole. They had a warrant for his arrest as a 'conman' and they heard that he was working for MI9. He had absconded with the funds from the sergeants' mess in his regiment and had disappeared into France. On meeting Langley, O'Leary showed him the abbot's letter regarding Cole's treachery, after which Langley immediately sanctioned the killing of Cole when he was found. Cole, it appeared later, was also on the run from the Abwehr as he had double-crossed some of its operatives.

The Resistance also ordered that Cole be killed at the first opportunity, but it was not until 1945 that the French police caught up with him and shot him while trying to 'arrest' him on other matters.

The number of escapees and evaders was growing by the day, creating a backlog, and other methods of extracting them were constantly being sought. One of these was the creation of a special unit known as the Coast Watching Flotilla (CWF). This was not a new idea; a similar idea had been used by the Polish to collect the large number of Poles who had been in France when the country had capitulated. It was being run by a section of MI6 under the control of Captain Slocum, who ran the Operational Section of the Secret Intelligence Service (SIS). The new CWF was put under the control of the captain commanding the 8th Submarine Flotilla in Gibraltar, which allowed the flotilla's depot ship of the dockyard to carry out any maintenance or repairs required on these craft. Some of these boats were painted to look like Spanish or Portuguese fishing boats, so if spotted from the air by enemy aircraft they appeared to be neutral.

In an effort to clear the backlog of escapees in the O'Leary Line, seven operations were mounted. In one operation alone, thirty-five escapees and evaders were picked up from St-Pierre-la-Mer, near Narbonne, followed a month later by a further thirty-five from the mouth of the River Têt at Canet-en-Rousillon. One of the vessels used by the CWF was just 47ft long and on one of its missions it managed to cram eighty-three persons on board, the majority of whom had to be accommodated on the deck.

The wireless operator that Langley had found and trained proved to be worse than useless. His knowledge of Morse code was barely adequate and the first time he transmitted he went to pieces. He was obviously not suited for this clandestine work, and so was returned to London. His place was taken by a young Belgian fighter pilot by the name of Alex Nitelet, who had been blinded in one eye during a dogfight. He was fully trained in the use of Morse and knew all about the escape line because he himself had been rescued by it some months previously.

Slowly but surely the O'Leary Line got back on track despite the earlier setbacks. The number of people willing to help hide the escapees grew and it was estimated that at its height more than 250 men, women and even some children were involved, from Belgium to Spain.

In Marseille the organisation was able to provide forged identity cards, travel documents and ration cards, all within three days of being asked for them.

Black marketers, who were rife on the waterfront, could provide food for the escapees at a moment's notice. One Jewish tailor, Paul Ulmann, could copy any uniform required within forty-eight hours of being asked. Throughout France and Belgium there were 'letter-boxes' that could be used to contact agents, and information came from such places as police stations, military establishments and even from inside Gestapo headquarters itself.

The O'Leary Line was now the biggest of its type in Europe and the most well informed. This also made it vulnerable to infiltration by the Gestapo, who, on a number of occasions, placed their own agents into the chain. One such agent was a Frenchman who was working for the Gestapo. He arrived at La Petit Poucet and offered O'Leary information about German counter-intelligence agents operating in the area. Ever suspicious about such claims, O'Leary made enquiries about the man and discovered that he had attempted to penetrate the Spanish end of the Line. Picked up by the Resistance, the man was questioned and eventually admitted to being in the pay of the Gestapo. He suffered the fate of all traitors – death.

The Line suffered a severe blow when two key members of the organisation, Alex Nitelet and the black marketer Gaston Négre, were picked up by the Vichy police while recovering an airdrop from MI9 containing a large sum of money and supplies.

As the war progressed the Germans decided that the Vichy government was not keeping a tight enough control of its citizens and the Resistance, and so in November 1942 the German moved in to take over control. This meant that patrols along the borders were increased; additional transmission detector vans were moved into the area, and more and more Gestapo agents began to infiltrate the Lines.

A new wireless operator, an Australian named Tom Groome, was parachuted in to take the place of Nitelet. The Germans' grip tightened and within weeks of arriving, Groome was caught in the middle of a transmission by one of the detector vans. There was some good news, however, when an active Resistance group rescued Nègre from prison by slipping a powerful sleeping draught into the wine of the warders. Further good news followed concerning Ian Garrow. He was about to be sent to a concentration camp in Germany when Paul Ulmann made a warder's uniform, which was smuggled into the prison by a jailer who had been bribed. Garrow changed into the uniform and walked out of the prison to a waiting car, were he was whisked away over the Pyrenees into Spain.

At the end of 1942, Louis Nouveau recruited a former Foreign Legionnaire, Roger Le Neveu, in Paris. At first he appeared to be the ideal person to be a courier, and he began to escort escapees and evaders down the Line successfully. Then during one trip, he arrived alone saying that his charges had been captured but he had managed to talk his way out of the situation. Some members of the organisation were having doubts about Neveu, and it transpired that these were well founded.

The Germans suddenly introduced special passes for travel just as the Line was about to move some of its charges. Neveu volunteered to get the passes and within hours had obtained them. In the rush to get the charges away on the train, Nouveau had not reflected on how Neveu had managed to get the passes in such a short time. It was when they changed trains at Tours, and a gun slammed into Nouveau's ribs as the carriage was invaded by German plain-clothes police, that he realised that they had been set up.

With Nouveau in custody, Neveu contacted Ulmann and suggested that he contact O'Leary and arrange a meeting in a café in Toulouse, where he could explain the circumstances surrounding Nouveau's arrest. O'Leary agreed and went to meet Neveu, but when he walked into the café the Gestapo were waiting for him. Both Neveu and O'Leary were arrested, although Neveu's arrest was a sham in an attempt to throw suspicion off him; it fooled no one.

Arrest after arrest followed but despite being tortured viciously by the Gestapo, O'Leary said nothing. However, the Line had been damaged beyond the repair. Le Neuve was tracked down after the liberation of France and executed by the French Resistance. O'Leary survived the war and was given the highest civilian awards possible by the grateful governments of France, Belgium, Britain and the United States.

THE SHELBURN LINE

The Shelburn Line stated life as the Oaktree Line in 1943. The idea was to organise the evacuation from the beaches of northern Brittany using motor gun boats (MGB) of the Royal Navy.

The place selected as the collection point was the beach at Anse Cochat near the town of Plouha, northern Brittany. To co-ordinate the mission, two men – Vladimir Bourysschkine, aka Valentine Williams, and Sergeant Major Raymond Labrosse of the Canadian Army, a French–Canadian – were parachuted in from an SOE Halifax of No. 161 Squadron, RAF. The two men landed in a field near Rambouillet, south-west of Paris, and within seconds the two shadowy figures raced for the safety of the trees. The two men shook hands with a group of figures, exchanged a few words and then left. The two men were to play a key role in the escape of 307 Allied airmen and secret agents out of Nazi-held territory.

Labrosse stayed in the area, while Williams headed for Brittany and the home of Countess Roberta de Maudit at the Château de Bourblanc, Chauny, near Paimpol, a town 50 miles north of Paris. It was just 15 miles from the headquarters of Field Marshal Erwin Rommel, the commander-in-chief of all German forces in the Atlantic sector.

The two men organised the Oaktree Line with the help of the French Resistance, creating an escape network that returned 175 Allied airmen back to England. Unfortunately the Gestapo had infiltrated the organisation and Williams was arrested, but Labrosse escaped and managed to join up with a group of escapees and evaders before crossing into Spain. After a brief stay in Gibraltar, Labrosse returned to England on 3 September 1941. Williams was interrogated by the Germans in Rennes prison and beaten on a number of occasions. While there he got to know some of the other inmates – Russian soldiers. Williams had been born in Moscow, but raised in the United States and spoke both fluent Russian and French. Together with a Russian officer by the name of Bougaiev they managed to escape during a very heavy air raid. During the escape Williams fractured his leg while jumping down from a wall. Despite this, he managed to evade capture and was picked up by the Resistance and taken to a safe house to be treated. After getting him to Paris he was taken to Brittany and placed in the care of what was later to become the Shelburn Line and returned to England.

Meanwhile, back in London, Labrosse had met up with another escapee, fellow French–Canadian Sergeant Major Lucien Dumais, at MI9, where they were assigned another mission. MI9's top secret section IS9 (d) was better known as Room 900 and was the War Office branch concerned with Allied prisoners of war. Its function was to aid their escapes, to supply agents and helpers with money, radio communications and supplies, and to arrange pick-ups by aircraft and naval evacuations from the coasts of France. Labrosse and Dumais's mission was to organise a new escape network code-named Shelburn, involving evacuation by sea by Royal Navy MGB from a beach at the Anse Cochat, near Plouha, Brittany, to Dartmouth, Devon. This operation was given the code name Bonaparte.

The MGB was a high-speed launch powered by three diesel engines that cruised at 33 knots, but with a top speed of 40. The launch was 128ft in length and carried a crew of thirty-six. Its armament consisted of one six-pounder gun aft, twin machine guns in turrets, which were mounted on either side of the bridge, and a two-pounder gun mounted in front of the bridge.

The two agents, Labrosse and Dumais, were given extensive training in operating, repairing and building wireless sets, then given a large amount of francs together with forged identity papers. Lucien Dumais became 'Lucien Desbiens' and Raymond Labrosse became 'Marcel Desjardins'.

The two men were flown to France in an SOE Lysander aircraft, which landed in a meadow 50 miles north of Paris. After meeting with members of the local Resistance, the two men separated. Labrosse travelled the countryside looking for various places in the area from which he could transmit and receive coded radio messages. Dumais also travelled, but his job was to find safe houses for the airmen who would be brought into the area by other escape organisations. In addition to the houses, he had to find doctors who would be prepared to treat any sick or wounded airmen; people who would be prepared to feed and clothe them; printers who would create false identity papers at short notice; and all knowing that they would be putting their lives of themselves and their families on the line if discovered.

Dumais (Desbiens), who had been appointed to command the whole Shelburn network in France, was now posing as a mortician. Labrosse (Desjardins), his second-in-command and radio operator, was a salesman of electrical medical equipment. Labrosse made most of his transmissions from the apartment of Monsieur Dorré, the stationmaster of the Gare Pajol, who, because of his position, was able to gain valuable information and give practical assistance to the organisation. Mr Dorré's daughter, who Labrosse later married when Paris was liberated, often assisted in the transmissions. With the help of dedicated and patriotic Frenchmen, the Canadians gradually pieced the organisation together.

A great deal of work still had to be done before the organisation's network could be up and running. Procedures and routes for the escapees and evaders had to be worked out, together with a system of relays and safe houses. Couriers had to be recruited, together with equipment and supplies.

When everything was in place, the escape organisation radioed London, asking for an operation. They would then select dates of moonless nights and, if agreed, 'Room 900' would then confirm the dates.

On the appointed day, a BBC message would be sent at 7.30 and 9 p.m. This would mean that the MGB had already left Dartmouth and was making for 'Bonaparte' beach. The airmen would then be collected for embarkation. The message was: 'Bonjour tout le monde á la Maison d'Alphonse' (Hello everyone at the house of Alphonse). If the operation were to be delayed twenty-four hours, another message would be sent by London: 'Yvonne pense toujours à l'heureuse occasion' (Yvonne always thinks of the happy occasion). For the next few months the two French–Canadians worked tirelessly, realising that everything had to be in place before the first operation could take place, which hopefully would be in the December.

Throughout France ordinary people were also needed to watch for downed airmen, to pick them up and send them on their way to Paris. Guides had to be provided to escort the escapees in stages to Paris and then to Brittany, and countless other details had to be looked into.

In Paris, Paul-François Campinchi was responsible for Shelburn's Paris sector. It was here that downed airmen were to be screened, processed and interrogated by security agents who could speak English. Somebody would also have to teach the Allied airmen to act like French workers and labourers.

Many Frenchmen, who refused to speak to the enemy, became ill humoured and sullen, and the airmen would have to be taught to behave in this manner. There were also certain idiosyncrasies Frenchmen possessed, how they smoked their cigarettes and some typical mannerisms. Fake identity papers and everyday items found in the average Frenchman's pockets would also have to be provided. They would have to be fully briefed for the various trips they may have to take, and all this under the very nose of the Gestapo and German counter-espionage organisations.

Security was paramount for the agents and their helpers to ensure maximum secrecy. Information was on a need-to-know basis and no one was told more than was absolutely necessary. The identity of the Resistance workers and their helpers were shared discreetly and even then it was limited to just one or even two names. The airmen were given no more than the bare essential information that they needed; they had always assumed that the French Resistance had been behind their escape. At the end of the war when the Gestapo records came to light, it became clear that they had no idea of the existence of Shelburn and its part in spiriting escaping airmen away.

The spot picked for the repatriation of the escapees was on the beach at Anse Cochat. When Lucien Dumais went to inspect the beach he met François Le Cornec, the leader of the Resistance cell at Plouha. The two men discussed the Bonaparte plan in great detail and Dumais found the group very well organised and well aware of what was expected of them. They already had plans in place to hide the airmen and help with the evacuation. The beach itself was located about 1½ miles from Plouha. Isolated and difficult to reach, it was perfect for such an operation. Taking the airmen from Paris to Plouha was going to take a great deal of planning. They couldn't take all the men in one go, as it would attract attention, so it was decided that they would not be brought to Brittany until three days before the evacuation was to take place. They would take the train that led from Paris to Plouha, but they would get off at the small town of Guingamp.

Guingamp had been chosen because the leader of the Resistance, Mathurin Branchoux, had among his men François Kerambrun, a local man who drove a small delivery truck for the Germans. He was allowed to use his truck for private business during off-duty hours and had been given special passes that allowed him to go almost anywhere. He was also well known to the Germans in the area and was almost never stopped and searched. So it was decided that he would collect the airmen from the station and drive them to hiding places at Plouha just before the operation. The day before they were due to be picked up, the airmen would go to the Maison d'Alphonse, a house that belonged to Jean Giquel, a member of the Resistance and was just a mile from the rendezvous beach.

In Paris, the numbers of escapees and evaders was growing, so it was decided that they would have to move some of them quickly. The network was in place and organised, and so Labrosse contacted MI9 to request an evacuation. The first operation was organised for late December, but bad weather and heavy seas made this impossible, so it wasn't until 29 January 1944 that the first evacuation took place.

Shortly before the appointed date, airmen were brought from Paris to St-Brieuc and then taken to half a dozen house in and around Plouha. A few minutes after the BBC announcer had given his cheery greeting, 'Bonjour tout le monde à la d'Alphonse', French guides, together with the airmen, came out of the houses and slipped in small groups through the woods behind the village on their way to the House of Alphonse. Getting the airmen all together, Dumais told them that they were just a mile from the evacuation point and many lives had been risked to bring them this far. He then explained that it was extremely dangerous and many enemy sentries and patrols were in the area. They had to maintain absolute silence at all times and do exactly as they were told.

He further explained to them the need to watch for small pieces of white cloth on the ground as they covered mines. If a situation arose and it became necessary to kill, they were expected to help, using knives, hands or anything else they could, but to be quick and above all quiet. Their lives and those of their helpers depended on it.

Led by guides, the group slipped out into the darkness. Shortly before midnight, they reached the path leading to the beach. Clutching, sliding and tumbling, they scrambled as quietly as they could down to a cove. From a position higher up the cliff, one of the Resistance men began flashing the letter 'B' in Morse code with a masked torch, repeating the signal every couple of minutes. For what seemed like ages, nothing happened. In the cove below, the men waited nervously, and then suddenly the dark shapes of four boats rowed by sailors appeared. An officer, with a cocked pistol in his hand, jumped out of the lead boat, stepped forward and gave the password: 'Dinan'. 'St-Brieuc,' came the reply. 'OK,' said the officer, 'get on board fast.'

A few seconds later, and after a last handshake, the boats were leaving with their 'packages for Britain'. Twenty minutes later the silhouette of a boat suddenly appeared out of the darkness; the MGB *503* made no sound as it stood out of the range of the German searchlights. Then as the men scrambled aboard, the reassuring rumble of the engines as they were started brought to boat to life. With the last man aboard and the rowing boats safely stored, the powerful gunboat eased its way out to sea and back to Britain.

It had taken just thirty minutes from the time the seventeen airmen and two French Resistance workers, who were both wanted by the Germans, were taken off the beach and placed aboard the MGB. With the 'packages' safely away, the Resistance workers made their way silently back to the 'House of Alphonse'. There they would wait until 6 a.m., when the Germans lifted the curfew and they could return to their homes.

Over the next few months Dumais and Lambrosse, together with their French and Belgian counterparts, organised the evacuation of 118 airmen. In July 1944 the use of the MGBs to evacuate airmen and agents came to an end. In total the Shelburn Line was responsible for the rescue by sea of 128 airmen and seven agents, a total of 135 men and women. In addition to those evacuated by sea, Dumais and Labrosse arranged for ninety-two men to be evacuated over the Pyrenees and into Spain. A total of 307 airmen owed their lives to Shelburn and its key operation, Bonaparte.

Dumais and Labrosse stayed in France after Shelburn was shut down and helped organise and equip a Maquis near Plouha. Late in July 1944, the Maquis joined up with a group of Breton Resistance fighters and attacked a German convoy of over 200 men heading for the Normandy front at Plélo, killing fifty-four and taking 136 prisoners.

After the liberation Dumais stayed at St-Brieuc for a couple of months under the name of Captain Harrison and helped track down the collaborators and agents the Germans had left behind.

The Shelburn Line, although it did not operate for very long, was the most successful of all the escape networks on the European continent as it never lost a single 'package'. The only casualty was the 'House of Alphonse', which was burned down by the Germans, who suspected it to be a Resistance hideout.

THE POSSUM LINE

On the same Lysander aircraft that brought Raymond Labrosse and Lucien Dumais into France to set up the Shelburn Line, a Belgian pilot by the name of Capitaine Dominique Edgard Potier and five escaping airmen were returned to England.

Potier was a Belgian Air Force pilot who had escaped to England when his country had been invaded and offered his services to the RAF. They considered him too old for combat flying duties and rejected him. Potier then approached MI9 and volunteered to go to France and help with the escape lines. Airey Neave accepted him immediately because of his ability to speak fluent French and English, which made him an ideal agent to be dropped into either occupied France or Belgium.

On 15 July 1943 Potier was parachuted into Florenville close to the Belgian Ardennes, to help set up an escape route called the Possum Line. Potier (code-named Martin), together with a French–Canadian radio operator by the name of Conrad Lafleur (Charles), were to arrange for the evacuation of Allied airmen brought to them by the Belgian section of the Comète Line. The airmen were to be evacuated by Lysander aircraft or by MGB from Brittany.

During the next four months a number of airmen were whisked away under the noses of the Germans, then in November Potier and Lafleur were recalled and returned to England. The following month, together with another wireless operator, Albert LeMaitre (London), and a former Comète Line courier, Baron Jean de Blommaert (Rutland), Portier parachuted back into Belgium, landing near Fismes.

Later the same month, Lafleur returned to Belgium together with a highly experienced female courier, Raymonde Beure, who also acted as his watcher. Despite all the usual precautions, the Gestapo homed in on the pair of them while they were transmitting from a house in Reims. After a gun battle in which some of the Germans were either killed or wounded, the two agents managed to escape, but Beure left her purse behind in the confusion. In it were a number of addresses and photographs, including one of her fiancé, Raymond Jeunet, and a hotel key.

Jeunet had been expecting his fiancée to call him, but because of the incident with the Gestapo she had not. Being a very jealous man, he was convinced that she was having an affair with Lafleur and so left his home in Fismes and went looking for her. On arriving in Reims, he was spotted by the Gestapo, who now had his photograph, and promptly arrested him. In his possession he had a photograph of his fiancée, which they took from him. They took him to all the hotels in Reims showing the receptionists the photograph of Beure until it was recognised by the proprietor of the hotel Jean d'Arc. The proprietor quickly admitted that the girl had rented two rooms at the hotel, at which point the Gestapo raided them. The first was empty, but the second contained Potier, who was immediately arrested.

After weeks of torture by the Gestapo, and close to breaking point, Potier managed to throw himself from a third-storey window onto the concrete below, so as not to be forced to betray his comrades. He was rushed to hospital but died three hours later without regaining consciousness.

The Possum Line, having been discovered, was disbanded and the agents, including Beure, assigned to other groups and tasks. Despite its short operational length, the line still managed to aid Allied airmen to escape and return to continue to fight against the Nazis.

There were a number of other smaller escape lines and organisations, such as the network Jade-Fitzroy set up by a young Frenchman by the name of Claude Lamirault, who worked with the Possum Line. Then there was the Hector Network created by Colonel Alfred Heurteaux, a former First World War pilot, and the Brutus Network organised by Capitaine Pierre Fourcad, which operated in the Lyon district. There is no doubt that there were many more, and although their names may have been lost in the fullness of time, their contribution and bravery will never be forgotten.

ESCAPE
STORIES

4. LIEUTENANT GEORGE PURYEAR, USAAC

THE FOLLOWING IS a report from notes taken by Second Lieutenant L.H. Thayer, United States Army Air Service (USAAS):

Lieutenant Puryear, it is believed, was the first American Officer to escape from captivity in Germany [during the First World War], and a narrative of his experiences is one of vigour and youthful audacity. From the time of his capture, partly due to his own eagerness in a moment of success, he made it his aim to escape from the clutches of the Hun, and in the face of tremendous obstacles accomplished his purpose.

On July 14 [1918], having completed his training in the United States, then at Issoudun and Cazaux, and having served for two months as a ferry pilot, he was ordered to join the 95th Aero Squadron of the First Pursuit Group. At that time the 95th was changing over from the Nieuport Type 28 machines to SPADs and on July 18 from the Saints aerodrome, Lieutenant Puryear made his first flight over the Château-Thierry sector. With a week of patrol experience behind him, he went up on the 26th with four other SPAD Scouts to patrol the lines from Château-Thierry to Neuf-le-Château. It was a day of mist and rain, so thick that two of the machines turned back. The other three had an engagement with a German bi-plane machine, but Lieutenant Puryear ventured on alone in spite of the bad weather. The Hun observer was shot and the pilot forced into a landing. Puryear in the enthusiasm of probable victory followed the German plane down, shooting continuously and thinking himself in Allied territory, landed not far from the wrecked Hun.

The strange experience that was awaiting him had not even occurred to him before, but it happened that the combat had gradually carried him into German territory. As he taxied around the field in his plane he suddenly realised that he might be behind the German lines so he headed his machine around to face the long way of the field and prepared to take off. As he was running up into the wind the machine struck a ditch and nosed over. That gave him something to think about. In the distance behind him and around him, machine guns were snapping, overhead he saw the white puffs from the bursts of other aircrafts' barrage, but still he was undecided as to his location. He jumped from the cockpit of his own machine and hunted around for the other planes. The German pilot in the meantime had pulled his dead observer out of his aircraft and taken him away. A gradual process of assessment convinced Puryear that he was behind the German lines and somewhere near machine gun emplacements.

The first man he saw was an unarmed German who accosted him in a friendly manner. As the man spoke French and wore no helmet, Puryear was suddenly taken with the idea that the man was an Italian. The American asked where he was. The Hun told him civilly the thing that he feared, namely that he was within the German lines and asked him if he were an American officer. Puryear replied that he was, whereupon the German saluted him at attention. A crowd of Germans began to gather about him from various sides, (presumably a German observation balloon had telephoned warning of his descent) and he was taken captive.

He was conducted straightaway to a house, which was being used as an emergency hospital, where he was relieved of his flying suit, belt, goggles and other leather equipment except for his helmet, which was taken later, and searched for firearms. During the search he chatted in English with the officer in charge. From this point he was put through a series of quizzes by Intelligence Officers who sought to enhance their knowledge of Allied aviation through all sorts of questions. Four different times he was quizzed and on each occasion in a separate office, but of all the questions the only one he considered to have any particular importance was the inquiry as to where his aerodrome was located.

After these inquisitions he was placed with two hundred prisoners, (including two French Officers) in a temporary concentration camp, where he was given his first German meal. The meal consisted of old German bread, sodden and stiff like a piece of bacon, and so unappetising that he was unable to eat it although it was then about noon and he had had nothing but a cup of coffee since the time when he tumbled out of bed in the morning and started from his aerodrome at 05:00 am. Thus he hungered until six o'clock in the evening when a German soldier in the guardhouse gave him some barley soup and some horsemeat, which his fatigue from marching flavoured sufficiently for him to call it good. There was here a private who was a German/American, quite familiar with Broadway and Brooklyn Bridge. The Hun treated him quite well, but food was scarce and unappetising. That night as he looked outside he estimated his chances of getting away and though he did nothing at that time, he first began to make his plans for escape which culminated in the bold venture of 6 October that opened the way to freedom.

The next morning he was taken along for an all-day march on a meal of so-called coffee, made from brown barley, and some unappetising bread. Upon reaching another town he was engaged by a third in the series of German Intelligence Officers who, after questioning him, told him in English that he would now be conducted to his 'room and bath'. The 'room and bath' were found to be an old barn with an insufficient layer of straw gathered in one corner. Here he seated himself and fed himself jam and bread, potato bread type which Puryear characteristically referred to as a 'clod of dirt', and finally went to sleep with a chill creeping up his back.

The following day he joined a large detachment of prisoners, which included four hundred French and eighty British, mostly Hospital Corps men, and twenty-eight Americans who had been captured from the 26th and 42nd Divisions during the Château-Thierry fight. The march to Laon that followed was one fraught with discomfort and suffering for many of the men. Puryear, although still possessing his officer's suit with insignia, was lightly clad and during the night of the 28th would have suffered much but for the generosity of a British Hospital Corps soldier who gave him food and a blanket. To add to his difficulties his shoes wore through during the long tramp and his feet became sore. It was during this trip he first made the acquaintance of Adjutant Andre Conneau, a French pilot, with whom he was to make his first attempt to escape. The next day, which was the third on starvation rations of soup and bread, they took a train into Germany, starting at 05:00 a.m. and arriving net day at 23:00 p.m. at Rastatt, Baden, where they were quartered in an old fortress overnight, and then introduced at the Friedrichsfeste camp.

The treatment of the prisoners on this long trip was one to aggravate them and beat down the morale. On the way Lieutenant Puryear made company with 1st Lieutenant Zenos Miller, who had been a pilot in the 27th Aero Squadron of his own Group, and with the following Lieutenants: Willard Bushey, Crawford J. Ferguson, H.W. Shea and Oats. Between them the men continually complained, 'kicked', swore and precipitated arguments with the more conservative members of the group as the philosophy of accepting the hardships of war with equanimity. About them the men saw German wounded lying without care, as if they were so many dead horses, a country savagely devastated by the wastes of war, British captive soldiers, starved, pale and unshaven, toiling for the Huns behind their lines, brutally discriminated against, and a few solemn looking French civilians. The atmosphere was anything but encouraging.

At the camp at Rastatt they first received passable food, which came through the British Red Cross. This food was distributed, after being inspected and checked by the Germans, by an American prisoner designated to issue it according to his own methods. At this point they discovered that they were only 160 kilometres from the Swiss border, and already strongly urged by a desire for freedom, Lieutenant Puryear made a mental calculation of the number of days travel that would be necessary to carry him to the border in case he should escape. He estimated that he could do it from seven to thirteen days. On the following day he discovered an easy way to get out of the camp. The method, so far as the writer knows, still remains a secret in the minds of those who employed it. As Lieutenant Puryear gave this story to the interviewer prior to the Armistice, he desired to keep secret the means of escape in order that he might do nothing that would reveal to the Germans how a number of Americans found their way out of Rastatt prison. Puryear decided to couple his chances with those of Conneau the Frenchman who, he said, looked mean, hard and game enough to do anything, and together they planned escape. Lieutenant Puryear depended upon Conneau, who appeared to have considerable knowledge of the country over which they were about to travel, and the only preparations which he personally made were to borrow a substantial pair of shoes from a British Captain to replace his own, which were in a very dilapidated condition. On August 5 at 11:30 p.m., Lieutenant Puryear succeeded in making his escape unnoticed. He preceded to a prearranged spot where he waited for an hour and a half, until after the next change of guard, when Conneau appeared. Together they started on their journey. The Frenchman had a map and compass that they used to guide them, and a heavy French leather and fur coat, which he loaned to Puryear from time to time to warm him. After a few hours they entered the Black Forest. About two o'clock it had commenced to rain, and from that moment, it seemed that the heavens never ceased to cast a deluge upon the fugitives. During three nights of travel there were about three hours when it was not raining hard. During the daytime they hid in the forest, resting on the Frenchman's coat, trying to snatch moments of sleep, but no sooner would they fall asleep than it would commence to rain, and they would have to take the coat from under them and crouch beneath it, using it as shelter from the rain. The Frenchman was a true comrade, and gave Lieutenant Puryear a full share of what he had. Under such circumstances they finally invented the method of thatching themselves in for the day with branches leaned against a tree, a method that succeeded in turning the rain.

After resting by day they would start at 10:30 p.m., when darkness had fallen, and travel onward.

Conneau however was mistaken in his direction and bore too much to the West, with the result that they found themselves on the second day still at the edge of the forest, with peasants working quite near them in the fields. Again on the next night they erred and at 3 a.m. on 8 August they came out on the banks of the Rhine. Realizing that they were off their course, they took a small road southward and just as they were intending to stop for the day at 4 a.m., they walked into a German sentry on duty. They knew the Rhine was well guarded and the troop concentrations thick, and they were so fatigued and discouraged that they made no attempt to run from the guard. The Hun turned them into the guardhouse, where they were equipped with blankets and passed a good night in rest. They found that they had been captured fifty kilometres from Rastatt and now, after being rudely thrust into cells for a night's rest at Kehl, they were sent straight to Rastatt. Without any quiz or trial they were sent into confinement for five nights and transferred to Rastatt. Puryear was searched and relieved of his helmet. This left him without a hat. The Commanding Officer of the camp questioned him closely as to his escape and Lieutenant Puryear disclosed everything except the means he had used to get out. Within a short time he was sent with fifteen other American officers to Landshut, Bavaria, where he was assigned to the old castle on the hill north east of the town that had been set-aside as a concentration prison for American aviation officers. There were eighteen of them there, ten of whom were Major Harry M. Brown and his pilots and observers of the 96th Aero Squadron, who had been captured on July 10 after an unsuccessful bombing expedition in thick weather. The newly arrived captives were quarantined and inoculated for cholera, typhoid and small pox.

The food here was good but scarce. They received meat once a day and white flour twice a week, occasionally pancakes and although the Red Cross food was excellent they found it scarce. There were no special facilities for entertainment and the days dragged. Under such conditions the minds of the officers were often turned towards the chance of escape, but it was 240 kilometres to the Swiss border, and this combined with the approach of fall and its cold nights, were strong persuasion against attempts to escape.

It was a congenial group however. Among the officers who were there were 1st Lieutenant Carlisle (Dusty) Rhodes, also of the 95th Aero Squadron, who had been reported dead, but had come down in a vrille [spin] in Germany, unhurt; Lieutenants H.F. Wardle, Herbert Smith, James E. Lewis, George Ratterman and Captain James Norman Hall who had previously been reported dead, and was the first American Officer captured by the Germans, all of whom Puryear had known. To pass away the time the men played cards, and an occasional package from home, received through the Red Cross, added to the comfort of all. The Commanding Officer of the prison camp was reported by Lieutenant Puryear as being one of the worst of the Huns, a man of mean disposition who 'bawled them out' in German every day by the clock, had their shoes taken away every night at eight p.m. and counted them in their beds with the guard. In spite of this some of the officers planned an escape, details of which are given elsewhere, and succeeded in getting out by cutting through the wooden wall, but they were recaptured.

Puryear's mind was still bent on escape, but he was wiser than to attempt it here. He applied therefore for a transfer to the prison at Villengen. There was in the employment of the Germans, a civilian by the name of Pasteur, who had been married to an American girl and who owned property in New York. He was apparently the intermediary between the prisoners and the Germans, and carefully reminded them: 'I am a German, be careful what you say'. Through this individual Lieutenant Puryear made his application for transfer early in September. Major Brown was also transferred. Another Lieutenant who had a hole cut through his wall preferred to remain and take his chances of escape. 1st Lieutenant Carlisle Rhodes, who was in the group that had left Landshut, pretended that he was sick and escaped from the train, whereupon, when Lieutenant Puryear actually became ill, he got no sympathy and nothing but 'hell' from the guards. Lieutenant Rhodes was later recaptured. Lieutenant Puryear and the party, after two days in stuffy cars, during which the German guards exercised the strictest rules, forcing them to keep their shoes off, giving them no food for one and half days and allowing them to go to the toilet only every five hours, arrived at Villengen. This was a new American Officers camp, fair according to the general standard, but better than others as it developed. It was September 15th when they arrived. The food supplied by the Red Cross was good and the clothing sufficient. After four or five days Puryear was informed by an interpreter that he had some good news for him. The news was that he was entitled to fourteen days solitary confinement for his previous escape and since he had served only five of the days he would be given the pleasure of nine more days in jail. From September 20th to the 29th, he spent the time in a six feet by 12 feet cell, with nothing but a bed, table and chair, with a small window above him that let in a few rays of the sun.

He was released on the 29th and by the 6th October he had escaped from the camp. In the interim he did considerable figuring. It was thirty-six kilometres in a direct line to the Swiss border, but to the point to which he later tramped and crossed into Switzerland it was sixty-five kilometres, and he estimated that he must have tramped a hundred kilometres in order to reach it.

But to return to the plans for escape. The Americans had determined upon concerted action, and decided that they would select a night and all attempt to escape from the camp at several points at the same time. Two of them were in such hurry that eleven others altered their plans and agreed to the same night rather than have their own chances spoiled by the special measures of discipline which would follow any one attempt. They waited for three nights for plans to develop before making the dash for freedom. Puryear had equipped himself with a hand-drawn map, made by a fellow captive, and with a small compass purchased from a Russian Officer at a price of one stack of coffee, one box of Red Cross meat, one package of hard-tack and an O.D. army shirt, the total of which looked like a million dollars to the Russian.

The men had carefully studied the defence of the camp. The barracks were located in an enclosure of about 800 by 200 meters, which was surrounded by a high board fence peaked with barbed wire. Outside of that was a wire fence, and still further on a ditch set with barbed wire entanglements. The main wire fence was about nine feet tall and on the inside was fastened with iron hooks intended to prevent persons from climbing over it. Both inside and outside the camp powerful electric lights and posts of guards of about one hundred German soldiers, men of some age and limited vigour, were set over the two hundred Russians and seventy-seven Americans confined there.

On the night of October 6th as stated, thirteen Americans were waiting impatiently, bent on escape. At 11:15 p.m. the lights flickered and went out (they had been short-circuited by an accomplice who had thrown chains across the wires at an agreed signal). Apparently there had been some suspicion among the Germans, who were prepared for the trouble, nevertheless the Americans made their rush from four different points of the camp. The extinguishing of the lights was a signal for action. Three of the men, including Puryear, had posted themselves in a barracks window on the south side. As the lights went out they pulled from the window its iron grating, which in advance had been carefully cut with a file, and Puryear jumped through to the ground.

Before this time they had constructed a 14ft ladder from bed slats, the rungs of which had been fastened in place with wire in the absence of screws. Puryear pulled the ladder through the window and placed it against the fence while Lieutenant Ticknor, a fellow captive, braced it at the bottom. By climbing to the top of this ladder it was possible to jump and clear the main fence, the low fence and the barbed wire ditch, in one leap. It was a starlight night, but dark. As Puryear scrambled up the ladder it squeaked and aroused the suspicion of the guard, who was but ten steps away. 'Halt', the German guard cried. Puryear was at the top of the ladder. 'Halt', came the warning cry again. The American jumped, got to his feet and dodged behind a tree four paces away. The guard had seen him before he sought protection of the tree. A second guard was approaching about thirty paces away. Puryear figured that he could not keep one tree between himself and two guards very long, but a desire to play fair and to still leave a chance for his accomplice who had not yet jumped from the ladder made him remain a moment in his place of hiding. Suddenly he ran past but eight feet from the guard. The stolid German followed his instructions and challenged him twice before shooting. The first time the fugitive was three steps away, by the time he could shout again Puryear was ten paces beyond and running a zig-zag course. The German fired and missed. Another shot from the other guard. The bullet whizzed by him in the darkness. On he sped until at length, just as both guns fired again, he stumbled into a ditch, which in the excitement he had forgotten.

'Forgetting about that ditch probably saved my life,' said Lieutenant Puryear later. 'The Hun thought he had winged me and immediately turned towards the others who were breaking out on every side. There was all kinds of excitement, guns were firing and men were shouting. I heard two more shots behind me, kept on running until my breath gave out about a quarter of a mile away. I went to a prearranged spot where we were to meet, and waited for fifteen minutes, during which time there were about fifty shots exchanged, I should judge. No one came, so I got down on my knees, prayed for luck and started off.'

In his travels toward Switzerland Lieutenant Puryear used the tiny compass that he had received from the Russian. Realising that he would be travelling by night and that it would be difficult to get his directions in the dark, he had contrived to make the compass points visible by scraping the phosphorescent material from the face of his wristwatch and applying it to the compass needle. By this means he was able to travel in the dark and still keep himself constantly appraised of his direction. Frequently he would hear Germans approaching on the road, whereupon he would step off and into the woods to avoid them, as he was travelling in a Russian coat and cap which formed a distinctive silhouette against the sky. One man, who caught him unawares, spoke to him in passing and Puryear replied 'Gute Nacht' in his best German.

The journey to the border was without unusual incident. On the night of Thursday, October 10, he came out south of Walshut about 11 p.m. Believing he was near the Swiss border, he climbed the mountain to assure himself, having seen a picture of the town. The only element between him and freedom was the Rhine. It was only 200m across but the current was flowing at a speed of several miles an hour and Lieutenant Puryear had not been in the water for two years. He selected a point near a bend where the current would assist in carrying him to the other shore. Then he went into the woods, stripped off all garments but his underclothes and breeches, and gradually crept down to the bank, shedding a garment every few feet. At 5.30 a.m. he sprang into the river and swam it. It was about a fifteen minute job, but the swift current was so great that eddies and whirlpools pushed him about and very nearly exhausted him before he reached the other side. He crept up the bank, stared back into Germany and cursed it. Several peasants approached, took him into their home and gave him food and clothing and he was later assisted by the American Red Cross.

Lieutenant Puryear was the first American Officer to escape from Germany according to available records, but was preceded by three days by an American private.

In general he regarded his treatment in Germany as fair. Men were paid sixty marks a month by the German government, but had to spend fifty-two of this for mess and with the balance they could only buy two mugs of poor German beer.

'It was an experience,' he said, 'which I am glad I had, but could not go through again voluntarily.'

5. LIEUTENANT COLONEL JAMES LANGLEY, MBE, MC

WHEN LIEUTENANT JAMES Langley's batman, Guardsman Birks, woke him up on 10 May 1940, saying that Germany had invaded France, Holland and Belgium, little did Langley know that this was to be the start of a series of events that would affect him for the rest of his life. Two days later the 2nd Battalion Coldstream Guards moved to take up a defensive position north-east of Brussels on the bank of the River Dyle. Within days they were experiencing their first taste of the fighting with sporadic sniping coming from the Germans on the opposite bank. At the same time they were trying to deal with the constant stream of civilian refugees crossing the bridge. However, with the increase in the fighting, the order was given to blow the crossing.

Further down the bank the British discovered a small château that overlooked the river, giving them a clear view of any movement on the opposite riverbank. This proved to be crucial when they spotted four pairs of Germans each carrying a stretcher, over which a Red Cross flag was draped. As they neared the river the flags were removed and four black objects started to inflate – rubber boats. British Bren guns opened fire from the château and all four boats and their crews were destroyed in a hail of withering fire. The Germans then opened up with field guns and a number of direct hits on the château forced the British to withdraw.

The withdrawal was greater than at first thought and the troops were told that they were going home via Dunkirk. Langley's No. 15 Platoon was then told that they were to be the rearguard action. They took up position in a cottage on the side of a canal and for the next few days watched streams of British and French troops heading towards the beaches of Dunkirk. Throughout the following days and night there were continuous raids by the Luftwaffe, bombing and strafing the beaches. The Germans were advancing all the time and shelling the cottage. Then one morning there was a mighty explosion as a shell ripped through the roof and Langley was thrown across the room. As he came to, a stretcher-bearer arrived and applied a dressing to his shattered arm and dressed his other wounds. He was taken to the beach, but because he was a stretcher case and took up the space for four men, he was returned to what was left of the cottage. Within hours of being there Germans appeared at the gate, so Langley asked to be carried out on the stretcher to meet them. The leader gave Jimmy a drink of water and offered him a cigarette. He asked if Jimmy was an Offizier and when told the he was, saluted and moved on – Langley was now a prisoner of war.

Langley was taken to a large hospital at Zuydcoote, near Calais, which was ostensibly a hospital for children with tuberculosis. There his wounds were dressed properly and for the next few days was looked after. After being transferred to the British ward of the hospital the wound to his arm became infected and he was told that it had become gangrenous and would have to be taken off. The British Army surgeon who performed the operation later told him that he had left enough of his arm so that he could tuck his evening paper under it.

With the fall of France, conditions in the hospital deteriorated and the British officers were moved to another camp at Lille occupied by the French. Among the officers who went with Langley was Major Oswald Phipps (Lord Normanby) of the Green Howards Regiment. The British officers were treated like criminals by the German guards and the French sergeant in charge of the kitchens told Langley, when he complained, that he had been instructed by the Germans that British officers were to be served last. This sometimes meant that by the time they got to the serving point there was no food left. With only water to drink and no food, and the sanitary facilities non-existent, things started to look bleak for the British officers. After a couple of days of this treatment, Major Phipps suddenly went ballistic and berated the German guards in fluent German. It turned out that Phipps's uncle had been the British Ambassador to Germany and that Phipps had lived there for some years and had learned the language.

The German guards, who had been subjected to this ferocious verbal attack, sent for the Kommandant, who in turn was told in no uncertain manner about the treatment to the British officers. Within an hour, Langley and Phipps were transferred to a French convent near Roubaix that had been turned into a temporary prison hospital for French naval officers. On their arrival they were greeted by one of the nuns and then told that more than half the French fleet had been sunk at Mers El Kébir in Algeria, with the loss of 1,300 French sailors, by the Royal Navy to prevent it falling into German hands. The atmosphere in the convent, which was full of French naval officers, was extremely hostile to say the least, and both the British officers feared for their safety. Then the senior French naval officer intervened and warned the other officers that the two British officers were to be treated with respect or they would answer directly to him. The British officers were moved a week later, but until that time they were treated with respect.

The two officers were taken to the Faculté Catholique of Lille University, which was an assessment centre for British wounded. Here German doctors decided whether or not the wounded could be sent on to POW camps or their injuries so bad that they could be repatriated back to England via Switzerland.

Examinations were carried out and the assessments made every three weeks. During one assessment one British officer complained that he could not lift his right arm above his shoulder because of a bullet wound. The German doctor, a stern-faced man, took a large bar of chocolate from his pocket and said to the assembled British officers and men that the first person to catch this bar of chocolate with his right hand could keep it. He then threw it in the air and the officer who had earlier complained about being unable to lift his arm caught it neatly as it sailed over his head. The German doctor roared with laughter, pointed at him and said, 'You will go to Germany, and you can keep the chocolate.'

When it came to Langley's turn to be assessed he was told that for him the war was over and that he was to be repatriated to Switzerland as soon as it could be arranged. Life at the hospital at Faculté Catholique was half prison, half hospital with a certain amount of freedom allowed. A number of incidents occurred during the following weeks, but one was particularly serious and was to have a profound effect on him. Some of the French women from the nearby town would throw small food parcels over the walls for the prisoners and had been warned on a number of occasions not to do so. Langley remembered with horror and disgust the moment when he was talking to an English-speaking German officer and rapid gunfire erupted suddenly. The German guards had repeatedly lost their temper with the women, who chose to ignore the warnings, and opened fire, killing a number of them and wounding many others. Langley looked at the German officers with contempt, turned on his heels and walked away. The officer could not understand why such an incident should cause Langley to react in such a way.

As the number of wounded prisoners dwindled, the food parcels, which up to now had been 'pooled', were now being given out individually. Also, a number of the more seriously wounded were 'adopted' by what became known as 'War Godmothers'. These were local French women who sent food and other necessary items to the prisoners in an effort to help ease their position. Madame Caron, who was one of the cleaners on the wards and the wife of the local gendarme, 'adopted' Langley. Her husband regarded his wife's support for the British with scepticism, and with some trepidation, knowing the Germans' attitude to fraternisation with the enemy. Every evening she would arrive with a cooked meal for him, and as Langley remembers, she never failed to provide him with good substantial food for the whole of the time he was at the hospital.

Then on 30 September word came down that the Germans were going to move *all* the prisoners to Enghien, Belgium, and from there to Germany. As his health improved and he got stronger, Langley looked towards planning his escape. He had decided that when he did he would do it alone, as he would travel faster by himself without having to worry about a companion. The concern was which route to take. The Germans controlled the countries from Norway to the Pyrenees, with the exception of Sweden, Switzerland and Portugal, all of which were neutral. The closest British soil that could be reached without crossing the sea was Gibraltar, and that was more than 1,000 miles away. To get there he would have to travel through 500 miles of hostile territory into Spain and 500 miles through Spain to Gibraltar. Although Spain was deemed to be neutral, General Franco, who had taken over the country just prior to the war, had done so with the help of Germany. So there were very strong pro-German sympathies within Spain's government, but within the Basque population many anti-Franco factions. It was these factions that were instrumental in helping to run the escape routes through Spain itself.

In October 1940 Langley approached Madame Caron and told her of his plan to escape, asking if she could hide him for a few days. She refused, saying that her husband would not agree to this, but she would find a safe house for him, which she duly did. Langley started to make preparations for his escape. That same evening two British officers escaped and Langley realised that if he were to go he had to do it the next day while there was a state of confusion. Madame Caron produced the address of a safe house, a password that would ensure his safety when he reached it and a map of Lille.

He had already found the safest point from which to leave, which was a porter's lodge used as a guardhouse during the day but for some unknown reason left empty at night. Langley collected his bits and pieces together: £30 in French francs, a small torch, twenty cigarettes in his silver cigarettes case, a box of matches and a couple of dirty handkerchiefs. An RAMC corporal agreed to help him. The man spoke fluent French and often used to slip into town for a drink and a liaison with a French girl via the porter's lodge. The corporal also provided some additional bandages for Langley's stump, which was still in the process of healing.

That night Langley, making use of the shadows, slipped out of his room and entered the porter's lodge where the corporal was waiting. The German guards were chatting up some of the local girls and were oblivious to what was going on. Langley climbed up onto the windowsill with the help of the corporal, clambered through the window and dropped the 12ft onto the ground. After making sure that no one had heard him, Langley examined his map of the town and headed towards it. He had memorised the map and the position of the safe house. On reaching the town he found the house and knocked on the door; three knocks, a ten-second pause followed by two knocks.

The door was partially opened by a young woman, who took his hand and pulled him inside. He was led into a room where a short elderly man, his wife and another young girl were seated. They smiled and welcomed him with a glass of wine, followed by a delicious omelette. They told him that two other officers had been there the night before and were now on their way with the help of the Resistance. Because there was a great deal of German activity in the town, and a number of houses had been searched, arrangements had been made for him to sleep in the upstairs part of a bombed-out house next door.

The next morning another young woman arrived carrying a bundle of clothes, all of which had seen better days. The main bulk of the clothes consisted of a shoddy black suit, which smelt strongly of cheese. The girl took him through Lille, where they boarded a tram, and then onto the village of Ascq, where she left him after giving him the address of another safe house. This turned out to be the home of the village priest, whose main worry was that the Luftwaffe band were billeted in the village and a large number of them were Roman Catholic. Consequently, they all turned up for mass in his church.

After several days in the village, Langley was returned to Lille, where he was once again taken to a safe house, this time on the outskirts of the town. Madame Samiez, who owned the house, hated the Germans with a vengeance. It was said that whenever she went shopping she always carried at least four German stick grenades hanging from her undergarments, which were covered by a voluminous skirt, and she had two Mills bombs in her shopping basket. It was also said that on more than one occasion she had dropped hand grenades over railway bridges onto German trains. She made no secret of her dislike for the Germans and was extremely vociferous on occasion. The problem with staying with such a person was that it heightened the risk of being discovered, as the Germans had made many searches of her house. However, somehow she managed to stay one step ahead and during the war hid many Allied soldiers and airmen.

Two days later a middle-aged man arrived to collect Langley and put him on a train to Paris. On the train he was introduced to a man called Georges, who was to be his guide, and two more escapees, both very large Scotsmen. The rule at the time was that civilians were not allowed on the train until all the Germans had embarked and were seated. The train was packed and Langley had to stand until it reached Amiens, where fortunately the majority of the Germans got off. On reaching Paris, Georges took the three men via the Metro to a safe hotel on the Left Bank. What became apparent was that almost all the couriers who guided evaders and escapees never revealed their names and remained 'faceless' people throughout the war.

The guide told them that the 'Old Comrades Association of the 1914–1918 War' would handle their escape, and they were to go to their offices, only to find them shut down by the Geheime Staatspolizie (Gestapo). On the door was a sign that said that any information regarding the association was to be made at the commandant's office of the local gendarmerie. They made their way to his office and explained their position. The commandant told them in no uncertain manner that he was not prepared to help them in any way and if they did not leave his office right away he would call the Germans and hand them over.

The three men returned to the safe hotel and explained their predicament to Georges. It was decided to contact Madame Samiez, as she was in contact with the Resistance organisation. A postcard was sent saying that all her friends were away and she did not know of any others they could call on. The reply that came back a few days later shocked them to the core. In big, bold letters, the postcard read in English:

AWAIT THE PASSWORD. HELP WILL COME. LONG LIVE THE ALLIES.

How the postcard slipped through without being spotted was a total mystery; one can only assume that the French postal workers concealed it somehow. Immediately plans were drawn up to move to the other side of the city. The three men then went to a small town called Romorantin, where Langley had been given the address of a friend of Madame Samiez who might be able to shelter them. It was at this point that Langley began to feel depressed and isolated. He was on the run in a foreign country, speaking and understanding very little of the language and just hanging around waiting for someone to help him. In addition, his two companions spoke no French, had Scottish accents that were so strong that sometimes even he could barely understand them, and they both stood out like sore thumbs because of their height.

Unable to find the woman's house, Langley and Georges approached the home of the parish priest and asked for directions. He knew the woman and thought that she was away, but said he would go and find out as it was unsafe to go out without proper documents. He returned saying the house was empty and because of the activity of Germans in the area Langley ought to return to Paris.

For the next few days the escapees stayed in their hotel, only venturing out occasionally during the day. Then on the fourth day word came that arrangements had been made to get them out of Paris. They were to go to the Gare d'Austerlitz at 6.45 a.m., where they should look for a man dressed in a black suit with a red handkerchief in his top pocket and carrying a newspaper. Langley was to approach the man and whisper the word 'Mozart' and then follow him out of the station. He would be given four tickets, and the four men would board the train for Bourges.

Entering the station, he saw the man waiting, but before he could say anything the man grasped him by the elbow and ushered him outside. Handing him the tickets, he explained that they were to board the train one at a time but to enter the same carriage. As the train pulled away from the station, James Langley felt a mixture of relief and trepidation. At Vierzon the train was stopped and everyone ordered off. At first it was thought that there was going to be a thorough search of the train, but then it was discovered that the French and German border officials had not arrived. Vierzon was the checking point for those people travelling on into unoccupied France. At Bourges the four men and their guide got off. The three escapees and Georges walked around the town until evening, when their guide established contact with other members of the Resistance and a lorry arrived to take them on to the border.

The lorry stopped at a café just 500 yards away from the border. The men entered the café, only to find it almost full of Germans. They were border guards, and it appeared that the guide knew most of them and appeared to be on friendly terms. After a few glasses of wine the four men settled down uncomfortably to wait for dark. Their guide did not seem to be fazed in the slightest with the German border guards, and joined in singing with them as more and more wine was consumed. As darkness started to descend the guards left and fifteen minutes later the guide took the escapees outside, where Langley discovered that they were not to be the only ones making the crossing into unoccupied France. It appeared that the guide also ran a rather lucrative business guiding people across for a fee – 1,000 francs per head. The group headed out some distance behind the German border patrol that had left some twenty minutes earlier. After crossing a field, they crawled under a hedge, into a ditch and then under a barbed-wire fence and into 'Free France', as one of the party exclaimed.

After spending the night in a local hotel, which had been pre-arranged by the Resistance, the four men caught the train for Lyon. On arrival, Langley went to see the American Consul, George Whittinghill, who looked after British affairs when no British Consul was available. The Consul admitted that he could not help personally, but he knew a man who could and Langley was invited to return to the embassy the following day to meet him. The following day Langley was introduced to Raoul Beaumine, who immediately told him that he had known his father. Beaumine then told him that his name had appeared on a Red Cross list of officers who had been wounded or were missing. The Red Cross had made enquiries and was told that he had been a POW but had escaped and was now on the run.

Beaumine then said that there were two ways out – through France, over the Pyrenees and into Spain, or to Switzerland. Before he could answer, Georges, who had arrived soon after Langley, intervened saying that he had another escapee outside. So it was decided to toss a coin for whoever went where, as Beaumine could only take one person with him back to Switzerland. The coin was tossed and Langley lost – he would have to go through France and into Spain.

Beaumine gave him the name and address of a family in Vichy who would be able to help him. He also gave him an address in Marseille, the Seaman's Mission, where his other two companions could find help and where he would go later. Langley and the other escapees headed for Vichy to await preparations for them to be spirited away through the Resistance underground. It has to be remembered that Langley now only had one arm and what was left of that still needed regular dressing changes and attention.

After ten days of waiting, word came and Langley headed for Marseille, while his former companions headed towards Lyon and Switzerland. Marseille was the only unoccupied port in France from which ships sailed to the French colonies and other parts on a regular basis. It was also the most crime-ridden city in Europe and was controlled in the main by gangsters. The local gendarmerie paid lip service to any loyalty to the Vichy government and was corrupt. Marseille was flooded with refugees trying to leave the country and was a hotbed for spies and informers of all nationalities.

Langley made his way to the Seaman's Mission, which was run by the Reverend Donald Caskie. The mission had started life as a club for British seamen when they entered port, but with the war no more British ships came. The Reverend Caskie had been the Presbyterian Minister of the Scottish Church in Paris but after the city had fallen had made his way to Marseille. He had reopened the mission there, where it was used to house and help refugees, evaders and escapees, and later used as a cover for escape organisations. After spending just an hour in the Mission, Langley decided it was not safe to discuss any escape plans as he suspected there were informers among the people staying there. He gave himself up to the gendarmerie by reporting to the guard on the gate of Fort St-Jean. This had once been the recruiting fortress for the famous French Foreign Legion, and had its motto carved over the entrance:

LEGIONNAIRES, YOU ASK FOR DEATH. I WILL GIVE IT TO YOU.

On entering the prison, Langley discovered that there were fifteen other British officers who had given themselves up. All were waiting for the Resistance to get them to the frontier with Spain and, hopefully, over the Pyrenees. The officers were allowed to come and go as often as they pleased providing they were present for the roll call on Monday mornings. Other ranks were confined to the prison, but British ingenuity prevailed and they regularly spent the evenings in Marseille via an escape route through the latrines.

The latrines were basically a recess cut into the outer wall that in turn led to a tunnel, which was cleaned by means of the tide as it rose and fell. An iron bar across the hole served as a seat and by tying a rope to the bar the prisoners, after placing their clothes in a waterproof bag, could lower themselves into the sewer tunnel that led to the sea. They then swam to the nearest jetty and climbed out, the swim having washed away most, if not all the sewage. They returned the same way.

After spending a week at the fort, Langley decided to take a room at a small hotel. As long as he turned up every Monday morning for roll call, there was no problem. In fact, the commandant used to issue a week's rations to all the officers and let them get on with it.

As the days passed it became obvious that to try to get over the Pyrenees in winter would be foolhardy to say the least. In Langley's case, as a *motile de guerre* (disabled serviceman) it would be doubly difficult climbing over the mountains with only one arm. He could be repatriated if he passed a medical board and be declared unfit for military service, so he decided to wait it out for this to happen.

Having decided that this was the simplest and obvious way out for him, Langley looked into different methods of aiding other, more able-bodied evaders and escapees to evade capture. Increasing pressure was being put upon the Vichy French government by the Germans to prevent escapees making it out of France via Marseille. There was no organised escape organisation as such in place at the time, as most escapes were made in pairs with the help of members of the French Resistance. What was needed was an organised network where co-ordination and control was the order of the day. A network of safe houses needed to be set up close to the border with Spain where escapees and evaders could rest prior to the arduous trip over the Pyrenees. One of these was a small French farmhouse in the Pyrenean foothills owned by Madame Kattalin Aguirre. Here escapees and evaders rested before making the dangerous and arduous trip over the mountains. Madame Aguirre was later denounced and sent to a concentration camp, but fortunately survived and returned to her family after the camp was liberated by American troops.

Two apartments owned by Dr Rodocanachi and Louis Nouveau were the main safe houses in Marseille, although there were a number of others that could be used in an emergency. Such was the secrecy surrounding the safe houses that Rodocanachi and Nouveau, although good friends, never knew that each other's apartment was being used by the escape line.

Forged papers and documents had to be made, civilian clothes obtained and more and more safe houses found in Marseille itself. Alternative methods of escape had to be considered and one of these was by sea. After all, there were a number of ships flying flags of neutrality and conveniently visiting the port on a regular basis. One of the biggest problems facing evaders was the language barrier. Those who did speak some French rarely knew enough to convince anyone that they were actually nationals. Some of the evaders volunteered to stay in France and help set up an escape organisation, but in order to do so only fluent French speakers would be of any use. There were, however, exceptions to the rule, such as Captain Ian Garrow of the Seaforth Highlanders.

In the formative years, a Captain Murchie had headed up the escape committee, but when he made his escape over the Pyrenees, he handed the mantle of responsibility to Garrow. Garrow had reached Marseille ay the end of 1941, after his 51st Division had been overrun at St-Valery-en-Caux. He spoke very little French, was tall and rangy, and looked every inch a Scotsman. How he managed to evade capture was a mystery, but he had an air of authority and confidence around him all the time, and appeared to be unfazed whatever the situation. Another of these 'exceptions' was a fighter pilot called Mike Maloney, whose aircraft had been shot down over northern France. He had been captured and interrogated after some days on the run, but had managed to escape and make his way to Marseille. The three men, Langley, Garrow and Maloney, sat down and discussed the possibilities of setting up an escape committee through which evaders could be helped.

Then news came through that the Mixed Medical Commission, as it was known, was to sit and decide who was unfit or fit. The unfit were to be repatriated. Those who were deemed to be borderline cases were warned by the American Consul General that the medical examination was going to be thorough. Three days before the examinations, the men started depriving themselves of sleep and going on drinking sessions that would leave them with the mother of all hangovers. They did not wash or shave and rubbed their wounds until red and inflamed. In short, they looked like human wrecks by the time they appeared in front of the medical board, which consisted of six doctors, two nominated by the Americans, two by the Swiss and two by the Vichy government. One of the doctors on the board was Dr Rodocanachi, so Langley had one ally when he appeared.

One week later came the news that all those who had been assessed had passed the board and were to be repatriated, including Langley. Langley's stump was still giving him cause for concern, so he approached a French doctor for help. Although it was an offence to give aid to an evader, the doctor grudgingly agreed. He was very rough in his treatment and when offered payment for his services, he refused. When Langley commented on how rough the doctor had been while treating and dressing the wound, the doctor replied that he had meant to be. He said he loathed the British because they had killed his grandfather at the Battle of Trafalgar and stolen a number of French colonies. When asked why then had he bothered to help him, the doctor replied that he hated the Germans even more than he hated the British and would help anyone who was fighting them.

The German authorities then put increasing pressure on the Vichy government to clamp down on the security of the port of Marseille, and the freedom experienced by escapees and evaders alike was to end. Even the gangsters who controlled the underworld in Marseille were finding it difficult to operate, although they still seemed to enjoy an unfettered lifestyle. After the war it was discovered that many of the gangsters were also members of the Resistance and they had chosen their way of life to the detriment of the Germans.

The creation of the escape line was greatly helped when Jean-Pierre Nouveau, the son of Louis Nouveau, made a successful escape to Spain over the Pyrenees. With Nouveau in Spain, arrangements were made to recruit guides who knew the mountains. These men had to be available to guide escapees and evaders through the treacherous mountains in all weathers. Among them was a Basque by the name of Florentino Goikoetxea. He was to become the most famous of all the guides, and after the war he was awarded the George Medal, Legion d'honneur and the Croix de Guerre among numerous other medals and awards.

When Langley was repatriated he was immediately contacted by Colonel Norman Crockatt, who wanted his help in setting up escape and evasion lines throughout Europe. The distinction has to be drawn between an escapee and an evader. Escapees were those who had been captured, even for just minutes or hours, and who escaped. Evaders were those who had never been captured and had evaded those who were looking for them.

6. COLDITZ CASTLE

ONE OF THE first escape attempts by British prisoners of war was made on 2 May 1941 from Colditz Castle when two British officers, Lieutenants Peter Allan of the Cameroon Highlanders and John Hyde-Thompson of the Durham Light Infantry, attempted to smuggle themselves out of the camp in two old straw mattresses that were being dumped. The two mattresses were taken from the loft by prisoners and taken into the yard. One of the mattresses was placed on a handcart, while the other was left lying on the stone courtyard. Seeing that the mattress on the ground looked unusually lumpy, one of the guards stepped on it. Feeling something hard beneath his foot, he tore open the mattress cover to find Hyde-Thompson inside. Immediately, guards surrounded the luckless soldier and escorted him to the guardroom. In the confusion that followed, the handcart, with Allan still inside the other mattress, was wheeled out of the gates.

Once outside the camp and in the countryside, Allan waited until the mattress was tipped off the cart onto a rubbish dump, then lay there until dark and made his escape. Travelling mostly by night, Allan, who spoke almost fluent German, made his way through Bohemia and Moravia (formerly part of Czechoslovakia – now the Czech Republic) until he reached Austria. He walked almost the entire way to Vienna, although at one point he scrounged a lift in Bohemia for almost 100 miles, in an SS staff car, until he reached the American embassy in Vienna. America was not in the war at this time, and the consul, who was unsure that he was genuinely an escaped British officer, refused to help and turned him away. The problem that faced the American Consul was that they were aware that the Gestapo used English-speaking provocateurs to try to get the consul to help them. Then, if they did so, the Gestapo would have the excuse to shut down the Consul, claiming that staff were abusing their diplomatic privileges by aiding enemies of Germany.

Totally depressed by this setback and extremely tired and weak from hunger, Allan realised that sooner or later he was going to get caught, and gave himself up to the local police after being stopped and questioned. He was immediately handed over to the military and returned to Colditz. Had he gone to the Swedish embassy there is no doubt that it would have taken him in and helped him escape.

Back in Colditz, escape committees had been formed and a friendly rivalry formed with the other nationalities as to who would get the first escapee away. Like many other POW camps, the influx of inmates brought together not only soldiers and airmen, but also men who had civilian trades such as engineers, locksmiths, tailors, artists, linguists and even criminals. Among the criminal fraternity were thieves, forgers and the like, who had lived most of their lives outside the law and could easily adapt to finding ways to 'acquire' materials and information that would be a great asset to the escape committees.

The first person to successfully escape from Colditz was a French officer by the name of Lieutenant Alain le Ray, who hid in a park during a game of football and slipped away under the cover of darkness. On reaching France, he joined the Resistance for the remainder of the war. The first British officer to make it home was Airey Neave. He and a Dutch officer by the name of Anthony Lutyen dressed in painted German officers' uniforms with cardboard insignias attached, clambered down through a trapdoor beneath a stage, made a hole in the ceiling into a storeroom, then went down the stairs and through the guardroom. Lutyen, who spoke fluent German, chatted non-stop as the pair sauntered out of the guardroom, past the sentries, and walked on to freedom. After returning to England, via Switzerland, Neave became an important part of MI9, and the story of his escape is described later in the book.

Among the British contingent of Colditz Castle was Captain Pat Reid, a notorious escapee. Very soon after arriving at the camp he became involved in the construction of a tunnel being dug by the French, but this was detected. The French Tunnel, as it was known, was constructed in 1941–42. Also known as Le Métro by the British, this was a truly amazing escape attempt. A group of French prisoners known as Société Anonyme du Tunnel, dug a shaft in the clock tower of the castle, tunnelled through a wine cellar, through the oak joints of the chapel and around the walls of the castle itself. The tunnel was started in March 1941 and was discovered by the Germans in January 1942 with less than 10ft to go. During the course of the digging, it is estimated that the tunnellers removed more than 40,000 cubic feet of rubble and managed to secrete it somewhere within the castle itself.

Then on 29 May, one of the most audacious attempts for a massive escape occurred. One of the guards who patrolled the area outside the canteen had been bribed with a promise of 700 marks if he was to turn a 'blind eye' to any activity. He had been given a down payment of 100 marks, but he reported the incident to his superiors and was told to keep up the pretence of going along with the plan. The problem was that the Germans had no idea how the escape was to be made and how many people were involved.

The potential escapees had loosened a drain cover in the floor of the canteen, had entered the drain tunnel, broken through a sidewall and dug a tunnel under the castle wall. The operation had been carried out at night, and had involved picking the locks of the doors leading from a staircase into a yard, and from there through another door into the canteen.

On the night in question, the Germans waited in the guardroom for the escape to be attempted. Searchlights flickered over the terrace beneath the walls of the castle, and the guards watched nervously for the first signs of movement, not knowing where it was to come from. Then there was a slight movement in the grass. Training his binoculars on the spot, the German officer leading the security team saw a square of turf slowly being raised up on a wooden frame. The turf was then placed to one side and the head and shoulders of a man appeared. Guards quickly occupied the canteen from where the escape was being made. While this was going on, the guards outside surrounded the tunnel exit and arrested Reid, the man coming out of the hole in the grass. In all, twelve men – ten British and two Polish – dressed in civilian clothes, with fake identities and carrying money in German marks, were discovered in the tunnel. The guard was allowed to keep the money he had been given as a bribe, promoted and given extra leave.

The escape attempt, although foiled, showed the lengths and ingenuity to which the prisoners would go to gain their freedom. Almost every day ingenious, and some frankly hare-brained, ideas were put before the escape committees and attempts were made almost every month by the French, Dutch or the Poles. The British at the time seemed to be more concerned with the setting up of escapes rather than actually taking part. This, of course, was extremely important, as every escape attempt had to be orchestrated to a certain extent, and required a great deal of planning and the co-operation of the other nationalities in the camp.

There were only three ways of getting out of Colditz: through, over or under the wire or the wall. Going under meant tunnelling, and Colditz was a castle on a hill, so although tunnels were attempted, none were successful. Going over the wire was the most dangerous method of attempting to escape because the escapee could easily be spotted and left exposed. Through the wire or the wall, i.e. hiding in carts or wagons that were delivering goods, or impersonating

someone who was permitted to go in or out of the camp was the most successful of all the methods.

It was left to a French cavalry officer, Lieutenant Pierre Mairesse Lebrun, to
carry out one of the most daring escape attempts. Lebrun attempted his escape
on 9 June 1941, when he hid in the rafters of a pavilion in the local park, where
prisoners were allowed out in small groups. The escape was arranged by using
a very small Belgian officer, who hid beneath the folds of a large comrade's
cloak when they left the camp. Lebrun, who had been counted out with the
others, slipped into the open-sided pavilion that was in the recreation area and
clambered into the rafters. When the group returned, the small Belgian officer
took Lebrun's place when the return headcount was carried out, making the
number tally with the number that had left camp.

Because the escape committee had approved the plan, Lebrun was given
German marks and a number of other escape aids. After waiting for the group
to leave the area, and ensuring that no Germans were hanging around, Lebrun
slipped down from the rafters and headed towards the local railway station.
Dressed in a grey flannel suit, which had somehow been smuggled in to him,
he offered the stationmaster a 100-mark note for a ticket. Unfortunately the
note was an old one that was no longer in circulation. Becoming suspicious,
the stationmaster, together with another member of staff, locked Lebrun into a
room and rang the prison camp.

The Kommandant told him that no one was missing from the camp. In the
meantime, Lebrun had forced open a window and leapt out. Unfortunately he
landed on top of an old woman, who was not well pleased and shouted at him in
no uncertain manner. On hearing the disturbance the stationmaster and some
of his staff chased after him and he was caught. On returning to the camp, the
Kommandant sent him into solitary confinement for a month as a punishment.

After completing this, Lebrun returned to his quarters, even more determined to plan an escape. On the morning of 12 July, he and a small party of
French officers were allowed to walk and exercise in the small park. Some
were playing football, others, like Lebrun were exercising and leapfrogging
over each other. The park was contained within an area surrounded by a 9ft
barbed-wire fence, which in turn was surrounded by a 9ft wall. Lebrun had
figured out that, with the help of fellow officers, he could vault the fence and
then climb the wall. He chose one section of the fence because behind it, by
the wall, was a small wood into which he could quickly disappear from sight.

As the party of French officers was quite small, so was the escorting party.
The guards seemed to take little interest in the officers exercising; they were
more interested in watching the others playing football. Suddenly, Lebrun

sprinted towards the fence, where two of his colleagues waited with their hands linked to form a stirrup. On reaching them, Lebrun placed his foot into their outstretched hands and in one motion, as he leapt, they propelled him upwards and over the fence. On landing, he sprinted towards the wall. The guards had by this time noticed what was happening and raised their rifles. Lebrun realised this and ran backwards and forwards alongside the wall to draw their fire. After firing, the guards stopped to reload and it was at this point that Lebrun scrambled over the wall and into the wood beyond.

He knew that within minutes the area would be crawling with soldiers looking for him. Leaving the wood, he saw a cornfield, and walking backwards into it, pushing the corn upright as did so, he made his way to the centre of the field and lay down. This clever ruse fooled the Germans, and despite them having a spotter plane flying overhead, they failed to spot him. Later that night he set off. Over the next few days he travelled at night and hid for most of the day. After he had covered around 50 miles, he saw a bicycle leaning against the wall of a farmhouse and took it.

Heading for the Swiss frontier, Lebrun pedalled for more than 200 miles, during which he changed his bicycle when his became unusable. When he reached farmhouses, he claimed to be an Italian making his way back to Italy. On another occasion he was spotted by some Germans but managed to make a run for it and escape. Close to the border a German who became very suspicious of him stopped him. Lebrun, realising that he was in trouble, knocked the guard over and hit him with a bicycle pump until he was unconscious.

Entering the woods close to the border he waited, watching the German patrols slowly cruising along the edge. At first he thought that he would be able to time the gaps between the patrols, but then realised that the timing was completely random. Crawling closer and closer to the border, he waited his moment as a patrol passed and disappeared, and then he dashed across and over the border fence.

Giving himself up to the Swiss police, he was taken to the French embassy where arrangements were made to take him via the escape line into France. After going through France he and a guide climbed over the Pyrenees and into Spain. Unfortunately his luck ran out and the police caught him as he travelled through Spain. He was locked in a castle to await his fate, but he jumped from a window into the moat. The fall broke his spine, and had it not been for the French Consul in the area, who insisted that he be given immediate hospital treatment, there is no doubt that he would have died. His war was over, but his escape showed the determination not to give up and that the spirit of the Allies was not going to be broken.

7. LIEUTENANT AIREY NEAVE

ON 24 MAY 1940, Lieutenant Airey Neave and his men found themselves fighting a rearguard battle against overwhelming German forces of the 10th Panzer Division in the town of Calais. Neave was part of the 30th Infantry Brigade, whose job was to try to slow down the German advance on Dunkirk so that the British and Allied soldiers trapped there could be got away. Running from house to house as the German tanks pounded the buildings, Neave realised that this was a hopeless cause, but continued to try to delay the German advance. As he ran across the road, tracer bullets from one of the German tanks followed him and one struck him in the thigh, sending him crashing to the ground.

Dragging himself into the relative shelter of a nearby house, he was picked up by other British soldiers, who took him to a small French hospital for treatment. All that day and the following night he and many other wounded men lay in the cellar of the hospital listening to the almost continuous bombardment of the town. Then, as he heard that the Germans were closing in, despite his painful wound, Neave decided that he was going to make a break for it and, regardless of protestations from the staff, tried to make his way out of the hospital. It was then, and only then, that he realised how seriously wounded he was and that there was no way for him to escape without help.

The offer of help came from a French soldier by the name of Pierre d'Harcourt, a medical orderly who Neave later discovered was a member of a tank regiment that had been decimated by the German Panzers. He had taken on the role of a medical orderly in order to effect an escape when he could. His idea was to substitute Neave with a soldier who had died in the hospital. The driver of the ambulance that took the bodies away for burial was a loyal Frenchman and was more than willing to help.

Unfortunately they discovered that the Germans examined very carefully every body that was being removed. Before any of d'Harcourt's ideas could be put into action, word came through that all wounded prisoners were to be transferred to another hospital at Lille. D'Harcourt decided it was time he left and headed for Paris. Some time later, when Neave returned to England and worked for MI9, he heard that d'Harcourt was helping run an escape line through France and had aided a number of Allied airmen and soldiers to escape.

The wounded from the hospital were placed in German trucks and the convoy headed for Lille. On reaching Bailleul, the truck carrying Neave broke down. The walking wounded were allowed to walk around a small town unaccompanied and at almost every house the door was opened and the men were invited in and offered food and wine. The generosity was overwhelming and, despite the risks, some people even offered to hide them and then help them to escape.

Neave accepted all the townspeople had to offer regarding food and wine, but not the offer to help him escape. He knew that his physical condition at the time would be a serious stumbling block in any attempt and it would probably cost those who helped him their lives if he were to be caught.

With the truck repaired, the journey continued on to the hospital at Lille. Within days of being there a young French nurse offered to help Neave and Corporal Dowling of the Durham Light Infantry to escape. Plans were made to obtain civilian clothes and some French money, but with no travel documents or identity papers it was going to be difficult. Somehow the Germans seemed to get wind of an escape attempt and told all the wounded prisoners, in no uncertain manner, that anyone escaping would cause severe reprisals to be carried out on those left behind. It was the threat of the latter that caused Neave and Dowling to shelve their plans for the time being.

The following week all the walking wounded were collected and the long trek to Germany started. After travelling through Belgium the prisoners were placed in a coal barge and taken up the Sheldt River and then into the River Waal. They passed under the bridge at Nijmegen in Holland, a bridge that was to pass into history some four years later when the 1st Airborne Division was involved in the Battle of Arnhem.

As the barge entered Germany, Neave felt the first pangs of despair, realising that any chance of escape was slowly disappearing with every mile covered by the barge. Two days later they reached the POW camp at Spangenburg near Kassel – Oflag Ix-a. Settling down to recover from his wounds, Neave started to look around at his surroundings with the intention of leaving at the first opportunity. A number of escapes had already been attempted, but none had been successful. In fact, some of the escapees had been captured and severely beaten by local civilians.

The morale among the junior officers was extremely low, mainly because of the negative attitude of some of the senior British officers. They considered that escape attempts were hopeless, disrupted the smooth running of the camp and upset the Germans, who retaliated by issuing meagre rations. However, the non-commissioned ranks in the Stalags, who went on working parties outside the camp, were given additional rations because of their work environment. These men also had access to the outside world and were able to assess the terrain, the roads and railway stations – in short anything that would aid an escape attempt.

Red Cross parcels started to filter through the system, which made life in the camps more bearable and raised morale considerably. Then in February 1941, the prisoners at Spangenburg were moved to an old fortress on the banks of the Vistula, just outside Thorn, Poland. The fortress was damp and cold and the rations barely enough to sustain them. The reason for the transfer was given as retaliation for the alleged ill treatment of German prisoners of war in Canada. This was, of course, total nonsense and was just an excuse to undermine the morale and well-being of the prisoners.

As the train pulled into the station at Thorn, German field police met the prisoners with snarling Alsatian dogs, while searchlights lit up the area brighter than day. Surrounded by tanks, the men were marched to the fortress and deposited in the dark, damp cellars. The conditions were harsh to say the least and the chance for exercise and fresh air were extremely limited. From a possible escape perspective, that fact that they were now in Poland lessened the chance because it was one of those countries of which very little was known at the time.

Neave then discovered that just 3 miles from the fortress was another POW camp, Stalag XX-a, for NCOs and other ranks. Among the inmates were a number of men from his own company who had survived Calais. Working parties from the Stalag came to the fortress every day and it was through them that Neave gradually discovered that there was an escape committee in existence.

The fact that he knew a number of the men personally helped him to devise an escape plan. It was intended that he and Flying Officer Norman Forbes would visit the camp dentist, a British Army officer, whose surgery adjoined the Stalag. They would escape from the surgery and hide in a hut occupied by warrant officers. They had already been approached with the idea and had agreed to help. The two men had obtained civilian clothes from Poles working with the work parties and the intention was that they would slip out with one of these groups.

With the planning in place, the two men, with a number of others, were marched the 3 miles to the dentist's surgery, which also adjoined the Kommandant's office and was opposite the main gate into the compound. The two men went to the surgery, removed their uniforms and slipped into the civilian clothes. They then picked up some bundles of wood and at a given signal walked into the Stalag compound while the other prisoners engaged the guards in conversation. Once inside the compound they were taken to the warrant officers' hut, where they stayed.

The Germans soon realised that two inmates from the fortress were missing and immediately started searching for them outside, not realising that they were hiding inside the Stalag. For the next five days the NCOs hid the two men. They watched with amusement as they stood just inside the wire, watching and listening to SS (Schutzstaffel) men being given orders on where to search for the two men, who were standing just literally feet away. During roll call they stayed under the warrant officers' beds.

When it became obvious that the Germans had scaled down the search, believing the men had escaped, the two men left the compound in a work party to fill mattresses with straw from a local farmer's barn. As the work party filled them, the two men slipped away and hid under the straw. Two others who had been hidden in a ration truck took their places. When the work was finished the work party returned to the Stalag with the same number of men as went out.

The two men slipped out of the barn under the cover of darkness with the intention of heading for Warsaw. There was an airfield nearby and as Forbes was a pilot they had considered sneaking in and stealing an aircraft, but as neither of them were navigators they decided to head for Warsaw instead. The terrain consisted of thick, dark forests and rocky, rough tracks. After four days of struggling through this terrain, exhausted and hungry, the pair found themselves at a control point and were promptly arrested.

Handed over to the Gestapo (Geheime Staatspolizei) they were taken to its headquarters in the town of Plock. Neave realised that he had a drawing of the airfield at Graudenz in his pocket, but managed to tear it up before it was found. Unfortunately he forgot about another one that he had in a matchbox, and that one was found. Neave was justifiably worried as the possession of this map made him look like a spy. The interrogators immediately started to ask questions and accused him of spying for the Russians. What Neave did not know was that the airfield at Graudenz was a bomber station and that preparations were under way for a massive bombing campaign against Russia, which was to take place two weeks later.

The two men were then taken in front of a civilian member of the Gestapo interrogation team. Dressed in a dark suit, the man had blond hair and cold, blue eyes, and spoke excellent English. He started by accusing them of working for the British Secret Service and when told that the map they had was to aid them to escape to Sweden he screamed that they were lying. They then told him that they had received the information from three Canadian pilots who, in home-made German Luftwaffe uniforms, had been captured trying to steal an aircraft from the base at Graudenz.

Only the Germans and fellow prisoners at the camp could have known the detailed information regarding the attempted escape by the Canadians. The Gestapo decided to check the story and Neave and Forbes were thrown into a cold, damp cell. They pondered their fate throughout the night, drifting in and out of sleep.

The following morning they were dragged from their cell and taken separately into interrogation rooms. Fearing the worst, Neave steeled himself, but was surprised when his civilian interrogator offered him a cigarette and addressed him as *herr leutnant*. Immediately suspicious, he listened as his interrogator told him that he too had been in the army and had been in the forefront of the attack on Poland. He had been transferred to the Gestapo because of his ability to speak English. His attitude was almost pleasant, but then he started to press Neave for information regarding the map of the airfield and how he managed to escape from the prison camp.

Determined not to give any information about the Polish farmer who had helped them, Neave repeated his story regarding the map and said that they had escaped from the dentist's surgery at the camp and lived off food from the Red Cross parcels. For the time being Neave felt that he was being believed and he was returned to his cell after another two hours of questioning. Up to this point neither man had been mistreated, but the interrogators had created a sinister and threatening atmosphere throughout their questioning, leaving Neave and Forbes wondering when the interrogation would become physical.

Up to this point, there had been no training given to British soldiers on what to expect when being questioned, so this was new territory. When Neave finally escaped and joined MI9, he made certain that troops were given information regarding the interrogation techniques used by the Germans.

The interrogation continued for the next ten days and all the time the threat of violence continued to build. At night both men, now in separate cells, wondered whether or not they would be shot as spies, as this appeared to be the underlying implication of the questioning. Then, after the tenth day, they were told they were being returned to the prison camp and that guards were coming to collect them.

On their return the Kommandant placed both men in cells deep inside the fortress and in solitary confinement. The cells had no ventilation or windows and were lit by a solitary dim electric light bulb. After spending a month in these conditions, the men were returned to the main body of the camp. Within weeks Neave had been transferred to another camp, Oflag IV-c – Colditz.

At the beginning of May 1941, Neave and Forbes arrived at Colditz, also known as a Sonderlager (special camp). The inmates of this infamous prison camp were deemed to be persistent escapees or enemies of the Reich. The huge castle near Leipzig, once the palace of Augustus the Strong, was an intimidating sight as it dominated the skyline of the Saxon countryside. The security in and around the castle was said by the Germans to make it impregnable, which immediately made the inmates all the more determined to prove them wrong and achieve freedom.

The only thing on the minds of most Allied prisoners of war was escape. Within days of the first inmates being incarcerated each nationality had formed its own escape committee. This was not because they planned all escapes according to their nationality, but because they were separated and imprisoned in different parts of the castle. They all co-operated with each other and helped each other in any way they could. For example, Captain van Doorninck, a Dutch officer, had once been a locksmith and was an expert in repairing instruments and watches, and he often did work for the German guards. Consequently, they allowed him to collect a large range of tools necessary for the work, the same tools he used to fashion keys for the cell block locks and other doors.

For weeks Neave observed the movements and mannerisms of the German guards. It was during one of these observations that he became aware that anyone entering the inner courtyard, where the prisoners were kept, was required to collect a numbered brass disc from the guardhouse and return it when they left. Then a visiting workman was bribed to part with his disc; however on leaving he reported to the guardhouse that he had lost it. All guards were then warned to be on the lookout for the disc or anyone presenting it.

With the obstacle of the disc overcome, the escape committee arranged for duplicates to be made in preparation for future escape attempts. Neave saw another problem, which was that all the German guards carried a rifle with a fixed bayonet, and making a fake weapon would be extremely difficult. The answer, as far as he was concerned, was to try to pass himself off as a soldier on special duty. This, however, required him to carry a bayonet in a scabbard. Fortunately one of the other prisoners was a skilled woodcarver and fashioned him one from a bed board. He then created a buckle out of tin foil and placed it all on a cardboard belt.

Neave had one advantage over most of the inmates in that he spoke German very well. The camp had a theatre in which most of the inmates put on shows but which also gave them access to costumes, paints, dyes and props. Neave put forward a proposal that he would dress as a German corporal, using a converted Polish officer's uniform painted with some scenery paint. The insignia was made out of cardboard and although very realistic at some distance, would not pass close scrutiny. He would take advantage of a theatrical performance, which large numbers of inmates and guards attended, and then just walk casually out of the main gate.

Everything was set and the evening performance started. Neave, dressed as the corporal, mingled with the other guards and slipped out of a side door. Walking past the first sentry on the inner perimeter, he approached the second sentry among the arc lights that illuminated the area. Speaking in fluent German, he handed over the brass disc and told the guard that he had a message for the Kommandant from the duty officer. The guard watched Neave march away then looked again at the number on the disc, then realised that the number '26' was the one that had gone missing. The guard then raised his rifle and shouted 'Halt'. The guardroom personnel were quickly called out and it was then that Neave saw to his dismay that the paint on his uniform had turned bright green under the arc lights, not the field grey that it looked like under normal lighting.

Bundled inside the guardroom, Neave was threatened with a firing squad for insulting the German Army. He was then taken to solitary confinement. The next morning he appeared in front of the Kommandant, who sentenced him to one month's solitary confinement in the town jail. He was also photographed for German police records as a criminal. He was then taken from the castle, over the drawbridge across a dry moat and into the jail. All the time he was being marched there, Neave was taking in the surrounding area and making a mental note of a possible escape route for future use.

That moment came on 5 January 1942 when, together with a Dutch officer by the name of Anthony Lutyen, he effected an escape. The two men, dressed in painted German officers' uniforms with cardboard insignia attached, clambered down through a trapdoor beneath a stage, made a hole in the ceiling into a storeroom and then went down the stairs and through the guardroom. Lutyen, who, like Neave, spoke fluent German, chatted non-stop as the pair sauntered out of the guardroom, past sentries and across the drawbridge. What Neave did not know until after the war was that there was a police photograph of him pinned to the wall of the guardroom.

As the pair stepped out of the guardroom they were met with freezing temperatures and driving snows that, although it aided them considerably as they walked past the guards, also numbed them with cold. After walking over the drawbridge, they clambered down into the dry moat and struggled up the other side, slipping and sliding in the frozen snow. On reaching the top of the moat, they then had to clamber over a 12ft outer perimeter wall. Neave stood on Lutyen's shoulders and grasped the ice-covered top. With great difficulty, but aided by the urgent desire to escape, he managed to pull himself on top of the wall, then reaching down he grasped the hand of Lutyen and pulled him up. The pair dropped heavily onto the ground the other side, their fall cushioned slightly by the deep snow.

Taking off the German greatcoats, they buried them as deep as they could in the snow, pulled their converted uniforms and ski caps made from blankets on, and set off through the driving snow. Their forged papers identified them as Fremdarbeitern (foreign workers) with permission to travel from Leipzig to Ulm.

After two days of travelling through the snow they arrived at Leipzig and bought two railway tickets to Ulm. They had acquired the money by selling Red Cross chocolates and cigarettes to the German guards back at Colditz. Cash from the escape fund of the escape committee had also supplemented them. Safely aboard the train, the two men settled down for the 100-mile journey and a chance to get warm. Once at Ulm, they went to purchase tickets to the small town of Singen, which was close to the frontier, but after showing their travel documents they were arrested by the railway police. Despite this setback, the two men managed to convince the police that they were genuine foreign workers and they were taken to the office that dealt with foreign workers.

Placed in a room while further checks were made, the two men quickly made their escape through a window. They hid in a forest nearby until the following day, when they jumped aboard a train going to the small town of Stockach, near Ludwig. They then headed across country and through forests towards Singen. The snow had ceased, but the temperature continued to drop. Hungry, frozen and on the point of exhaustion, they were stopped by some elderly woodcutters who were on their way to work. Neave and Lutyen identified themselves as 'Polis' labourers from a nearby labour camp, but this was met with disbelief because none of the woodcutters knew of any labour camp in the area. Realising they had been rumbled, the two men headed off into the forest, while the woodcutters went for the police. For the rest of that day and through the night the pair struggled through the deep snow.

As dawn broke, they stumbled across a small hut deep in the forest and, after smashing a window to get in, collapsed into a deep sleep. Waking at dusk, somewhat refreshed, they ate what was left of the meagre chocolate ration and planned their last leg of their journey to freedom. They had been given a rough map of the area by one of the inmates of Colditz just before they left. Looking around the hut, they discovered a couple of white coats and some shovels. Putting the coats under the clothes and carrying the shovels, the two men set off for the frontier, trying to give the impression that they were returning from the forest after work.

As they approached the lights of Singen, they were stopped by two young boys in Hitler Jugend uniforms, who demanded to know who they were. Lutyen explained that they were workers from Westphalia who were staying in Singen. All the time Neave gripped the handle of his shovel tightly and admitted later that he would have had no compunction in killing the two boys had there been no option. Satisfied with their explanation, the boys admitted that they were on the lookout for two British prisoners of war who were on the run and trying to cross the frontier that night.

Watching the boys cycle off through the snow, the men heaved a sigh of relief and, glancing down at their compasses, they headed to the north of Singen. They tramped through more forests, then swung south until they crossed the railway and then on to the road to Schafthausen. Then, in the light of the moon, they could see the German frontier post just 100 yards away. Putting their shovel down and donning the white coats, the two men edged their way closer. The temperature was falling rapidly and both men were beginning to suffer from exposure and frostbite.

Neave and Lutyen could hear the voices of the frontier guards clearly. To get to the frontier they would have to cross the road and then get across an area of no-man's-land before reaching the Swiss border. Suddenly clouds obscured the moon and the wind got up, blowing snow into drifts. Taking advantage of this the two men crawled across the road slowly, under the fence and through the deep snow covering no-man's-land. The white coats and the driving snow prevented the guards from spotting them.

After struggling for more than an hour, they suddenly reached the Swiss border fence and clambered over. A few yards further on was a road, which they knew led to the small town of Ramsen, Switzerland. With renewed effort, bolstered by the realisation that they had made it, they walked into the town and handed themselves in, with great relief, to a Swiss frontier guard. They were taken into a guardhouse and given hot drinks before the Swiss police arrived to take them away and place them under 'hotel arrest'. The following morning they were taken to Berne where, eighty-four hours after escaping from Colditz Castle, Neave was drinking tea with the British Military Attaché.

8. LIEUTENANT ALEXEI PETROVICH MARESYEV

IN APRIL 1942, Lieutenant Alexei Maresyev was tasked, together with other Russian fighter pilots, with escorting a formation of Ilyushin bombers on a raid on a German airfield near Staraya, Russia, a target that was well behind the German front line. As they approached the airfield, the fighters went in strafing the parked aircraft and Maresyev immediately sent bursts of machine-gun fire into two Junkers Ju 52s attempting to take off. The two German aircraft crashed back onto the runway, much to the delight of Maresyev. His jubilation was short-lived, however, as if from nowhere there appeared nine Messerschmitt Me 109 fighters from the feared Richthofen Geschwader. Seconds later the air was black with whirling, howling fighter aircraft and Maresyev found himself in the thick of it. Realising that they had taken heavy casualties, the Russians tried to fight their way out of the area. Maresyev was one of the last to leave and as he was doing so he caught one of the Me 109s in his gun sights and squeezed the trigger, only to hear a dull click. His heart stopped momentarily – he had run out of ammunition. Dodging and weaving in desperation, throwing his aircraft all over the sky, he tried to throw off the attackers, but then bullets from one of the Me 109s thudded along the fuselage of his Polikarpov I-16 and into his engine. Seconds later the engine stopped, smoke started to pour out from beneath the cowling and the aircraft started to spiral crazily out of control. A searing pain from his legs suddenly enveloped him as he realised that some of the bullets had smashed into his legs.

Glancing below, Maresyev realised that there was nowhere he could crash-land his aircraft even if he could get some semblance of control. Seconds later his aircraft crashed into the top of some tall pine trees and disintegrated. Maresyev knew nothing of this as his limp, unconscious body was thrown from the cockpit on impact. Slowly he regained consciousness and found himself lying in the snow in the middle of a pine forest. A sudden searing pain came from the area around his legs and the realisation of what had just happened flooded back into his numb brain. He looked down at his legs that were crumpled under his body and appeared to be at an unnatural angle and not belonging to him. His feet were still attached and in his heavy, fur-lined flying boots. Lifting his body up on his arms, Maresyev went to move his legs but a searing needle-like pain seemed to attach itself to every nerve in his body. Such was the pain that he slipped back into unconsciousness. Several hours later he slowly came to and started to take stock of his situation. Then he heard a rustling sound followed by a loud snort, and a huge bear appeared from the trees. It stopped a few feet away, sniffing the air, and then slowly raised itself on its hind legs. With the bear's eyes firmly fixed on him, Maresyev slowly pulled his service revolver out of its holster. For a fraction of a second he remembered the complaints about the unreliability of these service revolvers and wondered if his was one of those. Then the bear growled and moved towards him. Raising the revolver, Maresyev knew he had only one shot before the bear reached him and squeezed the trigger, realising that this would be the end if he missed. There was a loud bang and the bear stopped momentarily before collapsing dead at his feet with a sickening thud.

The cold was intense but despite this his body was soaked in sweat from the adrenalin rush of terror from the encounter and the pain. As he sat in the snow contemplating his next move, the pain in his legs was not quite as severe as the intense cold seemed to have had a numbing effect. But every movement caused a searing pain to shoot through his body. However, Maresyev realised that unless he wanted to just lie in the snow and die, he must to try to head back toward Russian lines. He had to get somewhere where there was warmth, food and medical attention, but trying to determine where he was was difficult as the dogfight with the German fighters had taken him deeper into German-held territory.

Maresyev found a fallen branch nearby and fashioned a crutch from it. Hauling himself up with great difficulty, he headed towards what he thought must be the east. He realised that if he were to be caught by the Germans he would be shot and as he started his torturous journey it was going to take every ounce of strength, willpower and stamina if he was to survive. For the next two days Maresyev dragged his now useless legs painfully through the snow without seeing a single person. Then as he made his way across a patch of open but uneven ground he saw a German patrol of four men emerging from a forest. Dropping to the ground in a deep depression, he waited as they crossed the open ground to his left. Subconsciously, he started to scratch at the earth beneath him in an attempt to dig a foxhole in which to hide but the frozen ground was unmoving and all he could do was to lie and wait to see if they would stumble upon him. He still had his revolver so he might at least be able to manage to shoot one of them before they got him.

He could hear them talking to each other as they got nearer and he gripped his revolver even tighter, ready to move the moment they found him. He chanced a look and saw them pointing towards the area he had just come from, and he wondered if they were searching for him. Gradually their voices started to fade and then there was silence. Maresyev waited for what felt like an eternity before daring to raise his head and look around him. He was alone. Slowly he dragged himself up and as quickly as his shattered legs would allow made his way into the cover of the forest.

For the next few days Maresyev suffered pain on a level he never knew existed. It was excruciating but he knew he dared not take his boots off to see what the injuries were because he would never get them back on again. Seven days had passed since the crash and now, even with the aid of the crutch, he could not stand and had to resort to crawling on all fours. In addition to the pain, he had not eaten for days and resorted to eating some hard sour-tasting berries he found on a bush. Once he stumbled upon the corpse of a German SS trooper and was able to recover the SS dagger from the man's belt. The following day he managed to kill a hedgehog and eat it raw. He knew that if he didn't get help soon he would die as he was slowly starving to death and his wounds had obviously become infected and needed urgent medical treatment.

He had been crawling across the barren, wind and snow-swept frozen ground for eleven days, reduced now to eating ants, when he heard children's voices coming from what had once been the little Russian village of Plavini. Desperately he tried to call out but not a sound came from his parched throat and at that moment his strength gave out and he lapsed into unconsciousness. A couple of hours later some Russian farmers came across his almost lifeless body and carried him into their homes deep in the forest. They had been forced out of the village by the Germans and were now living in caves deep in the forest.

The farmers dressed his wounds as best they could as Maresyev lay in a coma for three days and it was only when he awoke that they found out who he was and heard about his ordeal. Russian partisans were contacted and a message was passed to his fighter squadron. His squadron commander, Major Andrei Degtyarenko, immediately flew a transport aircraft to a nearby field to collect him. In the meantime the Russian High Command, on hearing of his ordeal, arranged for an ambulance aircraft to be waiting for him when he was flown back to his unit.

Maresyev was flown to Moscow, where surgeons amputated both of his legs below the knee. For an extremely active 26-year-old this was a huge body blow and he became very depressed. However, while in hospital convalescing he met an old army colonel who told him of the exploits of a Russian First World War pilot by the name of Karpovich who had flown during the war with a wooden leg. One year later Maresyev had been fitted with artificial lower legs and persuaded the commander-in-chief of the Soviet Air Force that he would like to fly again. After a number of months of practice, his old skills returned and he was sent to a Guards Fighter Regiment on the Kursk Front with a promotion to major. Once again he distinguished himself by shooting down another seven aircraft, bringing his total to fifteen, and he was made a Hero of the Soviet Union.

9. SERGEANT ALBERT 'BRUNO' WRIGHT, RAF

AS THE MANCHESTER bomber *'M' for Mother* lifted off the runway at Woolfox Lodge, Rutland, on 30 March 1941, the mid-upper turret gunner Sergeant Albert (Bruno) Wright, a Canadian serving with the RAF, settled down for the mission to Brest. The targets were the three German pocket battleships, the *Prince Eugen, Scharnhorst* and *Gneisenau*, all of which were undergoing emergency repairs in the French harbour of Brest. As the aircraft climbed higher the temperature inside the aircraft continued to drop rapidly and Bruno Wright struggled to maintain an even temperature with his electrically heated Irvin flying suit. As they approached the coast of Brittany, the skipper's voice came over the intercom warning everyone to keep their eyes peeled for night fighters.

In front of them the sky suddenly lit up with searchlights and anti-aircraft guns started to pepper the air around them with exploding anti-aircraft shells and tracers. The pilot was having problems with one of the aircraft's two engines and was struggling to get the Manchester above 9,000ft. This was not a good bombing height for such a well-defended area such as Brest, but determined not to abort the mission, he struggled on. As they approached Death Valley (as the area had been nicknamed by bomber crews) the searchlights picked them out and the aircraft was bathed in a blinding white light.

Attempting to take evasive action by weaving the aircraft about, the bomb-aimer was having difficulty trying to keep it straight over the target. The aircraft suddenly rocked violently as the starboard engine was hit. The pilot immediately feathered the crippled engine while the bomb-aimer kept the aircraft steady. Then came the cry 'Bombs gone' and the aircraft seemed momentarily to surge upwards, then just as suddenly started to lose height – they had been hit again.

The skipper fought to gain height as he powered the aircraft away from the area, but to no avail. Then came the order to abandon the aircraft. Wright clambered down from his gun turret, clipped on his parachute, grabbed the handle of the escape hatch and pulled it. It didn't move and Wright stamped on the hatch until it flew off into the void. The rear gunner had now joined Wright and the two of them prepared to drop out of the hatch. The pilot's voice suddenly came over the intercom declaring that they were too low to bale out and for them to prepare for a crash landing. The two men in the fuselage braced themselves for the crash, then heard the engines throttle back and the grinding sound of metal being twisted and shattered as the aircraft hit the ground. The Manchester bounced, then bounced again, throwing the crew around inside the aircraft like rag dolls. As the aircraft shuddered to a stop, there was an eerie silence for a fraction of a second then a loud 'whoosh' as fuel spilled onto the hot engine and caught fire.

Struggling to his feet, Wright grabbed hold of the handle of a side-door escape hatch but it had been twisted in the crash. It was also red hot and seared his hands as he did so. Kicking open another side door, Wright turned to see the rear gunner still lying on the floor of the fuselage, his leg broken. Grabbing the man by the arm, he pulled him through the door and dragged him away from the raging inferno that now engulfed the wreckage.

As the two men watched the fire engulf the entire aircraft, they realised that they were probably the only survivors. Wright made his colleague as comfortable as he could and told him he was going to try to escape. He couldn't take the other man with him for obvious reasons, but asked him to try to get a message back to his wife to tell her that he was alive and well.

With the ammunition and oxygen bottles exploding all around them, it wouldn't be too long before the Germans arrived and the rear gunner would be taken away. Rolling up his parachute and harness, Wright tossed them into the fire and then set off across the fields. After covering about a mile, he stopped beside a wall and took stock of his situation. Inhaling the fumes from the burning petrol had affected his lungs and he was having difficulty breathing after so much exertion.

Taking out his escape kit, Wright examined the contents: chewing gum, Horlicks tablets, rubber water bottle, fishing line, compass and a silk map. After resting for fifteen minutes, he checked his compass and set off in the direction of the Atlantic. He decided to stick to the road as long as he could, mainly because it was easier than walking across fields and hopefully there would be signposts.

Darkness fell, and it started to rain, so he looked for shelter. As he walked to the top of the hill, he saw the grey of the Atlantic before him. He also saw a German sentry with his rifle slung across his shoulder, scanning the horizon with a pair of binoculars. Quickly moving into a dense copse, he decided to settle down for the night. Fortunately he had kept his Irvin suit on, so was able to keep reasonably warm despite the drizzle. Unable to sleep properly, he dozed on and off until dawn, and then took stock of his situation once again.

The dawn brought no solution to his problems. Although he was reasonably close to the shore, he was also very close to the German guard and so decided to stay where he was until dark, before making his next move. He considered stealing one of the small sailing boats that were drawn up on the shore, but he had no experience of sailing and taking a boat out into the hostile Atlantic would have been tantamount to suicide.

Heading back the way he had come, he made his way along the road. A couple of times he dived into the hedgerow when he heard the sound of an engine. But then he ran into a group of cyclists in the dusk, who, on seeing his RAF uniform, greeted him with smiles and pats on the back. Although he did not speak French, he had a smattering of sentences he had learned, and they quickly made him understand that he should get rid of his uniform.

Leaving the group, he walked farther down the road and came to a farmhouse. In the courtyard he saw an old man fixing the harness on a horse. Attracting the man's attention he said, 'Je suis un Anglais avion.'

The old man turned and muttered something in reply, then turned away again. Wright repeated the sentence, but then out of the corner of his eye he saw a younger woman come out of a barn. She grasped him by the arm and pulled him into the barn. Moments later they were joined by a younger man carrying an English–French dictionary.

With the help of the dictionary and sign language he explained that his aircraft had crashed and that he was on the run. They in turn told him that they would help him, but he must stay out of sight. The young woman, who appeared to be the wife of the young man, disappeared and returned with a large bowl of milk and some bread and cheese. Wright quickly devoured the food and then the woman dressed his burnt hands as best she could, relieving the pain somewhat. Wright lay back in the straw to rest and the next thing he knew was that the young man was gently shaking him.

He was carrying a bundle of clothes and indicated to Wright that he was to change into the clothes and give him his uniform. Wright changed and handed the clothes over to him. The man then bundled them up, tied a large stone to them and dropped them down the well in the courtyard. The only thing Wright did keep back was the little gold caterpillar that he used as a tie clip. It was given to everyone who had baled out of an aircraft and returned home, which made him a member of the Caterpillar Club. Wright had been given this after a previous mission had gone wrong and he had baled out over England.

The French farmer's wife then led him to a hayloft where he could sleep. The young man told him that he would contact some members of the Resistance that he knew and arrange for help in the morning. Wright snuggled down in the hay and within minutes was fast asleep.

The following morning, the sounds of the farmyard woke him up, and minutes later the young woman appeared carrying a bowl of coffee and some bread liberally covered in butter. She told him that Germans had been at the house twice during the night looking for two airmen. Then he heard the sound of a light aircraft slowly buzzing over the area, which he thought was probably a Fieseler Storch spotter aircraft.

As he lay back in the straw, the memories of the previous day came flooding back and the burns to his hands started to throb. He knew he would have to stay in the barn until nightfall before he dared venture outside, and only then with the permission of the farmer. Wright also thought about the risk the family was taking because if German soldiers decided to search the premises and found him hiding then there was no doubt in his mind that they would be taken away and shot.

Later that same afternoon the farmer brought some more food and milk and told him that he was to be moved to Brest, where the underground Resistance fighters could take care of him and make preparations to get him away. The following morning two men with a horse and cart arrived to take him to the port. He was to pose as an Italian farm labourer who spoke no French. Wright turned to the farmer and his wife to express his thanks, when she suddenly threw her arms around his neck and kissed him on both cheeks. Shaking the farmer's hand, he then pulled a roll of French money from his pocket, but after seeing the expressions of their faces he pushed it back. Unpinning the gold caterpillar from behind his lapel, Wright gave it to the farmer's wife. The smile on her face when she took it said it all – this was a gift from the heart not from the pocket.

Climbing aboard the cart, the three men set off towards Brest. On reaching the town, Wright could not help noticing the number of anti-aircraft installations. He also noticed the number of spent shell cases, indicating that they had had a busy night. He also saw that there was very little bomb damage to the town, for which he was grateful because the French townspeople did not deserve to be punished for what the Germans had inflicted upon them.

The cart stopped on the side of the road and an old man and a young boy beckoned to him to get off. He turned to say thank you to them, but they had already moved off. The town was full of German soldiers and all the time he was walking he tried not to make eye contact with them. He followed the man and the boy from a discreet distance until they entered a small garage down a side street. Once inside, the boy introduced himself as Jean-Jacques Le Scour and the older man was his uncle, Monsieur Masson.

They showed him into a back room that housed a number of rabbits and in the corner was a pile of hay. Jean-Jacques explained in his schoolboy English that he was to sleep here but he wasn't to go outside during the day. Some minutes later two women, Madame Masson and Madame Le Scour, Jean-Jacques mother, came in with a basket of food. From their attitude they were delighted to see him and to be able to help, even though they were risking their lives in doing so.

The next morning a very attractive woman in her mid-thirties visited him. Elegantly dressed, she gave her name as Mlle X, a British spy who was about to leave for England by submarine that very evening. Unfortunately Wright did not have the necessary documents that would allow him to travel and in any case, he was told later, she was carrying important information and having an escaping airman with her would be a burden.

After the war Wright discovered that Mlle X was in fact Mathilde Carré, a British agent who later betrayed the French Resistance fighters she worked with and became an agent for the Gestapo. They used her radio and codes to set traps for British agents of the SOE. She was eventually caught and after the war was tried in France for treason and sentenced to death. It was later commuted to life imprisonment.

The next visitor was a young Jewish girl who was to escort him to a photographer so that photographs could be taken for his forged travel and work permits. The photographer had been told he was a deaf mute so he was to say nothing the whole time he was there. The shop was full of pictures of German soldiers and sailors and gave the impression that the photographer collaborated with them. When the prints arrived later that day, a 500-franc note accompanied them from the photographer. It turned out that the girl had to disclose Wright's identity to the man in order to get the photographs processed quickly. Having been given that information, the photographer pulled out all the stops to make it a priority and the money was to help Wright.

That evening Wright sat down with the Massons for dinner and to listen to the radio. They listened to the French section of the BBC and heard a number of messages being passed to the Resistance. The Massons said that they hoped to hear the message that said 'Bruno has arrived safely', which would mean that he had got back to England. As he was about to leave for his shed, a full-scale air raid took place as RAF bombers once again attacked the harbour at Brest. The fact that the Germans were feeling the full brunt of the attack never made it less frightening. The children in the house were crouched in the hallway terrified and tearful, and Wright's feelings were very similar.

One of the Resistance men told him of an incident just after an RAF bombing raid on the harbour, when another bomber, with all its navigation lights blazing, flew over the town and dropped bombs indiscriminately. The townspeople found out later that it was the Germans who had actually carried out the raid in an effort to get the Bretons to blame the British. In fact, all it did was to make the Breton townspeople despise the Germans even more – if that was at all possible.

Then word filtered through that the Germans were going ahead with Operation Thunderbolt, which meant that they were about to move the pocket battleships out of the harbour. An immediate clampdown on all travel in and out of the town was enforced, and anyone caught on the streets was subjected to very stringent scrutiny.

The following night a member of the Resistance came and told him he was to be moved to another safe house. Just before he left, Jean-Jacques handed him a wallet with French francs in it. He told him to use the money but asked that when he got to London he would try to see that his brother, Hérve Le Scour, who was an officer with the Free French Forces, got the wallet. Wright said he would, and true to his word, managed to get the wallet to the brother when he returned.

The new family was Jewish and very relaxed. The apartment in which they lived was part of a billet for the Germans, who lived in the apartment above. In one way the family was above suspicion because no one would surely have dreamed of hiding an Allied airman in such close proximity to the Germans. On the other hand, if he were to be discovered there is no doubt that the family would have been interrogated, tortured and then shot.

The father gave music lessons to children every day and was in the process of learning English, while the daughter, who was crippled, spoke excellent English. This, of course, made conversation considerably easier and instruction to Wright simple. It was during one of their conversations that Wright discovered that the family had a friend who was French–Canadian and who was working for Allied intelligence in France. If they could make contact with him he might be able to help lay the groundwork for Wright to escape via one of the escape lines. This was to be the first time that Wright would hear of the famous Pat O'Leary escape line.

The following morning, he was taken for a walk to a café, where he was introduced to a man called Labasse. During the walk Wright found it very interesting to note the number of German military personnel in the town. He was told later that it was in fact payday and the men were out for a good time; much like the boys back home, Wright thought.

On entering the café he noticed that the proprietor immediately closed the bar. Labasse told him that they were leaving Brest later that afternoon by bus and handed him a ticket. The two of them were to go to the bus station separately. The Jewish girl who took him to the photographers arrived and walked casually with him to the bus station. Waiting for the bus was a crowd of people, including a number of German soldiers. The charcoal-burning bus arrived and they all got on. It was standing room only by the time Wright got on, and he found himself tight up against a German soldier, whose regimental dagger kept digging into his side every time the bus hit a bump.

When the bus reached the fishing village of Le Faou, the two men got off and Wright followed Labasse to a large house on the outskirts, where a very large and harassed-looking man met them. His wife would not let them into the house because she had become an Anglophobe after discovering that her daughter had had an unfortunate affair with a British soldier and had been left with a small child to bring up. A new host arrived to take him to another safe house. The man, Michael Perrot, shared a two-room apartment with his grandmother and could not only speak English, but was fluent in German. He cultivated friendships with German soldiers and extract information from them that he passed on to the Resistance.

Later that night a man called André visited him and it was his job to ensure that he was not a Gestapo plant. Satisfied that he was a genuine evader, he told Wright that they hoped to get him away by submarine that night and that they would get a message to his wife saying that he was all right; however, the submarine was cancelled.

The next few days were passed in relative luxury. Michael had a part-time job as a butcher and was able to get a reasonable supply of meat. Michael's grandmother was an excellent cook, so the meals were something to be enjoyed. Their apartment was part of a big house, which also housed a dentist's surgery; consequently Wright had to maintain a very low profile and was confined to one room for most of the day. The evenings were spent talking with Michael about his part in the Resistance. Surprisingly, Michael once related an incident during a bombing raid on the harbour when he saw a Manchester bomber attempting to weave its way in and out of the flak before seeing one of its engines hit. Wright realised that Michael had witnessed the demise of his aircraft.

Then one morning Michael had to go on a mission for the Resistance and Wright was left alone. Suddenly he heard the rumble of trucks in the street below and, peering through the slats covering the window, he saw a line of trucks towing anti-aircraft guns leaving the harbour area. Later he discovered that the pocket battleships had made their famous 'Channel break' after leaving the harbour at Brest. The anti-aircraft guns were no longer required because there was nothing there to defend. It saddened him that all those bombing raids and the loss of life caused, both civilian and aircrew, was all for nothing.

Michael returned with news that the radio message to his wife had got through. It was now just a question of waiting until the Resistance organisation could get him away. Ten days later Michael returned home with an ashen face. In a small town called Quimper, just 50 miles away, there had been raids on the town by the Gestapo and a number of Resistance fighters had been arrested. The concern now was that the Gestapo would be spreading their net increasingly wider and soon they would be entering Brest. For the next two days the men lived on tenterhooks and worry for Michael and his grandmother became a serious concern for Wright. Escape by submarine was now out of the question, and if he was discovered hiding in Michael's apartment the reprisals would be severe. The tension was becoming almost unbearable and every time a car or lorry went past, they feared that a knock on the door was inevitable. Then word came through that Wright was to be moved to another safe house and that evening Michael and his grandmother had a leaving dinner for him.

At midday the following day, the local veterinarian arrived to collect him and Michael in his car. Because he was the local vet, he was allowed to have a ration of petrol. Wright was to be taken to the Château Tréfry near the small town of Quéménéven and his new hosts were the Comte and Comtesse de Poulpiquet. Their magnificent home was in a secluded area surrounded by acres of farmland, the perfect place for a fugitive to hide.

On their arrival, the Comte and Comtesse, who both spoke excellent English, greeted them. Wright was taken to a third floor of the château and told he was to stay here at all times unless told that he could leave. The three men were invited to stay for dinner, after which Michael and the vet left. That evening as dusk fell, Wright was invited to go for a walk in the extensive grounds of the château with the Comtesse. Wearing a hooded coat and clogs. Wright enjoyed the freedom and fresh air of the French countryside. The house was run by two servants, both of whom were aware of Wright's identity, but who were totally trustworthy, having been in the family for many years.

As the days passed Wright got to know his hosts and was surprised to hear that they were not de Gaullists, but favoured Marshal Pétain. They regarded de Gaulle as someone who had deserted his country in times of war and was asking his fellow countrymen to do things that he himself was avoiding. Although the Comtesse was not a member of the Resistance, she was a committed patriot and despised the Germans for invading her country. Her husband, the Comte, had fought at the beginning of the war at the Maginot Line, but was hospitalised with pneumonia that left him with asthma.

At times their talks were tense as they discussed areas in which the British had attacked the French, such as Mers El Kébir, when French sailors were killed by British shellfire, and St-Nazaire, when British commandos attacked the submarine pens there, leaving the inhabitants to suffer reprisals at the hands of the Germans. Despite these misgivings, both the Comte and Comtesse were fiercely dedicated to helping Allied airmen, and their home became a halfway house for escaping and evading bomber crews.

For the next two months Wright stayed at the château, on the one hand enjoying the luxury, but on the other impatient to get back to England and see his wife and baby son. It was all that the Comtesse could do to stop him setting off on his own to walk to Spain.

Eventually she came home with the news that she had made contact with a girl who worked for one of the escape lines. How she made contact is not known, but such was the secrecy surrounding all these people that even today the vast majority of them are still unknown.

The following morning, Wright and the Comtesse left the château to go to Quéménéven to board a train to the town of Angers, where a young woman by the name Yvonne would meet them. After changing trains at Quimper, the two of them settled down for the journey, but the Comtesse became concerned about a man who sat opposite them whose luggage, she noticed, bore Berlin labels. She was concerned because Wright spoke no French and if the man tried to engage him in conversation things could turn difficult. In the corner of the page of the book she was reading, she wrote lightly in pencil, 'Be careful, the man opposite is a German'. Manoeuvring the book slowly, she held it in a position so that Wright could read what she had written, aware that the man could be watching her.

Fortunately Wright showed no reaction, but turned his head away and looked out of the window, indicating with his eyebrows that he had read and understood the message. Nevertheless, the fear of being caught was with him throughout the journey and every time the train stopped at a station his blood ran cold when he saw a German uniform on the platform. He had acquired a pair of dark glasses, which he wore throughout the journey, so he was able to keep the fear from showing in his eyes. The train stopped at Lorient, the main U-boat base for the German Navy, and it was obvious from the devastating bomb damage that it had been the object of many bombing raids. It was at this point that the German left the train, much to the relief of Wright and the Comtesse.

On reaching Angers, they left the train, and outside the station there was a young girl of about 18 who saw them and greeted them as old friends. She took them to her parents' home just outside the town, where they were made very welcome. Two days later the Comtesse, who had made several trips into town, returned with news that Wright was to be on the move again. Preparations were under way for him to be moved into Vichy France.

The man organising the escape was Dr Vorch, an eminent physician. He had been organising it from the start, but because the Gestapo had penetrated his organisation he had moved to Vichy France and was operating his section of the organisation from there.

As a parting gift, the Comtesse gave Wright a pocket-knife, a necessary piece of equipment for his new identity as a French labourer. His new guide was a Jewish psychiatrist, and the pair left that afternoon. It was a sad moment for Wright, as he had become close to the Comtesse and knew he owed her more than he could ever repay, as indeed he did all the others who had assisted him.

The plan was to take Wright to Lyon and hand him over to the American Consulate, who was handling British affairs in Vichy France. Boarding the train, the two men found themselves in an empty carriage, which enabled them to converse in English. Travelling slowly through the countryside, Wright found it hard to believe that there was a war on. They stopped at the town of Tours, where they broke their journey and were the guests of a Roman Catholic priest for dinner. They continued their journey later that evening to a little town close to the demarcation line between occupied France and Vichy France. There they got off and spent the night at a farm a short distance from the station.

The following morning a young girl arrived to take Wright over the border. He said his goodbyes to the doctor and set off across fields and along hedgerows to a country road, where a car was waiting to take him to the town of La Haye-Descartes. It was here that he met Dr Vorch, who would take him on the next stage of his journey.

Because it was the weekend, there was very little travelling and so it was decided to wait until the Monday morning before setting off. The pair had an uninterrupted journey on the next stage to Montluçon, where Dr Vorch was to hand over his ward to another courier. But on reaching their destination, no one was to be seen, so it was left to the doctor to take him on to Lyon. This was to be a long journey and so the doctor bought sufficient food for them both. It was now that the knife given to him by the Comtesse was to prove its worth. Coached by the doctor, Wright learned to cut up bread and cheese and transfer the food to his mouth using the blade of the knife. This was a method used by all French farm labourers and one, if not done properly, would be spotted by Vichy French officials, who maintained a very close watch on all travellers.

Twice their papers were inspected and after travelling all day the train pulled into Lyon. Dr Vorch took Wright straight to the American Consulate, where the Vice-Consul George Whittinghill welcomed them. As soon as he was safely inside the Consulate, Dr Vorch said goodbye and was gone.

This was one of the problems Wright had to face constantly and he felt embarrassed not being able to say a proper thank you to all those people who had helped him along the way.

The first thing the Vice-Consul did was to send a cable on Wright's behalf, advising his wife that he was alive and well. He was then sent to the address of a Polish couple where he was to stay until such time that arrangements could be made to get him over the Pyrenees and into Spain.

There were problems within the escape lines as the Gestapo had penetrated the organisation and many of the key players had been captured and tortured. Then one morning, Wright was invited to the American Consulate and introduced to a smart, elegant-looking man. The man, a secret agent, came straight to the point and asked Wright if he would be prepared to use his skills as a trained wireless operator on behalf of the Resistance. If he agreed, they would contact London and have him reassigned. Shocked for the moment, Wright told him that his war was in the air, not on the ground behind enemy lines. Besides he didn't speak the language and the kind of wireless operation they required had not been part of his training.

Disappointed, the man left. The Consulate then told Wright that arrangements had been made to get him to Marseille and that he would be picked up that very afternoon. The man who had asked him to become a spy turned out to be his guide and this was to be his first dealings with the Pat O'Leary Line. As they left the train in Marseille, a non-descript man, with piercing eyes and a strong face, walked up to his companion and greeted him with a hug. Wright was then introduced to the man and this was his first meeting with the legendary Pat O'Leary, or Albert-Marie Edmond Guérisse, to give him his real name.

Wright was taken to an apartment close to the docks. This was the home of Louis Nouveau and his wife, and was, as he was to find out later, the assembly point of escapees and evaders trying to get into Spain. The bravery of these people cannot be emphasised enough; every hour of every day, they put their lives on the line for the Allies without hesitation. At the end of the war, Nouveau was awarded the George Medal by the British government.

That evening Wright was treated to a dinner of steak and kidney pudding, a real taste of Britain. The following day another evader arrived, a Polish wireless air gunner (WAG), followed the same evening by a British pilot. The next morning two more arrived, a Yugoslav major and his batman. The group was complete when a British sergeant by the name of Pendergast joined them. This last man was to become a cause of some concern for Pat O'Leary because of his accent. At first they were suspicious of him but the British members of the group identified his accent as being a thick Northern Irish brogue.

That evening. Working in pairs, they went to a coin-operated photograph booth and obtained the necessary photographs for their forged permits and travel passes. Wright became a Czech industrial worker and prepared for his trip to the Pyrenees. They would travel in pairs to the foothills, where they would be met by two guides who would take the party over the mountains. They were warned that this was to be the most arduous part of their journey and to be prepared for it.

Wright teamed up with the Irishman Paddy Pendergast and headed toward Toulouse. The pair booked into a small hotel near the railway station to wait for the remainder of their party. The group suddenly expanded when two young Belgians arrived, then two more RAF escapees. Their number now totalled thirteen, a large group to guide over the mountains. They arrived at the small farmhouse at the foothills where their guides were waiting. The guides were Basques; one of them was the legendary Florentino Goikoetxea, who had no love for the Spanish authorities.

Despite it being the middle of June, with warm days, the nights were decidedly cold. For the next two nights the party threaded its way through the foothills, their thin clothes giving them almost no protection against the biting winds that whistled through the rocky gorges. During the day they tried to sleep and rest, but managed very little of both. Their guides rested some distance from them because in the event of the group being discovered and captured the escapees and evaders would probably sent to a prison camp but the guides would be shot.

Then they reached the point at the bottom of the mountains where they were to start their climb. Water was becoming a problem, or to be more precise, the lack of it. The torturous climb took its toll as some of the less fit of the party struggled to keep up. This meant that the group had to move at the pace of the slowest man. Eventually after three days they started the descent into Spain. The Spanish Civil Guard had long since ceased to patrol the mountains because it was futile as there were so many places to hide. Instead they realised that any escapees or evaders coming over the mountains would be desperate to head for the nearest town or railway station, so they set up a 10-mile exclusion zone around the towns and railway stations in the area.

Their guides sat them down and coached them in the sentences in Spanish that they would need to enable them to purchase railway tickets. They also suggested they split into pairs and make their own way to the railway station at Gerona. Wright set off with the Yugoslav major and together they made their way to the station and purchased tickets to Barcelona. On the way they had passed a number of Civil Guards patrolling the area but, ignoring them, they had just kept walking at a steady pace, their hearts thumping every time they approached the guards.

As they left the station, they were stunned to see two of their party under arrest by the Civil Guard. It appeared that one of the two escapees, a Frenchman, had approached a local man and asked for directions. The man had become suspicious and had called the Civil Guard. Wright and his companion immediately headed for a small wood and hid. One hour later their two guides appeared with more bad news, Barker and Pendergast had also been picked up. They had been caught because Pendergast had picked up one of the mountaineering backpacks hidden by one of the guides. The guide had hidden the backpack because it would have been a dead giveaway to anyone walking along the border, but Pendergast thought it wrong to discard such expensive equipment.

The remainder of the party had joined them at this point. When the train arrived they split into pairs once again and made their way onto the train. After a few stops, the train was suddenly filled with Civil Guards examining everyone's travel and identity documents. They became suspicious of the party of escapees, mainly because according to their papers they were all Czechs. They were all arrested and placed in one compartment and their position was finally compromised when one of the young Belgians, fearful that he was going to be shot, blurted out who they were. He then pointed at Wright and told the captors that he was carrying escape equipment. Wright was immediately searched and his tiny compass and hacksaw blade were found.

On arrival in Barcelona the group were placed in cells while the authorities decided what to do with them. The problem lay in the Geneva Convention that stated that if someone had escaped from a prison camp and crossed into Spain, then that person was able to claim diplomatic asylum and be released into the custody of the British Consulate. On the other hand, if they had evaded capture and crossed the border into Spain, they were deemed to have been a combatant who had crossed the border into a neutral country and as such could be interned for the duration of the war.

These situations were notoriously long-winded, and so Wright was placed in a regular *carcel modello* (model prison), where his head was shaved and he was held among hundreds of other prisoners, many of whom were Spanish Republicans who had fought in the Spanish Civil War.

The unsanitary conditions and the very basic food made the prison more of a hellhole than a 'model prison', but food from the British Consul helped supplement the meagre rations. Then Wright was transferred to an interrogation camp at Irun where he knew he would have to convince the authorities that he was an escapee. Prior to leaving France, the Resistance had briefed him on this and prepared him with a story.

Once at the camp he was placed in a cell with a young German who claimed that he was under a sentence of death for refusing to serve in the German Army. He claimed that he had been born in the United States and was trying to get back there when he was caught. Wright felt sorry for him, until he started asking pointed questions about how much help he had received during his escape. There were questions about how much help he had received from the American Consulate in Lyon, and who had hidden him along the way. Wright quickly realised that the man was a Gestapo 'plant' and avoided him like the plague after that. It also showed that the Gestapo had a very long arm and was being allowed to operate in a neutral country.

The Spanish authorities questioned him for several hours, then told him that they were satisfied that he was an escapee and ordered his detention at a concentration camp at Miranda de Ebro. On his arrival he was pleasantly surprised to find six of the original party among the hundreds of detainees, the majority of whom were refugees from all over Europe.

The delivery of Red Cross parcels was the highlight of the week. The British Consul visited on a regular basis and on one such occasion brought Wright a photograph of his wife and baby, and news that he had been promoted to flight sergeant. He also brought news concerning the way negotiations were developing regarding the repatriation of the military prisoners.

Then, on 23 September 1942, news came through that Wright was to be released into the custody of the British Consul. After leaving the camp, he and two others were taken to Madrid and, after stopping at the embassy for a while, they were taken to the border with Gibraltar. There they were handed over to the military authorities, and one week later stepped aboard the Royal Navy's battleship HMS *Malaya*.

Their arrival in Greenock was almost secret and all the escapees and evaders were bedded down on mattresses in a deserted warehouse and kept under guard. However, the years of confinement and the skills they acquired during this time stood them in good stead, as they slipped out under the noses of the guards to visit the dockside pubs. After hours of interrogation Wright was given three weeks leave and sent home to his wife and baby.

Wright returned to the RAF and started flight training as a pilot. Then, just before the war ended, he heard that the Comtesse Genevieve de Poulpiquet was alive and well, but the Comte had died, Bruno received a bundle of notes and letters from the Comtesse, in which she recounted the time when Allied airmen and soldiers were hiding in her home. She remembered smiling at the German cars as they sped past her château and thinking, 'If only they knew who is at my house.'

d Cross package issued to prisoners of war.

Escape kit devised by MI9 as issued to British airmen.

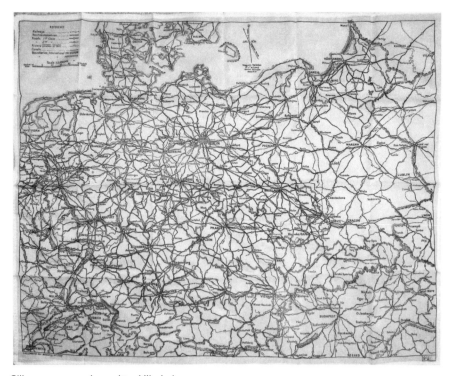

Silk escape map issued to Allied aircrew.

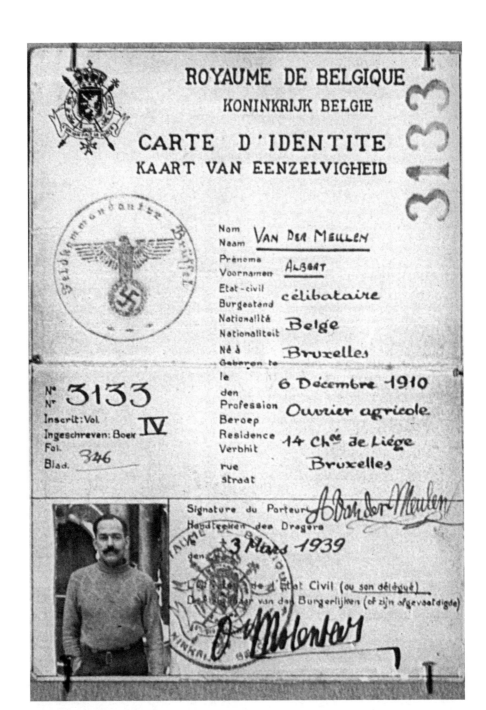

A fake ID card.

Goon-box, barbed wire, huts, German guards and the breathtaking beauty of a Sagan scene.

MGB *502* at high speed. The boats were used to help Allied soldiers and airmen escape when using the Shelburn Line.

SOE agents transmitting radio messages.

A British sergeant being interrogated by the Luftwaffe.

Baron Jean de Blommeart, one of the Resistance members involved in helping escapees and evaders in the Forest of Fréteval.

Lieutenant George Puryear.

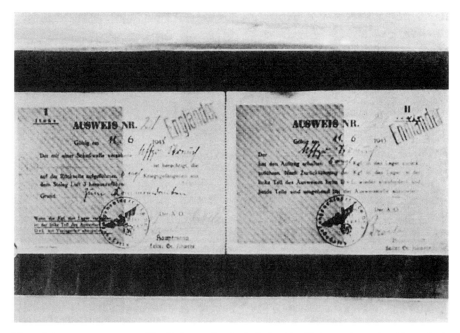

Two of the gate passes used by Bob van der Stok during the 'delouser' escape. These had been forged by another prisoner, Tim Walenn.

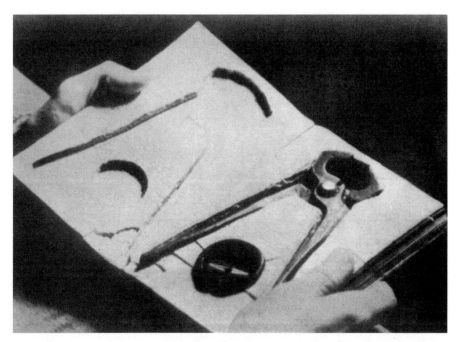

Seen here is a pair of pincers made by Travis and one of Al Hake's compasses hidden in a book. This was a commonplace method of concealing escape equipment.

Kommandant Oberst (Colonel) von Lindeiner.

Hauptmann Pieber speaking to the senior British officer, Group Captain H.M. Massey, DSO, MC. There's a German Unteroffizier in the background.

Leutnant Rudolf Frank.

Drawing of Stalag Luft III
showing the positions of the
three tunnels – Tom, Dick
and Harry.

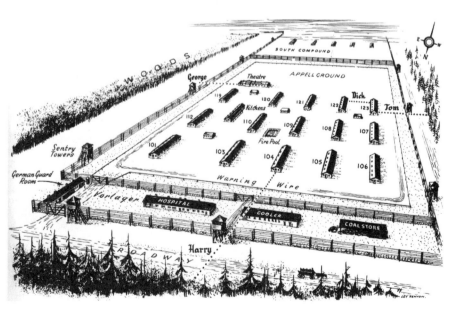

Looking up the tunnel Harry.

Looking down Harry.

Rubberneck congratulating a fellow ferret on the discovery of a tunnel.

Guard exiting Harry.

German guard demonstrating
the air pump used in the tunnels.

German guards demonstrating
the trolley used in the tunnels.

To all Prisoners of War!

The escape from prison camps is no longer a sport!

Germany has always kept to the Hague Convention and only punished recaptured prisoners of war with minor disciplinary punishment.

Germany will still maintain these principles of international law.

But England has besides fighting at the front in an honest manner instituted an illegal warfare in non combat zones in the form of gangster commandos, terror bandits and sabotage troops even up to the frontiers of Germany.

They say in a captured secret and confidential English military pamphlet,

THE HANDBOOK
OF MODERN IRREGULAR
WARFARE:

". . . the days when we could practise the rules of sportsmanship are over. For the time being, every soldier must be a potential gangster and must be prepared to adopt their methods whenever necessary."

"The sphere of operations should always include the enemy's own country, any occupied territory, and in certain circumstances, such neutral countries as he is using as a source of supply."

England has with these instructions opened up a non military form of gangster war!

Germany is determined to safeguard her homeland, and especially her war industry and provisional centres for the fighting fronts. Therefore it has become necessary to create strictly forbidden zones, called death zones, in which all unauthorised trespassers will be immediately shot on sight.

Escaping prisoners of war, entering such death zones, will certainly lose their lives. They are therefore in constant danger of being mistaken for enemy agents or sabotage groups.

Urgent warning is given against making future escapes!

In plain English: Stay in the camp where you will be safe! Breaking out of it is now a damned dangerous act.

The chances of preserving your life are almost nil!

All police and military guards have been given the most strict orders to shoot on sight all suspected persons.

Escaping from prison camps has ceased to be a sport!

Leaflet given to prisoners of war by the Germans.

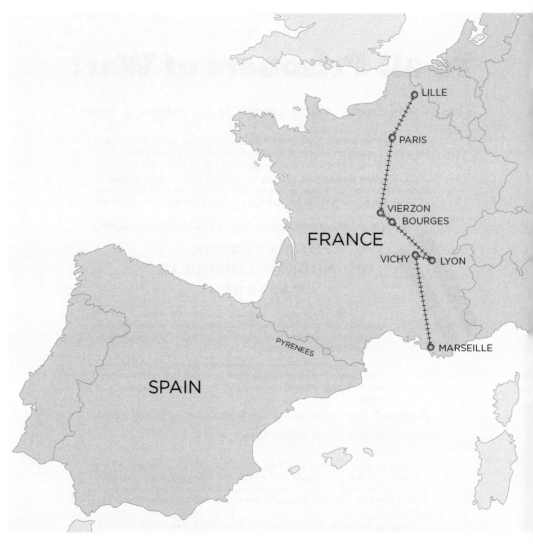

Rough sketch map of Lieutenant Colonel James Langley's escape, 1940.

Rough sketch map of Captain Airey Neave's escape, 1941–42.

Rough sketch map of Flight Lieutenant Angus MacLean's escape, 1942.

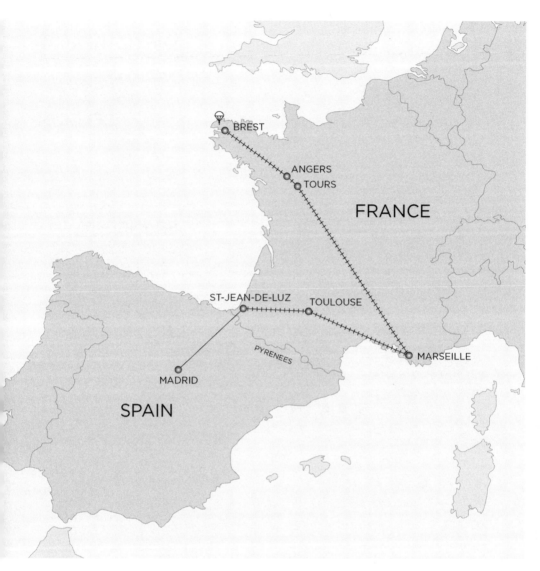

BREST

ANGERS

TOURS

FRANCE

ST-JEAN-DE-LUZ   TOULOUSE

PYRENEES   MARSEILLE

MADRID

SPAIN

Rough sketch map of Sergeant Albert 'Bruno' Wright's escape, 1942.

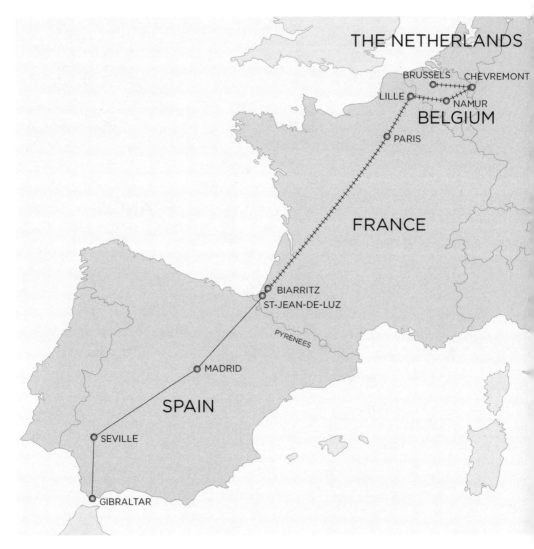

Rough sketch map of Group Captain W.S.O. Randle's escape, 1942.

10. GROUP CAPTAIN W.S.O. RANDLE, RAF

BEING AWAKENED AFTER only a few hours' sleep to be told that he and his crew were on standby was not the best start to the day for Sergeant Bill Randle. They had only just returned from laying mines at Wangerooge, an island off the coast of Germany, and this would be their second trip to Germany within twenty-four hours. That afternoon the crew air-tested their Wellington bomber *'Z' for Zebra* and checked out all the systems. Among the crew was an American, Sergeant Dal Mounts, serving in the RCAF, who was making his first trip. The target that night, on 16 September 1942, was Essen and the crews were told that they would be assisted by a 130mph tailwind above 15,000ft.

The last to take off, Randle set a course that would take them over the Dutch coast near Zwolle. As they crossed into the Netherlands at 22,000ft they could see anti-aircraft fire opening up and hear the flak as it exploded close to the aircraft. They continued on toward the Ruhr Valley, or 'Happy Valley' as it was known among bomber crews, which was lit up like a fairground. Searchlights swept the sky, while marker flares and bursting bombs laid a carpet of fire beneath them. Around them flak was bursting continuously, rocking the aircraft every few seconds. Struggling to maintain control, Randle set the bomber over the target, while the bomb-aimer released their 400lb bomb.

As Randle turned the big bomber away from the scene, the port engine shut down and Randle had no choice but to feather it. The aircraft had also suffered a considerable amount of flak damage, causing it to fly in circles. Randle knew he was not going to get the aircraft back to England on one engine and with the controls badly damaged. They were also flying into a 130mph headwind, which cut the aircraft's speed to just below 100mph, and it was losing altitude rapidly. Randle realised that the aircraft was slowly being pushed back into Germany.

Reluctantly he informed the crew that they should prepare themselves to bale out. The aircraft was continuing to lose altitude but Randle managed to keep it steady enough for the rest of the crew to make their exit. With the crew all gone, he set the controls and made his way to the escape hatch. Just as he set himself on the edge of the hatch, the aircraft lurched downwards. Randle felt a blow to the side of his head and then he was falling. He managed to grasp the D-ring attached to his parachute as he fell and pulled it. The next thing he remembered was floating down through the clouds into trees.

The situation felt unreal to Randle for a few moments; one minute he had been in an aircraft and now he was standing up beneath a tree supported by his parachute harness that had been caught up in the branches. All the talks and information given to aircrew who might find themselves in this situation now meant nothing. He felt lost and alone in a country whose language he only had a little knowledge, and he was now being hunted by German soldiers who an hour earlier had been subjected to bombing from his aircraft.

For almost an hour Randle sat beneath the tree collecting his thoughts. He was naturally scared, but then realised the only sound he could hear was that of a dog barking in the distance. He checked himself for injuries and felt a small cut beneath his eye and saw another on the back of his hand. He attempted to hide his parachute, but it was tangled up in the branches of the tree so badly that no amount of tugging or pulling could free it. He decided that he had spent enough time with this, so taking off his bright yellow Mae West he threw it on the ground beneath the tree, as there was no point in trying to hide that either.

He then headed off across the fields, keeping to the hedgerows and small wooded areas, hoping to find a road that had a signpost or something that would give him an indication as to where he was. As dawn approached he decided to find somewhere to rest up and take stock of his situation. Spotting a dense copse, he pushed his way in and curled up to try to get some rest. A few hours passed and then he was awakened violently by the roar of engines and as he looked up a Junkers Ju 52, with its flaps fully down for landing, passed no more that 50ft overhead. He had found a spot on the edge of a German airfield.

For the rest of the morning he waited, crouched inside the dense copse, listening to the sound of aircraft engines and road traffic going in and out of the airfield. Taking out his escape kit, he examined what it contained. There were silk maps of northern France, Belgium and Holland, together with currency from the respective countries, one penknife, a sewing kit, Benzedrine pills, Horlicks tablets, and two rubber water bottles. He also had on him a total of nine miniature compasses, one in a collar stud, one each of his cufflinks, two in the fly buttons and four sewn into the waistband of his trousers. There were also two passport-sized photographs taken in civilian clothes in case they were needed for permits or identification cards.

As darkness approached Randle navigated by the stars and headed away from the airfield as quickly as he could. He then set a north-westerly course, hoping it would place him into the western area of Belgium or the Netherlands. After walking for around seven hours, he realised that the landscape was beginning to change into more and more cultivated farmland areas. Having been brought up in the countryside of Devon, he suddenly felt more relaxed and at home. As a boy scout he had practised living off the land and this was to put him in good stead when acquiring food.

The clouds began to gather and then a slight drizzle set in. This also meant that he had lost the use of the stars and would have to resort to using one of the compasses. Keeping to the roads as long as he could, Randle continued walking. On a number of occasions he had to take cover as the hooded headlights of German vehicles sped along the roads. With the rain getting heavier and his clothes getting wetter, he thought it might be the right time to find some shelter. In the meantime pangs of hunger started to gnaw away at him. Entering a field, he selected some small turnips and some carrots.

In the corner of the field he saw a derelict cottage and, making his way to it, he was delighted to see that at least the roof had remained intact and the inside was quite dry. By this time he was literally soaked to the skin and his feet excruciatingly sore. Taking off his wet clothes, he spread them as best he could to get them dry. Then, peeling off his flying boots, he saw that his feet were covered in blisters, some of which were bleeding. Taking a needle from his sewing kit, he pricked each blister and drained them off, washing them with water from his water bottle.

Making a nest of sorts, Randle curled up in a corner of the room and fell soundly asleep. He awoke to sun streaming through one of the dirt-covered windows. The temperature had gone up considerably. So, taking the still very damp clothes, he placed them on the grass at the rear of the cottage. He then went back inside and peeled the turnips and carrots. Deciding against building a fire in case it attracted attention, he chopped the turnips and carrots into small pieces and ate them, washing them down with water.

Deciding to wait until dark before setting out again, Randle rested as best he could, aware that he might be discovered at any time. As soon as darkness fell he got dressed, thankful that now his clothes had dried out. Putting on his flying boots was extremely painful, but once on he steeled himself against the pain and started off. He realised that soon he would have to look for help as there was no way he could continue much longer because of the state of his feet. Each step was very painful, but he still kept going. All through the night he walked down the country lanes, glimpsing lights of farmhouses in the distance. He heard the drone of bombers in the distance and saw searchlights scanning the skies for them. Then, because his attention was not on the road, he collided with a man on a bicycle.

The man stared at Randle for a few seconds, during which time he had regained his composure and said, '*Morgen, Guten morgen.*' The man stepped closer and looked at Bill's RAF wings on his battledress. 'RAF, RAF?' said the man excitedly. 'Yes,' replied Randle. The man hurled himself at Randle, giving him a bear hug and kissing him on both cheeks. He then shook him vigorously by the hand. Indicating that Bill should get on the crossbar of his bicycle, he set off pedalling furiously back the way he had come, constantly jabbering in a language that sounded Dutch, but turned out to be Flemish.

On the outskirts of a village, they came to a large house. Randle was taken inside into the kitchen and was greeted by the smell of bread being baked. Within minutes the room seemed full of people slapping him on the back and wanting to shake his hand. They were all speaking the same guttural language and not one word could he understand. Then a smart, slim woman entered the room and asked him if he spoke French. Bill replied that he could a little, but she would have to speak slower because his schoolboy French was not that good. She turned out to be the village schoolteacher and as such seemed to take over the proceedings.

Randle told her, in his fractured French, that he was a bomber pilot and had been shot down while on a bombing raid over Essen. He added that he had been walking for two nights trying to reach the coast. It was his intention to try to contact one of the escape organisations that might be operating in the area. The latter part of the conversation she obviously did not understand and left the room. His hosts then took him into another room where on the table was a large plate of ham and eggs and some large chunks of freshly baked bread.

Invited to eat, Randle made short work of clearing the plate of food, and no sooner had he finished than the schoolmistress returned, this time with three men. One of them turned out to be the local doctor, who examined his cuts and bruises. He was then taken upstairs to a small bathroom, where he climbed into a warm bath. In the meantime, his uniform was taken away and, as he found out later, burnt. The doctor then examined his feet and treated them. Putting on a dressing gown, he made his way downstairs where the other two men were waiting with the schoolmistress. She explained that there was no Resistance organisation in the area, and that they would have to get him away from the village that afternoon because there was a curfew in force in the evenings and the Germans searched the area regularly.

Tired and exhausted, Randle felt total despair. Here he was in a foreign country, not knowing the language and having no idea what he was going to do next. He asked if he could stay there overnight, but a shake of the head told him that that was not possible. Getting to the coast was not an option either, because the Germans were building coastal defences and the area around them was restricted.

The only option was to head for Marseille in the south of France, but that was hundreds of miles away and the only practical way to do that was by train. Randle was taken into another room where there were some clothes: a dirty grey shirt without a collar, a pair of striped trousers that were far too big in the waistband and too short in the leg, a thin jacket, a workman's cap and a pair of shoes – which surprisingly fitted very well.

Looking at himself in the mirror, Randle looked like a tramp down on his luck, and this, together with an unshaven face and a black eye, completed his disguise.

The schoolmistress then asked him for his dog tags from around his neck. He was reluctant to give them to her because these were the only things that would identify him as a British airman. She explained that if he was captured and the dog tags found, he would more than likely be shot as a spy. Randle asked about his uniform and was told that it had been destroyed.

The schoolmistress explained that they were taking him to the railway station and that she had already acquired a ticket for him to a small town called Namur but he would probably have to change at Tirlemont. Going outside, he was surprised to see a number of people waiting to see him and almost all shook his hand or slapped him on the back. Then one Belgian woman came up to him and thrust a bundle of Belgian banknotes into his hand. Embarrassed, Randle mumbled his thanks and then set off towards the station with his hosts.

Within minutes of arriving at the station, the train pulled in and he climbed aboard. Waving goodbye, he realised that he never knew the names of any of his hosts, but if he were to be captured later maybe that was a good thing. Settling back in the corner of the carriage, he watched the countryside slip by, but all the time he felt very apprehensive. At one stop a woman got into the carriage and, on seeing him in the corner, looked disdainfully down her nose and sat as far away from him as she could.

The train pulled into Tirlemont and all the passengers disembarked. Leaving the station, Randle found a timetable, which told him that the next train to Namur was in two hours. Deciding to walk into the town, Randle saw his first

Germans and followed them into the town square. They entered a large build-ing, outside which fluttered a large Swastika flag. All around the town there were posters warning the inhabitants that the penalty for helping *terrorfliegers* was death.

For the next two hours he sat opposite the building on a bench in a small park. Ten minutes before the train was due to leave, he made his way back to the station. The journey to Namur was uneventful, except for a number of unexplained stops. But on reaching Namur, he was alarmed momentarily when he saw German Feldgendarmerei (field police) stopping people in the queue of people leaving the train. It was only when he got closer that he saw they were examining the passes of German soldiers.

Handing in his ticket, Randle quickly made his way out of the station. Time was getting on and he knew that he would have to get away from the town and find a place to stay before the curfew came into force.

Walking out of the town, he quickly found himself in the country. Fortunately the weather was warm and he headed towards the French border. As the sun started to set, he realised that soon he would have to find somewhere to sleep and he was becoming increasingly hungry. Dusk was settling fast when he saw an old man digging up potatoes in a field. Going up to the man he said in his schoolboy French, *'Monsieur, je suis un aviator Anglais. S'il vous plait. Aidez-moi. J'ai faim.'* For a moment the man continued to dig and said nothing, then looking up he replied, *'Restez là, mon ami.'* Randle went over to the side of the road and sat down wearily. When it was dark the old man stopped digging, put the potatoes and spade into a wheelbarrow, beckoned to Randle to follow him and set off down the road.

On reaching a small farmhouse, he was taken into the kitchen and introduced to the man's wife, his son and his daughter-in-law. The two women became somewhat alarmed about his presence, but the old man insisted that a plate of stew be placed on the table and indicated that Randle should join them. They asked him questions during the meal, and it was the son whom Randle found easier to understand. When he told them that he had been bombing Germany when he had been shot down, they all shouted joyfully, *'à bas les Boches!'* and the tense atmosphere disappeared. The next minute, the meal having been finished, a large bottle of cognac appeared and toasts all round became the order of the day.

Then the son left and the old man's wife took him upstairs so that he could have a wash. Returning downstairs, the old man led him out to a barn with a bed of straw and within minutes of lying down Randle was fast asleep. He was suddenly awakened by the sound of the barn door creaking open. Lying perfectly still, but now wide awake, he suddenly felt a pair of hands grab his shoulders and a bright light was shone in his face. Something was shouted at him in German and, terrified, he blurted out that he was English. A calm voice then said in English, 'It's all right. Calm yourself. We are here to help you.'

One of the men lit a lantern and Randle could see three men, one of whom was the farmer's son. The English-speaking man told him that they were going to take him to a safe house in Namur and that he was to follow him. Bidding a grateful farewell to the farmer's son, Randle stepped out into the yard and followed one of the men. The other man walked behind and the three walked across fields in silence and in single file until they reached a large house on the outskirts of town.

One of the men rang a bell and a small, barred window opened in the door. A conversation took place and then Randle was told to climb over the wall, which he did with the help of the two men. Dropping to the ground on the other side, he was shocked to come face to face with a cowled monk. The man took him by the hand and led him inside the house.

Randle awoke with a start the following morning and for a moment he thought he was in a prison cell. He looked around and saw a narrow slit window at one end of the tiny room and a big heavy door with a grille set in it. Then he remembered that he had been given sanctuary in a monastery and this was obviously a monk's cell. On a small table stood a washbasin together with some toiletries. On the wall was a picture of the Virgin Mary and child under which were the words, 'Notre-Dame de Chèvremont'. Looking round, he saw that his clothes were missing but on the back of a small wooden chair in the corner was a brown robe.

Getting out of bed, he washed and shaved and slipped the robe over his head. After a few minutes the door opened and in walked a short, tubby monk in his late forties carrying a tray of food, which consisted of sliced cheese and ham, some bread and a large glass of milk. In good English he told Randle to eat and when he had finished he would return. Randle enjoyed the food and then the monk returned and introduced himself as Father Marcel and said that Father Abbot had given him the responsibility of looking after him.

Randle asked Father Marcel where he was, but the only reply he got was that he was in good hands and that the less he knew about his whereabouts, and them, the better. The two men talked for most of the morning, during which Randle discovered that Father Marcel had once been a soldier in the Belgian Army and that he had an intense hatred of the Germans. German soldiers had murdered his mother, father and grandfather during the looting and massacre of Dinant in 1914. He had joined up in 1935, fought during the Blitzkrieg and had been defending the Albert Canal when he was shot and wounded. He had been captured and taken to Germany as a POW. There he had studied to take Holy Orders and was released after completing his studies.

When Randle asked what would become of him, Father Marcel replied that he did not know at present, but others were dealing with that side of things. Father Marcel then left, saying that he would try to find some books for Randle to read and if he wanted to he could join the brothers in prayer at any time.

He returned just after lunch saying that there had been some disquiet regarding him being there. Most of the monks were Belgian, but there were a couple of Germans, an Irishman and some Spaniards, who objected to his presence. They had sent a petition to the Father Prior stating that either Randle was to leave or be handed over to the Belgian police. The latter option would have meant that he would have been handed over to the Germans. The monks were concerned that if the German authorities found out they would all be arrested and the penalty for harbouring a British airman was death.

Randle immediately asked for his clothes and said that he would go and take his chances; he did not want to be responsible for the possible deaths of such good men. Father Marcel put his mind at rest by saying that Father Prior had remedied the situation by admonishing those who had petitioned him, saying that it was their Christian duty to help those in need. He also added that they appeared to be concerned more for their own safety than the safety of others, and as such they were to be sent to the monastery at Chèvremont for an indefinite period, where the brothers there were bound by a vow of complete silence.

With the pressure removed, Randle settled down to a monastic life for a time, enjoying the good food and company of Father Marcel. He began to enjoy the traditional chants that the monks sang on a regular basis and the exercise of walking within the safety of the walled gardens. However, despite the peaceful lifestyle, he was impatient to be on his way and get back to Britain. Every time he asked Father Marcel for information, none was forthcoming, only a shrug of the shoulders and an assurance that everything was in hand.

Then one morning Father Marcel asked Randle for his dog tags. They were wanted by members of the Resistance so that they could verify that he was who he said he was. Randle told him that the dog tags had been destroyed along with his uniform when he had been sheltered in a house in Flanders. Father Marcel then asked Randle if he could give some information about his squadron, his crew, his aircraft and what kind of bomb load it carried – anything that would show that he was in fact a British airman and not a Gestapo 'plant'. Randle replied that he could only disclose his number, rank and name. Father Marcel said he did not think that this would be enough to satisfy them and could he give just a little bit more. Randle replied he could not.

The days passed and still nothing from the Resistance, but then one warm, sunny afternoon, when he was dozing in the orchard, Randle was wakened by a hand on his shoulder, Father Marcel told him it was time for him to leave and to follow him. Returning to his cell, Randle saw that there was a smart dark suit laid out on the bed together with a shirt, tie and some shoes. Quickly getting dressed, Randle said goodbye to Father Marcel, who gave him a small gold crucifix and chain, saying that he would like him to wear it and that it had been blessed in his name.

Vowing to return after the war to say thank you properly, Randle followed Father Marcel to a small side door in the monastery wall. Randle was told that there would be a man outside who he was to follow. Saying a final goodbye, Randle stepped outside to where a thin-faced man was waiting. Without saying a word, the man turned on his heel and walked away with Randle following at a discreet distance.

As dusk was only just approaching there were still a number of people about, including German soldiers, as they entered the town of Namur. After walking for about twenty minutes, the man stopped outside an empty house. Glancing around for a moment, he entered the garden and made his way around to the back of the house with Randle following. After mounting the stairs they entered a room in which there was a long trestle table with three men sitting behind. His guide nodded to the men, then turned around and left.

For a few moments no one spoke and then the man in the middle of the three asked Randle in perfect English if he had anything that could prove that he was a British flyer. Bill replied that all his uniform and identity discs had been destroyed, and all that he was obliged to give was his number, rank and name, which he stated were 1385872 Sergeant W.S.O. Randle.

There was silence, then the man told him that they would need far more than that to convince them – or else. The implied threat sent a shiver down Randle's spine. It was quite obvious what was meant and he knew that these men were more than capable of carrying out the 'or else'. There was a need for him to answer more questions and at that moment Randle realised that he was going to have to comply. For the next hour the questions came, ranging from questions on cricket, his schooldays and the names of teachers, his parents and grandparents and where they were born. Finally they appeared to be convinced and the tense atmosphere relaxed. He was to be taken by a guide to an apartment in Namur and from then on, wherever he went, there would be a guide in close proximity, who he was on no account ever to approach.

One of the men got up from the table and beckoned Randle to follow him. Leaving the empty house, the two men walked in single file into the town.

The centre of the town was bustling as last-minute shoppers bought goods from the market. Leaving the town centre, they walked up a tree-lined avenue until they reached a large house with a short driveway. The moment they knocked on the door it opened and the two men entered. This was the house of Madame Davreux and her two daughters, where Randle was to stay for the next four days. He was to discover later that he was in the safe hands of the Comète Line, one of the most successful of all escape organisations.

The following morning Randle and one of the daughters, Madeline, went into town for his photograph to be taken. These were to be used in forged travel documents and permits that he was going to need for his journey to Spain. It was quite obvious that the photographer knew why the photographs were being taken and appeared to be very nervous from the moment the pair entered his shop. He, like all the others who appeared on the fringe of the Resistance, risked his life almost daily trying to help – but help he did.

While they were waiting for the photographs to be developed and printed, Madeline took Randle into town for a coffee. She bought him a copy of *Der Spiegel* (*The Mirror*) and while glancing at the pictures inside, he noticed out of the corner of his eye a young German soldier who had entered the café just after them smiling and approving of Randle's choice of reading material.

With the photographs collected, Randle and Madeline headed back towards the house. The photographs were collected later that evening and by the next morning Randle's *'laissez-passer'* (free-movement pass) was ready, showing a stamp stating that the pass had been issued in Antwerp. Randle was now Andre De Voulgelaar, a Flemish commercial traveller in agricultural machinery and fertiliser. The pass also contained a permit to travel in France, the Low Countries and, of all places, Biarritz.

With all the documents in place, the Davreux family set about re-educating him about his manners and how to conduct himself. It was customary in Belgium when having finished a meal to leave the knife and fork east to west across the plate, not south to north as was common in England. He had to alter the way he walked, not like the military man he was, but more like a tired traveller.

On the day he was to leave, Bill was introduced to a young girl who was slightly older than himself. Her name was Andrée de Jongh, also known as Dédée, and she was to be his guide for the first part of the journey. Her English was very good and she made it clear from the start that if anything went wrong during the journey he was on his own and was to try to make his way back to Namur. She gave him a railway ticket to Brussels and told him that he was to follow her to the station. When the train came in, he was to sit in the same carriage but well away from her. When they arrived in Brussels, there would be another courier to take him on to the next stage. He would then be taken to a large Catholic church where he was to sit in the third row of chairs in the right-hand side aisle. A man wearing a Belgian red, black and yellow *boutonnière* would contact him.

The family asked him if he had ever been in a Catholic church, to which he replied no. They then went through the ritual of how he should dip his fingers in the holy water on entering and then make the sign of the cross on his chest in front of the altar, while bending his knee.

Saying his grateful farewells to the Davreux family, Randle and Dédée set off on what was to be a potentially hazardous journey. On entering the station they boarded the train and seated themselves at either end of the carriage. The journey to Brussels was uneventful and the train only had two stops before arriving dead on time. They disembarked and walked out of the station. Dédée was met by a young woman who embraced her, then they walked away arm in arm. Randle followed at a discreet distance until they reached a crossroads, where they separated. Randle followed the other girl, who led him through the town towards a church in a market place.

The church was the Notre Dame du Sablon, and walking up the steps behind her, Randle went through the ritual that he had been shown by the Davreuxs. Once inside, he made his way to the third row on the right-hand side of the altar, passing the young guide who sat with a headscarf on appearing to be at prayer. The moment he sat down, Randle noticed that his guide got up and left. After what seemed like ages, but was in fact only minutes, a portly looking gentleman sporting a Belgian *boutonnière*, sat down beside him.

Without saying a word the man glanced at Randle, got up and left. Randle waited for about a minute then followed him. As he walked out into the sunlight, he saw the man on the other side of the road and he indicated with a slight gesture of his hand for Randle to follow him. They walked through a park, then across a busy main road and finally into a block of flats. Because the lift was out of order, they had to walk up the stairs until they reached the fifth floor. The guide knocked on the door, which was quickly opened, and he stepped inside, gesturing for Randle to follow him. Randle was then introduced to a middle-aged lady called Madame Marechal.

After inviting him into her sitting room, Madame Marechal explained the rules of living in her home. She reminded him that he was staying in an apartment that was situated in a block of apartments in the middle of Brussels. She also said that the apartment block was frequented by Germans who were visiting certain young women who lived in the block. She explained that although most of the girls were all right, it was known that there were a few collaborators among them. Taking him on a tour of the apartment, Madame Marechal showed him the various rooms and warned him always to stay away from the windows and to move about the flat as quietly as possible. She was supposed to be a woman alone and anyone hearing extra voices coming from her apartment might become suspicious. With a wide grin, she then pointed to a trapdoor in the ceiling and tapped on it with a bamboo pole. Randle was surprised to see the trapdoor open and even more surprised when the face of his rear gunner, Bob Frost, appeared.

Frost swung down from the loft, quickly followed by Dal Mounts, the American member of the crew. Then another body appeared, a blond haired, Germanic-looking young man. He introduced himself as Freddy Frankowski, a Polish bomber pilot who had been shot down during the German invasion of Poland. The Resistance had picked up Frost and Mounts just a day after they were shot down.

Randle was told that 'guests' were only allowed to eat in the kitchen. They could only flush the toilet once a day because excessive use might cause questions to be asked. The four men took it in turns with the sleeping accommodation, two downstairs in the bed and two on the mattress in the loft.

After he had settled in, Dédée visited. She took Randle to one side and asked him to check out the Polish pilot's story as her Resistance colleagues were a bit concerned about him. Randle discreetly questioned him during the evening and when Dédée visited the following day he told her that he was satisfied the man was genuine.

For the next three days the four men relaxed as best they could, conscious of the fact that they would have to be vigilant at all times concerning the way they moved about the apartment. Then on the third evening, Dédée arrived to tell them that they were being moved to Paris the following morning. She would be their guide and they were to travel in pairs. Randle paired up with Frankowski and Frost joined with Mounts.

The following morning they said their goodbyes to Madame Marechal and set off for the station. Dédée had briefed them fully the night before, but she went over it once again after handing them their tickets. She told them that there would be a three-hour wait at Lille and the only slight problem that she could foresee was at the border crossing at Bassieux, where customs officers checked everybody and everything. They were not, however, looking for escaping airmen.

As the train pulled in, a very attractive woman suddenly joined Dédée and the pair of them got into the carriage. The train was packed but two German soldiers gave up their seats for the two women. Randle and the other three men found themselves crammed into the packed carriage standing among a number of German sailors and their kit bags. Fortunately the sailors appeared to be off the same ship and talked excitedly between themselves and ignored everyone else. At one of the stops the sailors got off, leaving the carriage almost empty.

As they approached the frontier, a conductor came through the train making everyone aware of the fact. At the border the train stopped and everyone was ordered out onto the track. This was because the station platform was very small and was taken up by rows of tables where customs officials waited, each with a German soldier standing behind him. As they shuffled along the track towards the platform, Randle and Frankowski had attached themselves to an old lady, who was struggling to walk, and carried her luggage. By the time they reached the customs officials Randle was helping and fussing over the old lady, giving the impression he was a relative. Suddenly there was a disturbance by one of the tables when a man in a trench coat suddenly raced down the embankment and up the other side, heading towards a clump of trees. A shot was fired after him, but he was long gone before any of the officials could react.

The four men went through without any problems as the officials were still distracted by the episode with the man in the trench coat. Getting back on the train, the party settled back for the journey to Lille. The remainder of the trip was uneventful and on reaching the station they all got off. The two women parted company and Randle watched as Dédée walked across the road to another group of men who were dressed very similarly to him and his companions. He immediately realised that this was another group of evaders on their way down through the escape chain.

Dédée briefed her party again, saying that they had three hours to wait before the train to Paris was due to leave and so she arranged for them to get a meal at a restaurant close by the station. She told Randle that because he could speak a little French he was in charge of the group and handed him a generous amount of French francs. They were to be outside at 2 p.m. precisely, ready to go to the station.

The four men entered the restaurant and were shown to a table upstairs close to a fire exit. Randle ordered the meal for all of them and included a bottle of wine. The only other two people in the upstairs room were two German soldiers, who barely glanced up as they were eating their meal.

The meal was served and promptly devoured with great relish and as the coffee was being served Mounts whispered to Randle that he needed to go to the bathroom. Randle indicated that it was behind a curtain that was situated behind the cashier's desk. Mounts went behind the curtain, then the next moment there was a woman's shriek and the curtain was thrown back, revealing Mounts struggling with the lavatory madame outside the female toilet. A hushed, embarrassed silence fell over the room. Randle quickly got to his feet and went over. Mounts by this time had recovered his composure and was indicating to the woman by pointing to his ears and mouth that he was deaf and dumb.

'*Mon ami est idiot,*' said Bill to the woman, slipping a 1-franc coin on her plate. Taking Mounts by the arm, he led him into the men's toilet. Laughter replaced the embarrassed silence as everyone realised that a mistake had been made by the simpleton, but Randle decided that the party should leave. Paying the bill, Randle apologised once again and started downstairs. Suddenly a hand was placed on his arm and a voice whispered in English, 'You really must try to do better or you will never get back to England.' Randle never looked round, but just kept on walking down the stairs and out into the street, a cold sweat running down his back.

Crossing the road, they met Dédée, who had heard what happened and was not amused. Angrily, she led the way back to the station just in time to board the train to Paris. By the time they reached Paris her anger had faded and she was back to her normal happy self. Leaving the train at Gare de l'Est, the group proceeded down the Metro, where they were given a book of tickets and instructions on how to use them. Boarding the Metro train, they headed out of the city to a district called Oudinot. They were to go to an apartment house in a quiet residential area and upstairs to a suite of rooms. This was to be their safe house and was where they met Dédée's father, Frédéric de Jongh.

It was from this apartment that all the final arrangements were made for evaders and escapees to make their journey across France and into Spain. This was the Comète Line's holding facility for all Allied soldiers and airmen attempting to get back to England. The long journey by train to St-Jean-de-Luz was fraught with dangers, so specialist guides had to be recruited and only so many evaders and escapees could be taken at any one time. It was a human conveyor belt system that held dire consequences for everyone should anything go wrong.

The group was told that it could be some time before their turn came, so in the meantime they were permitted to go out and see the sights of Paris. They were told to keep away from the restaurants and to take sandwiches or buy snacks. They would eat all their main meals in the apartment. Randle described the experience of sightseeing in Paris with hundreds of German soldiers doing the same thing as completely surreal. The group was aware that the more relaxed they became, the more chance there was that they would become careless.

This was no more apparent than on one trip when Frost and Randle were crammed into a carriage on the Metro and Randle found himself face to face with a Luftwaffe Leutnant. As the train pulled into the station, the train lurched and Frost shot forward into the German. An involuntary 'sorry' came from his lips. The German was stunned and an incredulous look appeared on his face. Then the doors opened, and Randle and Frost forced their way out and up into the streets, expecting any minute to hear either shots or a hue and cry starting up behind them, but fortunately nothing happened. The two men quickly got themselves swallowed up in the crowds.

This was a timely and salutary lesson for them both, and on their return they reminded the others to be on their guard at all times. One more slip like that could spell disaster for them and the group.

Another time Randle and Frost went to the cinema and after making sure their seats were close to the exit, settled down to watch the film. Before the main feature came on, there was newsreel footage about a detachment of French SS troops on the Russian Front. There were a large number of Frenchmen in the audience who took exception to the newsreel and made it quite clear how they felt, with shouts and derogatory remarks aimed specifically at the German members of the audience. The whole auditorium descended into uproar and fights broke out between the two factions. Randle and Frost quickly slipped out of the cinema just before the police arrived.

During the evenings Randle took the opportunity to talk to Frédéric de Jongh about the reasons why he and all the others risked their lives almost every day for the Allies. He explained that those in the Comète Line felt they were soldiers too, although they never wore a uniform, and that by helping them to escape and enable the airmen to get back into the war, they would be playing their part in defeating the German Army.

Then one morning they were told that they had to be ready to move that evening. First-class railway tickets had been purchased for them and they were to stay in the apartment until it was time to leave. The group spent the day practising their responses to questions that might be asked of them by French officials. This was to be one of the tensest journeys they had experienced. Entering their compartment, they discovered that there were three spare seats. One was taken up by a young Frenchman who smiled at everybody, then settled down to read his book. Minutes later two German officers entered and the train set off. Randle noticed that the two Germans kept staring at the young Frenchman and muttering to each other. He could see that the object of their attention was the book the Frenchman was reading. Randle glanced at the book and was staggered to see that it was a copy of George Bernard Shaw's *Man and Superman* – the English version.

The Germans spoke to the young Frenchman and he replied in fluent German, the next minute the three of them were conversing in what appeared to be a friendly and intense manner. Pleased that the attention was away from them, the group settled down and pretended to sleep. At Tours, the two Germans got off and when the train stopped at Orleans so did the young Frenchman. With only the members of the group left in the compartment, they settled down to sleep. They were awakened by Dédée telling them that they were about arrive in Biarritz, where they had to change trains.

Disembarking from the train, the group moved to one end of the deserted platform and waited for Dédée, who had left the station. She returned with a young woman and introduced her to the group as Nadine, who was to lead them on the last leg of their rail journey to St-Jean-de-Luz. The train pulled in a few minutes later and the group got on. The train stopped at every station, and a few wayside halts, and then after about an hour it arrived at the last station on the line.

Excitement was growing within the group as they could smell the sea air and the taste of freedom. The small town of St-Jean-de-Luz was having its market day and the streets were crowded with local people buying and selling fish and vegetables. Nadine led the party around harbour to a house in the Rue Gambetta.

For the next three days the group enjoyed the sunshine and were encouraged to spend as much time in the sun as they could in order to acquire suntans. Dressed in the local manner of denims, black beret and rope sandals, the suntans would help them blend in with the local inhabitants. One thing puzzled the group was that they saw no Germans in the town, but they were warned not to trust the French police as they could be as dangerous as the Gestapo and just as unpleasant.

The group was informed that when their time came they would go by bicycle to a farmhouse at the foot of the Pyrenees, where they would be met by a Basque guide who would take them over the mountains and into Spain. They would take their suits, shirts and shoes in backpacks to change into when they reached Spain.

The following morning the group was told that they would be leaving that afternoon and to prepare everything for an arduous journey. There was unbridled excitement within the group as the smell of freedom was getting stronger. That evening bicycles were suddenly produced and the group set off at a leisurely pace, enjoying the sunshine and the scenery. They left the main road and went along some rough tracks for a few miles before stopping for something to eat and drink. The countryside around them became more barren and deserted. The group continued on until dusk, when they reached a deserted farm on the edge of the tree line leading to the foothills.

The guide showed them where to leave their bicycles and told them to rest until their next guide came. After a few hours the door of the farmhouse suddenly opened and in walked Dédée and a large, heavily built man with a deeply suntanned face. The man, as Randle was to find out later, was the legendary Basque escapee smuggler Florentino Goikoetxea. Dédée introduced him to the group by saying that he was the most experienced guide there was and everybody was to follow his instructions without question. He had made more than 100 trips across the Pyrenees and had never lost anyone. She would be in charge of the group right into the safe house in Spain and would make sure that they were handed over to the right people.

Just before the party set off, Dédée explained that the only danger area, apart from the mountains, was the Zone Interdite (Forbidden Zone). This was an area than ran 2 miles wide on either side of the border and anyone seen or caught within that area was likely to be shot on sight. The actual border, she explained, ran alongside the River Bidasso and all the natural crossing areas were heavily guarded by Spanish border police. In the unlikely event of anything going wrong, they were to head into Spain and make sure they were at least 20km (12 miles) inside the country before making any attempt to contact anyone. This way if anyone was caught they would be held by the Spanish authorities, otherwise they would be handed over to the French, who would in turn hand them over to the Germans.

The group set off with Goikoetxea leading, Dédée close behind, then Randle, Frost, Mounts and, bringing up the rear, Frankowski. For the next two hours the party climbed higher and higher, the airmen struggling to keep up with the pace being set by Goikoetxea and Dédée. Then up in front their guide raised his hand and everyone stopped quite still, holding their breath, as they heard the gentle tingling of bells just ahead of them. Then a flock of sheep crossed the winding track in front of them and the party relaxed.

After another hour the group stopped for a rest. Goikoetxea, however, had moved on ahead and twenty minutes later came back and spoke to Dédée. She turned to the group and whispered that they were thirty minutes or so from the border, so they had to be aware of patrols. The group started climbing again but soon their track started downwards and became easier. Suddenly Goikoetxea froze and everyone stopped. He signalled everyone to get down as voices were heard coming towards them. Quickly Goikoetxea ushered the group back along the path and into a small pine forest. Silently they made their way through in another direction, the pine needles beneath their feet deadening the sound of their footsteps.

At last they stepped out of the forest and saw the river. All the four men looked at each other with grins on their faces as they realised that the border was only a few yards away. Goikoetxea ushered them back to the forest edge, while he went ahead to make sure that the way was clear. He had to find a safe place for them to cross, as all the main crossings were well guarded. Minutes later he returned and beckoned for them to follow him. Keeping close to the tree line the group made their way along until they reached the crossing point picked out by Goikoetxea. They then walked down a steep embankment and stopped alongside the river.

Goikoetxea placed a rope around his waist and then instructed everyone to do the same, making sure that they were all linked together. Then a light was suddenly switched on, followed seconds later by music. They were just 50 yards away from a Spanish border guardhouse. They all froze momentarily, but Goikoetxea waded into the river and signalled for everyone to follow him and take shelter under some overhanging willows. Getting waist deep in the cold water took their breath away for a few moments, as the party prepared to cross. This time it was Dédée who took the lead and the group walked steadily across to the other side. The noise coming from the guardhouse was a blessing in disguise because any sounds they might have made would not have been heard.

Once across, Goikoetxea and Dédée set off at a fast pace, determined to put as much distance between the group and the border as possible. It was 1 a.m. and they knew that there would be no one about, enabling them to make up some miles quickly. The problem was that by setting such a fast pace the airmen were struggling to keep up, which frustrated the two guides. A couple of times Goikoetxea sent Dédée back to urge them on as daybreak was fast approaching. She told the group that it was vital to put more distance between them and the border and there was no time to rest.

Goikoetxea followed Dédée and, after a slightly heated conversation with her, started back the way they had come without looking or saying a word to anyone. Dédée looked at them wearily and led them into a small wood. She explained that they were to stay there and rest, but should leave someone on guard and she would be back later. Shame-faced, the four men prepared to rest, Randle taking the first watch.

About midday Randle, who had been dozing, heard the sound of an engine and peering out through some branches he saw a Renault taxi pull up alongside the wood. In the taxi sat Dédée, beckoning to them. The four men piled into the back and the taxi pulled away. One hour later they arrived in San Sebastian and were placed in a safe house.

Once they had settled in, Dédée told them she had to leave and go back over the mountains that night as she had another group to bring over. They all tried to find words to thank her, but they were insufficient. The gratitude and admiration they felt for the young woman were beyond words, and then she was gone.

The group was now in the hands of the British Consul, and although they were now safe from the Germans, they still had to be careful about the Spanish authorities. They spent the evening and night at the British Consul's house and the following morning were taken to Burgos, where they stayed with a British family for the night. The next day a large Bentley arrived to take them to Madrid, where they were taken to another safe house, only this time the safe house was the British embassy.

The Ambassador, Sir Samuel Hoare, told them that it would be a few days before arrangements could be made to get them to Gibraltar. In the meantime they took the opportunity to bathe and relax in the old Roman baths that were situated underneath the embassy.

Three days later they were told that they were to be given false identities and in the company of a junior secretary they were driven to the border to be handed over to the British Army. The group left the embassy in the Ambassador's official Bentley, stopping in Seville for the night before proceeding to Algeciras and finally Gibraltar. Fifty-five days after being shot down over occupied territory, in November 1942, Randle finally stepped onto British soil.

11. FLIGHT LIEUTENANT ANGUS MACLEAN, RCAF

TAKING OFF FROM RAF Driffield, Yorkshire, on 25 July 1943, the crew of the Halifax bomber *'H' for Harry* were blissfully unaware of what lay before them. The pilot, Flight Lieutenant Angus MacLean, RCAF, was on his seventh mission over Germany and their target was the Krupp steel works at Essen in the heavily defended Ruhr Valley. Flying over Holland, all appeared peaceful but as they approached the Ruhr Valley the flak started to rise to meet them and was so thick that it gave the appearance of a solid mass. Searchlights swept the air in front of the aircraft and then suddenly they were caught in the beams and pinpointed by three of the searchlights. Shrapnel from exploding anti-aircraft shells started to rain around them, perforating the wings and fuselage. Suddenly the aircraft was thrown onto its back and went into a steep dive as one large shell exploded close by. Struggling to maintain control, MacLean brought the aircraft out of its dive and back to its operational height. It was then that he realised that the ailerons had been damaged, jamming them in a left-hand turn position. Realising he could not make the primary target, MacLean set a course for the secondary one, all the time trying to clear the jammed ailerons.

Circling over the designated area, MacLean's aircraft was coming under increasing attack from the ground. Then, somehow, he managed to clear the problem and he was back in full control of the aircraft. All the time they were being swept deeper and deeper into Germany. With the flak increasing, they remembered that the intelligence officer (IO) had told them of the German recognition flare, and so they fired the appropriate one. The flak eased measurably and the Halifax continued on its way. Over the secondary target, they dropped their bombs and set a course for home.

Climbing to a new height, the crew settled back as the flak diminished, but were still aware of the possibility of night fighters jumping them out of the darkness. As they approached Holland, MacLean saw a stream of red tracers streaking up towards them. He realised immediately that these were markers and that night fighters had been vectored to intercept them. Alerting the crew, they all waited nervously for the first of the Messerschmitt Me 110s to attack. Seconds later they heard the unmistakable crack of cannon fire as an Me 110 raced into view. Then came the crackle of machine gun fire from his own gunners and he saw the German fighter suddenly engulfed in flames and hurtle towards the ground. They had scored a vital hit, but so too had the Germans as both port engines suddenly stopped.

Frantically MacLean tried to keep the crippled aircraft in the air, as in the distance he could see the outline of the Zuiderzee. However, MacLean realised that it was a hopeless cause and when the aircraft descended to 1,200ft he ordered the crew to bale out. One by one the crew left the aircraft until only MacLean was left and, setting the controls to level flight, he scrambled for the escape hatch and dropped out.

No sooner had he left the aircraft than he pulled the ripcord of his parachute. Second later the parachute deployed fully and MacLean hit the ground on his back. He lay there for a few minutes unable to feel anything. His first thoughts were that he had broken his back, but then the feeling started to return to his legs, then his back. His elbow was bleeding badly and almost all the skin had been stripped from his upper left arm. One of his flying boots had been ripped from his foot during the descent and the wet grass was beginning to soak through his clothes.

Looking around, he saw he had landed in a field. In the next field the remains of his Halifax bomber was burning furiously and oxygen bottles and ammunition were exploding all over the place, scattering the cows that moments earlier had been grazing quietly in the field.

Realising that the countryside would soon be swarming with German soldiers, MacLean struggled to his feet, collected up his parachute and hid it in a drainage culvert as best he could. The he looked around to see if he could find his other boot, but to no avail. He crossed over the culvert and started walking around the edge of the field. Dawn was starting to break when he saw a sign on the side of the road. It wasn't in German or French, so he assumed he must be in Holland.

He continued walking, but by now his back was extremely painful, to the extent that he could barely walk, and his other injuries were causing him concern. He then decided to look around for a place to hide and consider his position. Looking behind him, he saw to his horror that where he had been walking across the field he had left a track in the dew-laden grass. Seeing a small herd of cows close by, he chased them over the area where he had been and then moved them along in front of him.

He crawled into a thick hedge and pulled out his escape kit. Inside was a compass, money of different nationalities, glucose tablet and a collapsible rubber bottle. Taking the bottle, he moved slowly to one of the cows and milked it. Settling back into the thick hedgerow, he drank the warm milk and then fell asleep. He was awakened by the sound of voices and for a moment lay in the hedgerow totally confused, but then pain in his back brought him quickly back to reality. The voices grew louder and they were in German. Peering through the hedge he could see two young girls picking blackberries. As they got closer, he decided to show himself and stood up.

Stepping forward, he pointed to his uniform and said, 'RAF – Englander.' The younger of the two girls suddenly turned and ran. MacLean looked around desperately for somewhere to run, but then the other girl touched the Masonic ring on his finger and gabbled something in German. MacLean heard the word 'Freemason', then she pointed to a house in the distance. From the house he saw the younger girl approaching with a much older man.

With promises of help, the old man took him through the village, where he was visible to all and sundry. MacLean's feet by now were blistered and very painful, and after indicating this to them, he was led into an orchard to rest. With promises of food and clothing the villagers left him to spend the night there. Throughout the restless night he waited but no help was forthcoming. In the morning two labourers from the village came to cut the grass and shared their meagre ration of coffee and rye bread with him.

Throughout the rest of the day he waited, but by the evening he realised that no one was coming. He felt both let down and angry, but then realised the position the villagers must have felt they were in, in helping an Allied airman. The penalty for this was well known – death.

Using his silk escape map, which he had shown to the villagers, he had a good idea where he was. He was on an island in the Netherlands between the towns of Zaltbommel and 's-Hertogenbosch. The problem was that if the Germans found out that he was in the vicinity it would be simple for them to seal off the island. Moving cautiously in the fields, he headed for the River Meuse and hoped that the bridges were not manned by German control posts. If he could get off the island he would head for the port of Rotterdam with the intention of smuggling himself aboard one of the neutral ships.

After covering about 6 miles, he was moving down a small path when a tall gaunt man confronted him. The man looked at MacLean and the RCAF uniform and shook his head. Gesturing to him to sit down just inside the field, he left. Too tired and exhausted to think straight, MacLean resigned himself to whatever fate awaited him. Then after about half an hour the man returned, this time with an elderly woman. He was carrying a bundle of old, worn clothes and his wife handed MacLean a large bowl of warm milk and a thick wedge of rye bread.

After gulping down the food, MacLean gratefully took off his uniform and slipped into the tired-looking suit, a worn shirt, an old hat and a shiny pair of boots – the latter was obviously the man's Sunday best. The old couple took his uniform and explained by means of sign language that they would burn it; they then indicated that he should leave. Holding back tears of gratitude, MacLean shook hands with the couple and set off.

As he approached a village, he could see in the distance the heavy ironwork of a bridge. As he approached the bridge he could see that there was in fact a pontoon across the river, but no German guards. His attention was suddenly drawn to the sound of a lorry coming down the road. Stepping behind a hedge, he watched as two German motorcycles and a lorry with German soldiers in the back came hurtling along. They screeched to a halt in the village and an officer got out of the lorry and spoke to a woman. They then turned around and went back the way they had come. MacLean wondered if they were looking for him. Moving towards the bridge, he joined a large number of people making their way across. It was only as he approached the bridge that he spotted a German soldier on the other side examining everybody's papers.

Then came the sound of a barge whistle, and round the bend in the river came a long line of barges. The barriers went down to the pedestrians and the swing bridge moved to allow the barges to go through. This, of course, caused a build-up of pedestrians on MacLean's side of the river. Looking round, he saw a young woman carrying a parcel and with a baby in a pram. Moving alongside her, he smiled first at the mother, then at the baby. Just then the bridge swung back and the barrier was raised. Grasping the handle of the pram, he again smiled at the young mother and started to push the pram across the river.

He watched carefully as the German guard started to examine only some of the papers, as there was a large number of people coming towards him. Keeping his head down, MacLean walked at a steady pace past the guard and onto the road the other side. About half a mile further on, MacLean spotted a side road and, touching his hat to the young woman, he bid her farewell with a smile. He never knew if she suspected him of being someone who was trying to escape from the Germans or not.

Finding himself at the river's edge, he decided to follow the riverbank as far as he could, hoping that it would lead him to Rotterdam. The sun had slipped below the horizon when he came across a houseboat moored alongside the bank. In great pain, tired and hungry he decided to approach the boat and seek help. Approaching the boat, he could see a woman scrubbing at some clothes in a washtub on the deck.

The woman looked up and saw him standing by the gangplank. MacLean gestured to himself and said, '*Englander – kommen Sie mir hilfen bitter?*' (Are you able to help me please?) The woman looked around then grasped his wrist and without saying a word led him onto the boat and down into the living area. In the living room were her husband and their four children, three girls aged 11, 18 and 21 and a boy aged 15 – the Pagie family. The eldest girl, Jane, spoke some English and was able to translate. The father questioned the exhausted MacLean until he was satisfied that he was who he said he was. The Gestapo often used Germans who could speak English fluently to trap people in occupied countries who helped escapees and evaders.

The father placed his home at MacLean's disposal once he was sure of him. The mother treated his wounds and for the first time in days he was able to have a bath and make himself presentable.

For the next four weeks he hid on the houseboat, slowly recovering from his injuries, and by the end of this time he had almost recovered to his normal self. During this period the family had shared their meagre rations with him, without complaint. It has to be remembered that every minute of every day the family risked their lives in helping MacLean, something he never ever forgot.

Word came through that the Germans were aware that there was an Allied airman on the run in the area and MacLean could often see parties of soldiers scouring the riverbank. There was even a reward of 500 guilders for his capture, but nothing would have tempted the Pagie family.

Sundays were not the best of days for MacLean, for this was the day that relatives and friends came to visit. Because the houseboat was not all that big, a locked door would be of some concern to them, so he had to spend the day in a small closet with nothing to do but wait until they had all gone.

One morning MacLean woke in alarm to the sound of German voices. Peering through the curtained windows, he could see some German officers on the opposite bank studying a map. As he looked along the bank of the river, he could see German soldiers lying down in the grass with machine guns and rifles pointed across the river. Then he heard the loud explosive chatter of machine guns and he instinctively threw himself to the ground, expecting to see bullet holes puncturing the sides of the houseboat at any moment. His first thoughts were that he had been discovered, but when no bullets seemed to hit the houseboat and the firing continued he looked out again and realised that he was witnessing a mock battle. He discovered later that a German infantry school was close by and these were trainees on exercise.

MacLean was now becoming restless, his injuries had healed and he felt that sooner or later he was going to be discovered. If that happened it would have meant a death sentence for the whole Pagie family. Albert Pagie, the father, had made several trips to Amsterdam to try to make contact with the Dutch Resistance, but to no avail. It was Jane Pagie who came up with the answer. She worked in a clothing factory and had confided in a former Dutch Army officer. He visited the houseboat and told MacLean that he knew of no Resistance organisation in Holland, but he knew of one in Belgium. If MacLean could get into Belgium he would stand a good chance of escaping. The officer arranged for a guide, a priest, Father Kluge, who was leaving Zaltbommel for Weert. Because a number of people had been caught helping Allied airmen by Gestapo agents who pretended to be fallen flyers, the priest wanted proof. MacLean gave the officer one of his RCAF dog tags that he wore around his neck.

He was to meet the priest at a railway station some 20 miles away, and so Jane suggested that they cycle to the station giving the impression of a young couple on an outing. It was then that MacLean confessed that he had never learned to ride a bicycle. There was no time for MacLean to start, so the poor girl had to ride the 20 miles to the station with MacLean perched on the handlebars. Taking the back roads so as to avoid German patrols, the pair received a mixture of curious looks and grins from passers-by.

At the station, where Albert Pagie had arrived earlier, the three of them waited for the train until a middle-aged man approached speaking good English. He gave MacLean a ticket and asked him for his parents' name and address in Canada, saying that he would try to get a message to them. Then, as the train arrived, the priest, a slim, mournful-looking man, appeared. Jane told him that this was the man he was to follow and, quickly saying his goodbyes to the Pagies, he boarded the train.

The train was crowded and MacLean settled himself in one of the carriages away from the priest. Then, a couple of stops down the line, the priest appeared at his shoulder, opened his hand and gave MacLean his dog tag back without saying a word. The train rumbled on and later that evening pulled into Weert, just 5 miles from the Belgian border.

As the train pulled into the station, Father Kluge spoke to him for the first time, telling him that a young man with two bicycles would be waiting for him outside the station. Before he could explain that he could not ride a bicycle, the priest was gone. Walking outside, he saw a young man with two bicycles and approached him. After MacLean explained that he could not ride a bicycle, the exasperated young boy put one of them into a ditch and gestured to him to sit astride his crossbar. After about an hour of travelling they dismounted and the boy pointed across to a house, indicating that they were now at the border.

Crouching down in a field, the two waited and as dusk came they saw a woman emerge from the house and hang a washtub on the wall. This was the signal that all was clear and that they could cross. The two sprinted across the field, past the house and onto the road. The boy explained that their underground contact was in a tavern on the edge of the town of Molenbeersel.

When they reached the tavern, the two sat at a table and ordered a couple of beers. Looking around the busy tavern, MacLean saw two men seated by the door. One of them got up and with a barely perceptible move of his head indicted that he wanted MacLean to follow him. MacLean's companion nudged him to go and with that the airman got up and walked out of the door. Once outside he followed the man down a dark alleyway, where the man told him that they were going to his father's farmhouse some miles away so that arrangements could be made to contact one of the escape lines. Once again a bicycle appeared, and once again MacLean had to explain that he could not ride it! It has to be remembered that this was the only transport available to ordinary people during the war years, and even today it is still the most popular form of transport in the Netherlands and Belgium.

MacLean heaved himself up on to the crossbar and once again subjected himself to the painful bumping up and down as they pedalled along the rough side roads. They had been joined by a second man, who took turns with his companion in giving MacLean a lift on the crossbar. After two hours they reached the farmhouse, where the Peeter family welcomed him.

For more than a week MacLean rested at the farmhouse. His guide, Albert Peeter, was a very active member of the Resistance, but his group was a sabotage unit and had no connection with any underground escape organisation. Through their chain of connections they made contact with a group in Brussels, so arrangements were made to get MacLean to the city. One of these, a man called Mondo, collected him and together with Peeter they set off for Brussels. The journey by train was uneventful, except when a crowd of German soldiers going on leave entered their carriage, but fortunately they chose to ignore them.

On arriving in Brussels, Peeter left them and Mondo took MacLean to an apartment occupied by a Mr And Mrs Neve, who welcomed him. Immediately, MacLean felt relaxed and that he was now in experienced hands. Unknown to him at the time, he was in the hands of the Comète Line.

Even though he had convinced the priest that he was a Canadian pilot trying to get back to England, the Comète Line needed to be even more certain. The next morning the Neves told him that they would be out for the day, but he was to expect a visitor. Duly, a tall, very well-dressed, executive-looking business-man arrived. He started to ask MacLean some questions regarding the RCAF and the base he was operating from. When MacLean began to get wary, the man answered the questions for him, showing that he had the information and that he knew all about the RAF base at Pocklington. Now more relaxed, the two men chatted for more than an hour before the other man got up, appear-ing to be satisfied that MacLean was who he said he was. It was only then that MacLean learned that the man had had a gun in his open briefcase, which had been on his lap throughout the interview. The man was one of the Comète Line's executioners, and had he been suspicious of MacLean he would have shot him dead there and then; such was the fear that the Gestapo might have penetrated their organisation with an English-speaking agent.

As the man was leaving he told MacLean that he would be taken to another refuge the following day. The following afternoon a very attractive woman by the name of Peggy arrived and took him to a flat on the other side of Brussels. Two Frenchwomen, Madamoiselles Liégeois and Warnow, lived in the flat and MacLean was placed in a room in the basement, where he stayed for a week. The two girls worked during the day, so MacLean stayed by himself during this period. The only contact he had with the two girls was when they fed him in the morning and evening.

When they returned late one night, they had company with them and MacLean felt apprehensive when they stopped outside of the door of his room. There was a soft tap on the door and the key turned in the lock. The door opened and three men stepped inside. Seeing MacLean in the corner of the room, the men hesitated. MacLean greeted them in French, to which one of them replied in English saying that he had hoped to meet someone who spoke English. MacLean grinned and introduced himself. The two shorter men were pilots like him; the tallest man, however, was Prince Albert de Ligne, one of the senior members of the Comète Line.

The next morning the two French girls took the three men to the railway sta-tion, where they were introduced to their guides from the Comète Line – Count Georges D'Oultremont and Eric de Menton de Horn. The two other airmen would follow de Horn, while MacLean would follow the Count. Identity papers had been arranged for all of them and they took their places aboard the train. At the border the train was stopped and searched. German soldiers and French officials examined everyone's papers, and the train proceeded on to Lille, where they all changed trains for Paris. MacLean heaved a sigh of relief when the train pulled into the Gare du Nord, but this quickly turned to panic when two gendarmes stepped out and stopped the Count. They took him into the police office, while MacLean kept walking. Once outside the station he crossed over the road and sat down on a bench to see what would happen.

Now alone in a strange city occupied by the German Army, MacLean pondered his position. Then suddenly he saw the Count walking down the steps of the station. The man walked past him, indicating as he did so for him to follow. Later when they were alone, the Count explained that because of his frequent trips to Paris the police suspected him of carrying black market goods, but having found nothing they released him. MacLean had been briefed earlier that a new guide would pick him up. As the Count walked down the street, with MacLean following at a discreet distance, a grey-haired man, who had been looking in a window, suddenly fell in behind the Count and indicated to MacLean to follow him. The man led him to an apartment, where the other two men were waiting.

The following day MacLean was taken to the home of Monsieur and Madame René Coache at 71 rue de Naunterre, Asnières. Here he would stay until preparations had been made for the Comète Line to move him. Two days passed before the next guide appeared, the Comète Line's founder, Dédée.

Using the train and bus service, Dédée took him to a large château on the outskirts of Paris at St-Maur. This was the headquarters of the Comète Line and was a huge building with large gardens that were surrounded by very high walls. Within these walls operated one of the most sophisticated underground escape systems in Europe.

The two other airmen joined him at the château and new identities and travel passes were provided, as well as clothing. The documents were those of French labourers who worked for the Germans, and had been stolen from a German control post close to the border with Spain. A man called Fernand de Greef, a small, quiet, shy man who acted as an interpreter for the Germans had achieved this. What the Germans did not know was that de Greef's wife was a senior officer in the Comète Line's south of France operation. The signatures on the passes had to be those of the Kommandant in the area and Dédée became very adept at forging these.

After ten days of preparation, MacLean and some of the others were told that they were on the move, and late in the afternoon, with Dédée, Frédéric and the Count as guides, the party split up and set off. It was decided to use the Metro. The journey was nearly over before it had started when MacLean handed his ticket to the inspector at the turnstile. The man glared at MacLean and broke into a torrent of abuse in French. The man became more and more agitated, waving the ticket in the air. Then suddenly a very calm Dédée appeared at his side and produced another ticket. Speaking to the inspector, she placated him by saying that she had given her friend the wrong ticket and that it was her fault, not his. The inspector calmed down, smiled at the pretty young woman and waved them both through.

Once on board the train, MacLean relaxed and fell into a fitful sleep. The other escapees were on the same train but in different carriages. The trip was uneventful and the following morning the train pulled into St-Jean-de-Luz, a little town close to the Pyrenees. They were taken to a small farmhouse belonging to a Basque family. There they were fed and given a change of clothing, which included Basque berets and rope-soled sandals. They had to look like the locals, as the following day they had to walk 5 miles to another farmhouse where another guide would be waiting.

The following evening the party set off and by nightfall had reached a farmhouse at the foot of the Pyrenees. There they were welcomed by the woman who owned the house and given food. Hardly had they started eating when the door opened and a very tall, large man entered; this was their guide Florentino Goikoetxea. Without saying a word the man looked at each of the escapees carefully and then nodded to Dédée, who looked visibly relieved. As MacLean was to discover later, there was a very good reason for this. The journey over the Pyrenees was going to be both torturous and arduous, and only those physically capable of doing it could be considered. In the event of one of their party being unable to do it, they would have to stay behind until they were fit enough, or to be taken out another way.

Outside the house the wind lashed the rain against the windows and Goikoetxea looked out at the ever-darkening skies. This he said would be the time to go as the Germans would not venture out in this weather, and if they did, their dogs would not be able to pick up any scent. Shouldering an enormous pack onto his back, he led the party out onto the road and towards the mountains. The men struggled to keep up with him as he strode along, then after covering just a few hundred yards, he left the road and started up a narrow winding path. At first the climbing was relatively easy, but then the path became steeper and the rocks slippery. The rope sandals they had been given gave them extra grip, but soon the thongs that held them began to cut into the flesh.

After two hours MacLean and the rest of the escapees were breathless and exhausted, and felt like giving up, but the young Dédée, although soaking wet, looked as fresh as she did when they started out. Goikoetxea, out in front, did not seem to be out of breath. The climb up was relentless and sheer agony for the party of escapees, but they still carried on. Hour after hour they climbed upwards, every muscle in their tired bodies screaming for a rest, and then suddenly the ground started sloping downwards. By this time the rain had ceased, but cascading water could be heard.

Dédée explained that they were close to the Spanish border, but first they had to cross a river. The river had been swollen by the rain and the current was very strong. One of the escapees had been wounded when he was shot down, and his wound had only partially healed. Dédée explained this to Goikoetxea, who took off his pack, handed it to MacLean, then picked the wounded man up, put him on his back and plunged into the river. Dédée quickly followed him and then came the remainder of the party.

MacLean was last, and as he plunged up to his armpits into the icy water, the cold took his breath away. Struggling across with Goikoetxea's pack on his back, he went under twice, before strong hands hauled him out on the other side. The party flopped to the ground on the other side trying to regain their breath and rest their tired limbs. The last stage of the journey was now upon them; they had to cross a railway line and a road before they reached the border itself, which was heavily patrolled by both German and Spanish guards. The latter had a tendency to shoot first and ask questions afterwards.

Silently, Goikoetxea made his way down the mountainside to the railway track. The others watched as he looked up and down, then he raised his hand for them to come. After crossing the railway line, they hid while he went ahead to scout the road. Then his hand was raised and one after another they limped across the road as fast as their tired legs would let them. On the other side of the road was a steep slope that they knew they had to climb without stopping. Once over the top they raced down through trees and into a clearing where a grinning Dédée and Goikoetxea were waiting. They were safe.

The pace now relaxed and after another two hours of walking through the mountains they arrived at a mountain cabin owned by a Spanish family who were sympathetic to the cause. The party of men collapsed in front of a roaring fire and as one fell asleep where they sat.

It was noon the following day before they were awakened by Dédée, who was to take them to the next stopping place, San Sebastian. On the outskirts of the town they were taken to a large family house, where they were fed and able to rest. The following morning Dédée took the party to a crossroads just outside of town and told them that a car from the British embassy in Madrid was on its way to pick them up. She said she was leaving to go back to bring some more Allied airmen to safety. The men looked at her in awe, all mumbling totally inadequate thanks, and then she was gone.

Thirty minutes later a large black Buick arrived and the men piled in and were whisked away to Madrid. There the Air Attaché settled them in and prepared forged papers that would get them over the border into Gibraltar. MacLean was given the identity of a Captain Collie of the Staffordshire Regiment, who had gone absent without leave and was being returned to his regiment to face a court martial. The embassy car took him to the border, and, looking convincingly crestfallen – to the obvious delight of the Spanish border guards – he crossed over into Gibraltar. It was seventy-four days after his aircraft had been shot down.

On 7 October 1943, he was flown back to England to the RCAF headquarters. MacLean was not allowed to fly on operational missions again because, in the event of him being shot down again he knew too much about the escape lines and the people who ran them.

At the end of the war, MacLean, now a wing commander, became a member of a team set up to try to find out what happened to some of the aircrew who had gone missing but were never found. On a trip to Belgium, he was invited to attend the wedding of the youngest member of the Peeter family and it was while there that he learned of the imprisonment of Albert Pagie. Pagie had been arrested after the war by the Resistance and accused of collaborating with the enemy. MacLean immediately went to the authorities and put the record straight, saying that the only reason Pagie had collaborated with the Germans was to draw attention away from the fact that he was hiding Allied airmen aboard his houseboat. Pagie was released almost immediately and everyone was made aware that the accusations against him were untrue.

12. THE WOODEN HORSE – STALAG LUFT III

ONE OF THE most dramatic and daring escapes made from a prisoner-of-war camp during the Second World War was the one made from Stalag Luft III in Sagan, eastern Germany, in October 1943. This was to be the site of the famous escape using the 'Wooden Horse'.

Stalag Luft III was a POW camp for air force personnel in Poland. When the first inmates arrived they found a camp situated in a bleak inhospitable landscape that, on the face of it, offered very few opportunities to escape. The camp had been built in a clearing inside a pine forest that stretched for more than 20 miles.

Stalag Luft III was meant to be the most secure of all POW camps, a Sonderlager (special camp), one that had been set up to house those prisoners who had a record of attempted escapes. The prisoners were kept in barrack blocks that had been built on concrete pillars with just a 3in gap between them. The huts were some 300ft from a 10ft inner perimeter wire that was topped with razor wire. There was a 7ft gap between the inner and outer wire, which in turn was again topped with razor wire. The gap between the two fences was also layered with razor wire, and strategically placed seismographs detected any tunnelling that might be going on. Then, 15ft in front of the inner wire was a trip wire that the prisoners were forbidden to cross unless permission was given to do so.

Guard towers, manned continuously by two men, were fitted with machine guns and searchlights and placed strategically along the perimeter. This gave the guards an overall view of the camp and enabled them to spot any unauthorised movement by the inmates. Between the 'Goon' towers, as the prisoners called them, guards patrolled day and night.

It was to this camp that Flight Lieutenant Eric Williams and Captain Michael Codner came. Williams and Codner had been inmates of another camp and had escaped, but had been recaptured in Poland. They immediately started to make plans to escape again, as most of the other inmates did, but soon realised that this camp was not going to be an easy one from which to gain freedom.

The location of the barracks in relation to the outer perimeter wire made the idea of tunnelling out of the question. A number of tunnels had been tried and failed, but if they could find a way of making a tunnel shorter then it would be feasible. Ideas for escape were always welcome and would be given consideration by the escape committee. If they merited further investigation then plans would be put into action to see if they were feasible or not. Most were dismissed out of hand because they were either too complicated or too bizarre. There were also 'ferrets' – German soldiers who constantly searched the camp looking for clues that might lead them to an escape attempt. At night they would even climb over the perimeter wire so as to enter the camp without anyone knowing. They then would look and listen for any information that might help them. Some even had a sense of humour and would report to the 'duty pilot' as they left. This was a prisoner whose job was to watch the main gate constantly and report who went in and who went out.

Then one of the major tunnels that were being started in the washhouse was discovered. It was an ingenious idea because the washhouse was in constant use and watch could be kept on the guards without attracting attention. A section of the brick floor had been removed and a shaft dug. The lid to the tunnel consisted of a wooden frame with bricks attached that would be placed over the hole at a moment's notice. It was discovered by the ferrets after the prisoners had already dug a tunnel some forty feet towards the wire.

It was Williams who came up with the idea of a 'Trojan Horse'. His plan was to build a vaulting horse 4ft 6in high with sloping sides down to a base 5ft long and 3ft wide. The top would be padded with bedding, and there would be four slots in the sides, which enabled two poles to be inserted to carry it out into the compound.

The idea was that the 'horse' would be carried out into the compound and placed at a predetermined spot. Inside the horse would be one of the inmates, who would then start burrowing down. There would be a rota of 'diggers' and they would dig down to a depth of 5ft, and then dig a further 70ft to beyond the wire. The German guards, conscious of anything out of the ordinary, looked upon the project with deep mistrust. After all, every one of the prisoners was a known escapee from other POW camps, and so it was felt it was in their nature to try to escape.

The escape committee met and after a long and detailed discussion decided to give it a try. A great deal had to be considered; after all, what were they to do with the earth that was removed from the tunnel? Arrangements had to be made to disperse the soil in such a way that it wouldn't be spotted by the guards. Dumping it under the barracks was out of the question, as the guards made regular examination of the ground beneath, and they would soon spot any additional sandy soil deposited there.

Williams and Codner set to work 'acquiring' the tools required to build the horse. The materials came from the partially finished shower block that the Germans had been in the process of constructing for the past eighteen months. During the night, guards with dogs patrolled the whole compound, so to get to the shower block a distraction had to be arranged. One of the prisoners created a disturbance at the far end of the camp to draw off the guards and their dogs. While this was in process, the two men slipped out of their hut, over the wire surrounding the building site, and quickly picked up what they required. Red Cross tea chests were also used for the construction.

Dragging the timber behind them, they dodged the searchlights and carried it all back to their hut. As they reached their hut, the shutters were flung open and willing hands were ready to grab the timber and nails if needed. Fortunately they made the hut in darkness and the two men slipped underneath and buried the timber and nails in the sand.

The following morning Williams went to see the camp CO, Wing Commander Cameron, and explained his idea to him. 'Wings', as he was known, was enthusiastic and set about designing the horse on his drawing board. With this done, Williams and Codner set about constructing the horse using the tools that had been acquired or borrowed. In the meantime a gymnastics class had been organised with a large number of volunteers who were prepared to do two hours of exercise every morning and sometimes in the afternoon.

Williams and Codner questioned two prisoners who had escaped and been recaptured at the port of Danzig. They wanted to know the best method of travelling and it was decided that this was by train. One of the two men, an Australian, emphasised that the best method was to get aboard a goods train, because the travel documents that they made in the camp would not pass close scrutiny. The passenger trains were always kept under close watch and the identity and travel documents of foreign workers were examined closely.

Then came a stroke of luck. One of the Australians had cultivated a relationship with one of the guards, keeping him supplied with cigarettes and chocolate. He had even persuaded him to bring some eggs in exchange for chocolate. The guard, not the brightest of people, had been wounded fighting on the Russian Front and was terrified of being sent back. The Australian gradually weeded information out of him regarding the trains and the requirements for travelling foreign workers. They needed a special permit to travel as well as one from the chief of police in the area in which they lived and from the firm for which they worked. After much wheeling and dealing, the Australian finally threatened the guard with exposure for trading with prisoners. This offence meant he could be sent back to the Russian Front or even shot, so the guard was persuaded to bring the passes for him to see. Obviously they could not keep them, but one of the prisoners was an excellent artist and he made very detailed drawings.

With this additional information, the plans were set to go into full swing. With the horse finished everything was set for work to begin. One sunny morning the canteen doors opened and a group of prisoners dressed in shorts and shoes ran out and lined up by the trip wire. The four strongest men of the group carrying the vaulting horse followed them. They placed the horse at a spot 10 yards from the trip wire and slipped out the carrying poles. The instructors, Williams and Codner, then demonstrated to the rest of the men the kind of vaulting they wanted them to do. They then leapfrogged over the horse, followed by the rest of the class.

The German guards watched with increased curiosity and suspicion, wondering what the prisoners were up to. They were aware that this might be an attempt to divert their attention away from somewhere else where an escape attempt was being made. The guards in the towers scanned the surrounding areas within the compound but could see nothing unusual. The Kommandant made a brief appearance but, satisfied that it was a harmless activity to keep the men fit and occupied, returned to his office.

The job now was to convince the guards that there was nothing untoward about the activities surrounding the horse. So as to alleviate any lingering suspicions, one of the men had been primed to be awkward, and was constantly making a mess of his vaulting. Then when he attempted to make a two-handed straddle of the horse, he clattered into it and knocked it over. Everyone laughed, including the guards, who could see that the inside was empty. This happened several times during the following two hours, before the men called it a day and returned the horse to the canteen. Just before leaving, the last of the men to leave tied a thin black piece of cotton thread across the door. In the morning it was discovered to have been broken; the Germans had been and examined the horse.

For the next couple of weeks the horse was carried out and the men performed their routine of vaulting, and once again the same man, who appeared to be getting better, occasionally clattered into it, knocking it over. By this time the guards had lost interest and only occasionally glanced over to watch. Then one morning the horse was carried out and the men were warned that under no circumstances were they to knock it over. This time Williams was inside and he was to start digging the escape tunnel.

The statistics had been worked out with regard to the length of the tunnel and how long it was estimated that it would take. The calculations were that it was around 45ft to the trip wire, 30ft to the perimeter wire, a further 8ft to clear the wire, another 30ft to clear the guards' patrolling area and a further 7ft in case of any obstructions. This was a total of 120ft and digging 3ft a day should take six weeks – well that was the theory.

The moment the men started to pound up to the horse and then vault over it, Williams started digging. Taking away the top grey layer of sand, he placed that in a box and then started digging down into the yellowish sand beneath with a trowel. With each scoop he placed the sand into cloth bags that had been made from trouser legs, and when full hung them on hooks inside the horse. Also inside the horse with him was a Red Cross tea chest that had the top and bottom panels removed, and this was to shore up the shaft.

After two hours of continuous digging, Williams managed to sink the shaft to a depth that allowed the tea chest to be slid in position 6in below the surface. He then placed the lid over the top and covered it with the grey sand he had placed in the box. With this done, he tapped on the box to let the instructors know he had finished. The poles were then pushed through the holes and the horse lifted up, only this time the four men had to carry not only Williams, but also twelve bags of sand back to the canteen. Once inside, Williams got out and the twelve bags were removed. The sand was then transferred into long sausage-like bags that six men had attached to their waists and beneath their trousers. The men would then wander all around the camp, and by means of a cord that opened the bottom of the bags, distribute the sand as they walked.

The next day Codner took his place inside the horse and continued to dig the shaft. The two men alternated while the shaft was dug and after almost a week of digging, it had been sunk to a depth of 5ft. In order to keep the shaft shored up, the tea chest was placed on bricks, the latter having been stolen from building works that had been going on in another part of the camp.

Now came the difficult part, digging the tunnel. Because of the narrowness of the shaft and the tunnel, the diggers had to lie on their backs to carry out the work. Boards were removed from the bottoms of beds so that the tunnel, as it progressed, could be shored up. Above the heads of the diggers, the pounding of the gymnasts' feet confused the sound of the digging for the microphones.

As the weeks passed the tunnel progressed towards the wire, the two diggers shoring up as they went. Then after reaching 20ft, which placed the tunnel past the spot above where the vaulters landed, it was decided not to bother shoring up, but just to continue tunnelling. Working in the confined space, the air became foul, but the tunnellers could not make air holes in case the guard dogs discovered them. Then one afternoon disaster struck when there was a cave-in.

Immediately as the hole appeared, one of the vaulters threw himself across it, complaining he had broken his leg. Williams, who had gone to the canteen to fetch some water, saw the vaulters had stopped and were crowded around one of their men. Another of the vaulters whispered to him that the tunnel had collapsed, so Williams told him to fetch a stretcher. Crouching beside the 'injured' man, Williams thrust his hand down the hole and whispered to his colleague in the tunnel, asking if he was all right. Codner replied that he was and was in the process of shoring up the tunnel, but he needed Williams and the other men to buy him some time to do so, and for them to then fill the hole in when he finished.

In the meantime one of the men had gone to fetch the first aid kit, and for the next fifteen minutes Williams made a big fuss of binding the 'injured' man's leg to the stretcher. All the time the men were becoming aware that the guards were now taking more than a passing interest in the incident and that any moment they would be coming over to see what was going on. Suddenly there was a soft tap from inside the 'horse', signifying that Codner was back inside. The men quickly shuffled around the hole and filled it with the grey sand of the compound.

The tunnelling was becoming more and more arduous and two days after the cave-in incident, both men collapsed with exhaustion. Out of the 100ft required to take them under the wire and into the space close to the trees, they had only completed 40ft, and that had taken more than three months. With 60ft still to go, both Williams and Codner had reached the point where they felt like quitting. The main problem was the lack of air and lighting. Once in the tunnel they were working in the dark and it was difficult to keep the tunnel level. In addition to these problems, the further they got, the longer it took to drag the sand back, consequently each foot dug was taking progressively longer.

It was also a one-man operation once down there, but then Codner came up with a suggestion. If they both worked down there it would be quicker. In addition to this system, they built a little trolley that the tunneller took with him to the face, but this wasn't the success they had hoped for, so they replaced it with a basin that had a hole drilled at each end and a line attached to both ends. The tunneller took the bowl to the face and filled it with sand; it was then pulled back to the shaft, where the contents were placed in bags.

The two men went down the shaft and dug out a workstation in which they placed thirty-six bags of sand. At the end of the shift, they both got back inside the 'horse', but with no bags of sand. In the next shift one man went back down and brought back twelve of the bags. The following shift the other tunneller went out and collected twelve of the bags, then on the next trip the last twelve bags were collected.

With all the bags collected, the two men then went down again and dug out another thirty-six bags of sand and the routine would start again. However, at this point the gymnasts were starting to weary of doing the same exercise, and with both instructors now down the hole tunnelling, interest in the project started to wane. It was then that Flight Lieutenant Oliver Philpot stepped forward and said that he would organise and instruct the class.

Williams and Codner knew of another tunnel being dug, one that had previously been discovered, but was now being reactivated. Suddenly, while the team that was helping to build the tunnel were dispersing the sand in various places, including under the floor of the barber's shop and the kitchen area and in the roof space above the huts, a truckload of German soldiers came hurtling through the gates and stopped outside the canteen. It was quite obvious what was going on; they had somehow got wind of an escape plot and were about to search everywhere. This meant that if they found the other team's tunnel, then there was a good chance they would look for others.

The men were called out for parade while the camp was searched. Suddenly the ceiling in one of the huts collapsed on top of the searchers and moments later the entrance to the other tunnel was discovered. This seemed to satisfy the Germans, and after disciplining the POWs' senior officer by sending him to the 'cooler' for a week, the camp settled back into a semblance of normality.

Williams and Codner decided to let the atmosphere in the camp settle down before recommencing work on their tunnel. The two men took the opportunity to arrange for the clothing they would wear when they got out and the documents they would need. Because Codner could speak reasonable French, it was decided that they would both be French draughtsmen working for the Arado Aircraft Company just outside the port of Stettin. The two men intended to try to stow away aboard one of the numerous Swedish merchant ships that used the port. They knew this would be risky because the Germans constantly searched the ships using dogs.

They were also given the address of a brothel in Stettin, which was used by foreign workers, but banned to Germans. Operated by two Polish girls, it was said that they had offered refuge to Allied soldiers in the past. As tempting as it might have been, it was decided not to take advantage of it because it was felt to be wide open to scrutiny by both the German Army and the Gestapo, and raids upon the establishment were more than a possibility.

Work started on the other tunnel and the 'Gymnastic Club' kept up its relentless pursuit of fitness. To their dismay, Williams and Codner found that the sand and the ground above had dried up, causing a number of falls within the tunnel. These, of course, had to be cleared and the tunnel made safe before any more excavating could take place.

Another problem arose; because of the small diameter of the tunnel, the longer the tunnel became the amount of air available decreased. They did find, however, that as the bowl was pushed up, it forced additional air up to the tunneller at the face. It was under these horrendous conditions that the two men worked. All through the summer they toiled in the tunnel and above ground the vaulting gymnasts kept up their relentless exercise routine. As the summer days started to close in and the first signs of winter started to appear, problems arose regarding the weather. If it started to rain, the vaulters could not continue and it would look suspicious if they left the horse while they took shelter. They couldn't bring the horse in while the two men were in the tunnel because this would leave the shaft exposed. So it was decided to check the weather every day and if it looked like rain, they would not dig, but the vaulters would carry out their regular exercise and bring the horse in if it started to rain.

As winter neared, it was decided to try to find out exactly how long the tunnel was. They knew it was under the outer perimeter wire, but how far out they did not know. Williams crawled the length of the tunnel and slowly pushed a 4ft-long thin metal poker up and through the soil above. One of the vaulters standing by the horse kept a wary eye out for where he thought the poker might appear. Then suddenly he spotted it just 3ft beyond the perimeter fence – 15ft short of their proposed target.

An emergency meeting was hurriedly called to decide what to do. The problem was that the railway timetable they had acquired expired in just one week, so it was decided to continue digging for another 9ft. This was because just at this point there was a ditch, and it was noticed that at night, when the searchlight was played around the compound, this was the one place where it cast a shadow, so if they opened the tunnel there they could slip out and roll into the ditch. Two days before the timetable expired they had reached their objective and the decision was made to go.

Then a simple oversight nearly put an end to the attempt. Three men were going to make a break through the tunnel, which meant that the three had to be taken to the trapdoor in the horse. This in itself would cause a problem because of the additional weight. The stumbling block was that once the three men went down the shaft and into the tunnel, who was going to close the trapdoor behind them?

It was decided that the obvious way was that when the horse was taken out on the morning of the escape, two men would be inside. On 29 October, Codner and Williams were carried out in the horse. A bulge had been made in the end of the tunnel to allow for their escape gear. Codner went into the tunnel with his escape gear and, on reaching the end, made an air hole and settled down to wait for night. Williams closed the shaft, crawled back inside the horse and was taken back to the canteen. There, he and Oliver Philpot dressed themselves in black combinations, collected their escape gear and got inside the horse together with another of the prisoners. With the two escapees holding the other inmate between them, the poles were pushed through and the horse, with three men now inside, was lifted up and carried with great difficulty to its spot in the compound.

Once over the spot, the cover of the hatch was opened and Williams and Philpot slipped down the hatch into the tunnel. The other man then closed the hatch, covered it with dirt and climbed back into the horse. After the vaulting had finished it was taken back to the canteen, leaving the three men in the tunnel to wait for night to fall.

As Williams crawled up the tunnel, he suddenly came to a wall of sand and realised that Codner, in digging out the final 6ft, had pushed the sand behind him. Forcing his hand through the wall he was met with a strong smell of foul air and sweat. Realising that he would have to get the sand back to the shaft, he signalled Philpot to send up the bowl so that they could transfer the sand. For the next hour, the three men worked tirelessly, not only to move the sand back, but also to dig upwards to just below the surface. Their work was further hampered by the fact that the original tunnel had been dug when the two tunnellers wore no clothes. Now they were fully clothed, making fitting in the tunnel even more difficult and claustrophobic – if that was even possible.

As darkness fell, the men in the tunnel broke through the thin layer of dirt and into the fresh air. They then became aware of the pre-arranged singing and banging of tins coming from the other prisoners in the compound. Slowly Codner poked his head out of the hole, looking around he could see no movement as the searchlight swept by. The noise coming from the compound was drawing the attention of the guards in the towers and they knew this was the moment they had to make the break.

Pushing his escape kit in front of him, Codner crawled out of the hole and along the grass, and then rolled silently into the ditch. Then came Williams, followed by Philpot. The three men looked back towards the compound, and as the searchlights from the guard towers swept across it, they ran into the pine forest.

Inside the forest they changed into their civilian clothes, checked their documents for the umpteenth time and headed towards the railway station. Williams and Codner looked around for Philpot, but he had already gone. Taking their black combinations and their kit bags, they buried them in the woods and liberally sprinkled pepper over them. This would be to deter the guard dogs that would be sent to pick up their trail when their escape had been discovered.

Luck was with the two men, for as they arrived at the station the train pulled in and, after purchasing tickets, the men boarded. The train was going to Frankfurt and was crowded, and the two escapees stood in the corridor until it pulled into the station. In Frankfurt they made their way out of the station and into the town. They decided to find a cheap hotel, but after trying several they found them all to be full. They decided to move out into the countryside to find somewhere to sleep for the night. After a restless night under a hedge, Codner and Williams made their way back to the railway station. They discovered that there was a train to Kuestrin in an hour so they decided to get a coffee and went into the waiting room. The room was full of workers and German soldiers, but it was warm and helped them thaw out after the cold night in the open.

The coffee was made from acorns and tasted foul, but it was hot. Looking around the room, Williams noted that none of the workers or indeed the soldiers looked particularly fit and healthy, whereas both he and Codner appeared very well in comparison – after all, they had been exercising while digging the tunnel for the past nine months.

They took the next train to Kuestrin, with the intention of getting to Stettin, where they hoped they would be able to get aboard a Swedish ship. Once again fortune smiled upon them as there was only a short delay before their train arrived, but it was crowded with German soldiers to the point that there was barely enough room to stand. The train stopped at every station and slowly but surely the crowd thinned until finally they were able to get some seats. Within a couple of hours the train pulled into the station.

The train to Stettin was not until the evening, so they decided to go into town. After walking around Kuestrin, which was very small, they realised that if they continued to walk around people might begin to wonder what they were doing there. Finding a bar, they had a beer and then realised that this was a *Stammegericht* (basic meal) café, a place where you could get a coupon-free meal of stew, which was made with generous helpings of potatoes, carrots and swedes. After finishing their bowls of *Stammegericht*, the two men felt much better, but decided that they would go to the cinema they had passed earlier and stay in there until it was time to catch the train.

At the station, the clerk demanded to see all their papers and after scrutinising them he seemed satisfied and gave them their tickets to Stettin. When the train arrived they were pleased to see it was so full that no one could possibly carry out an inspection of passes and travel documents. After one stop, a large number of passengers got off, allowing the two men to find seats in a carriage. They dozed off but were wakened by shouting; a ticket inspector, accompanied by two policemen, had boarded the train demanded to see everyone's tickets. As the officials made their way through the carriage, the police picked on certain people and examined their travel passes and ID cards. Codner got the tickets ready and handed them to the inspector, who glanced at the tickets and then at them. With a '*weiter*' (carry on), he handed back the tickets and moved on followed the policemen. The train pulled into Stettin and once again there were no checks on passes, just ticket collectors. As the two men left the station, the cold wind from the Baltic lashed the rain against them, but the fact they had got this far without any real problems, filled them with warmth and hope.

Once again their search for a hotel proved fruitless and so, with the rain continuing to pour down, they looked for somewhere to shelter for the night. Sleeping outside was out of the question, so looking into a back garden, they saw an air-raid shelter and decided to hide in there for the night and pray that there wasn't a bombing raid due.

The following morning they awoke early and ate what was left of their biscuits before heading towards the docks. They would have to find somewhere else to sleep that night so they approached a French worker and, taking a chance, asked him if he knew of a cheap hotel. They were directed to the Hotel Schobel and, passing themselves off as Frenchmen from the nearby French labour camp, booked in for the night. Once established in the hotel, they made their way down to the docks again in an effort to find a Swedish ship. The docks were heavily guarded and the two men watched from a safe distance as the German guards paced up and down, watching and checking all the comings and goings off the ships. They appeared to be constantly checking the papers of seamen embarking and disembarking.

Going back to their hotel, Williams slit open the bottom of his mackintosh and pulled out a map that had been drawn by one of the escapees who had been caught in the area. It showed a map of the docks, and, more importantly, the dock where the Swedish ships berthed. The two men made their way over to the dock, only to find it enclosed by an 18ft-high barbed wire fence and guards everywhere, but there berthed alongside the dock was a ship flying the Swedish flag. The plan was to return that night and get over the fence by climbing on top of a railway wagon that was close by it. That night they made their way to the docks, only to find that the ship had sailed that evening.

For two days Williams and Codner watched the docks, but the routine of the guards did not vary and so they decided to approach their escape from a different quarter. They had made contact with an English-speaking French barber and he told them of a man, by the name of René, in the French labour camp who had connections with the Danish Resistance organisation called Spediøren, which ran an escape route in Denmark. In the meantime, they had to get passes to get them into the dock area. One of the Frenchmen lent them two of the passes and Williams set about copying them. He had brought some of his 'forging' equipment with him – mapping pens, red and black ink and a rubber stamp of an eagle carrying a swastika made from the heel of a boot. The passes were on a pink card and cheaply printed, so there was not going to be a need for any finesse as regard to copying. After diluting some red ink with water, he soaked a piece of card in the solution until it was almost the same shade of pink. When the card had dried, he set about copying the details. When he finished, although they were not perfect, he was confident that they would pass scrutiny in the half-light of the dock area.

The barber approached them and told them it would be safer for them if they went with him to the French labour camp, where they could stay while arrangements were made. He told them that the hotels in the area were not safe as the proprietors had to declare their residents to the German authorities if they stayed more than two nights.

After spending two nights in the camp, the barber returned to tell them that he had arranged for them to meet a member of the crew of the Danish cargo ship *S.I. Norensen*. The crewmember, a man named Sigmund, was also a member of the Danish Resistance organisation, they discovered later, and with great difficulty he managed to get them both on board the cargo ship which was bound for Copenhagen.

Just before the ship sailed, Codner and Williams were made to hide in a cramped corner of the bows where the anchor chain was situated. This was because just prior to sailing, the ship would be searched by German soldiers with dogs. Then one of the soldiers would stay aboard until they reached Swinemunde, where he would leave the ship.

For the next six hours they crouched in the tiny locker and waited. As the ship pitched and rolled, the temperature inside the locker dropped considerably and the insides of the steel hull were running with condensation. Both Codner and Williams were seasick and the cold had reached a stage where it was becoming almost unbearable. Then the engines slowed and the anchor chain rattled around inside the locker as it was dropped. After about twenty minutes there was a bumping and then the engines started up and the ship got under way again. The locker was opened and the grinning face of Sigmund looked in.

Once the ship had set sail, Williams and Codner felt they were free and both relaxed. That was until the captain received a radio message saying that the German SS were waiting in Copenhagen to arrest Sigmund. The message also said that a small fishing boat would rendezvous with them some miles from the port, and take Sigmund and the two escapees off. They would be put ashore at a remote point, where other members of the Resistance would be waiting.

About 5 miles from Copenhagen the cargo ship slowed as a small boat pulled alongside and the men transferred to it. They were taken to shore, where they were met by other members of the Resistance and provided with bicycles. The three men cycled with a guide to a remote farmhouse, which turned out to be the regional headquarters for the Resistance. Their departure from the cargo ship was not a moment too soon as it turned out, for thirty minutes after they had gone, they discovered later, German E-boats arrived to search the ship for Sigmund.

After spending a relaxing two days at the farmhouse, Sigmund took Williams and Codner to Copenhagen, where they were hidden in his sister's apartment. They were to stay until the *S.I. Norensen* was ready to leave for Sweden, but Sigmund, who had been reconnoitring the docks, returned to the apartment and told them that the area was crawling with German guards examining everything and everyone.

It was decide to abandon the idea of getting back aboard the cargo ship and so Sigmund bought three tickets for the electric railway that would take them to a small coastal village. Sigmund knew where he could find a small sailing boat, as the only option available to them now was to sail across the Kattegat, the stretch of water between Denmark and Sweden.

As darkness fell they approached the bridge that would take them across to the little island where Sigmund knew the boat was moored. They were also aware that there would probably be guards. Suddenly Sigmund froze as the figure of a German sentry moved onto the bridge. Codner and Williams decided that there was no time to waste and hurriedly devised a plan to draw the guard to them. Codner staggered out onto the bridge and then collapsed. The sentry challenged him, but on receiving no reply from the crumpled figure, moved closer. As he reached Codner, Williams crept out and struck the guard on the back of the neck with a sock filled with sand. As the guard staggered, Codner grasped him by the legs and pulled him to the ground. As he did so, the guard managed to strike him with the butt of his rifle, knocking him unconscious. Williams then killed the guard by grabbing him around the neck and throttling him.

In the meantime, Sigmund had slipped over the bridge and found the sailing boat. Williams revived Codner and they arrived minutes later to find that Sigmund had the boat prepared. Climbing aboard, they pushed the boat silently away from the island. They tacked along the shoreline for a few miles and then struck out across the Kattegat to Sweden. The following morning, the little sailing boat with three tired men aboard sailed into Swedish waters.

After surrendering to the authorities, the two men were sent to the British Consul in Gothenburg. On arriving, they asked if there was any news about Philpot and were told that he had arrived a week earlier. That same evening the three men were reunited and celebrated their successful escape. They were returned to England three days later and went quickly back to operational duties.

It is a fact that of all the Allied servicemen picked up by the Danish Resistance during the war, not one was ever taken by the Germans. The remarkable story of the Danish Resistance and their part in saving more than 74 per cent of their Jewish population is a story in itself.

This was not the only escape from Stalag Luft III. In March 1944, eighty officers of the RAF attempted to leave via one of the most elaborate escape tunnels ever built. Of the eighty who went, seventy-six escaped the camp; the other four were caught at the mouth of the tunnel when the attempt was discovered.

13. THE GREAT ESCAPE – STALAG LUFT III

THE GREAT ESCAPE from Stalag Luft III was the greatest mass escape from a prisoner-of-war camp ever known. It caused the Germans serious problems and great embarrassment, and tied up thousands of troops and civilians in the search for the prisoners.

The arrival of the charismatic Squadron Leader Roger Bushell at the camp was to be the spark that ignited the flame needed to focus everyone on the need to escape.

Bushell had been born in South Africa but educated in England. He had been shot down over Dunkirk attempting to protect the soldiers on the beach from Stuka dive-bombers. After crash-landing in a field, he had been captured and taken to a Dulag Luft (Durchgangslager Luftwaffe) transit camp.

Unfortunately for the Germans, Bushell had been a barrister in civilian life with a reputation of being belligerent, as the interrogators found out from his acid tongue. On realising that they were getting nowhere, they turned him loose into the camp. There he met up with his fellow inmates, among whom were Wing Commander 'Wings' Day, Major Johnny Dodge, Lieutenant Commander Peter Fanshaw and Jimmy Buckley of the Royal Navy.

Within days of arriving, Bushell had organised the digging of a tunnel. Cutting a trapdoor under the beds of one of the inmates, they burrowed their way out of the hut, under the compound and the wire, but with less than 8ft to go they hit a spring and the tunnel was flooded. The Germans discovered a second tunnel shortly after it had been started. A third tunnel was begun but the onset of winter put it on hold. Walking more than 120 miles towards a friendly border in snow, with very little food and in a hostile country, was not to be recommended.

In the spring of 1940 Bushell escaped by hiding in a tumbledown goat shack tucked away in the corner of a field. The prisoners had been allowed out to a field adjoining the compound and had started a mock 'bullfight' with the goat so as to draw the attention of the guards. While this was going on, Bushell slipped into the goat shed and hid.

After the prisoners had been returned to the camp, Bushell waited until midnight before making his way across the fields. Meanwhile, during the previous months, another tunnel had been successfully dug and seventeen of the prisoners made their way quietly into the woods just outside the wire. Escaping prisoners were on a learning curve and, once free, found it difficult to find their way without a compass, money or sufficient food to sustain them. All seventeen were caught the following day.

In the meantime, Bushell had got within 30 yards of the Swiss border when a German border guard challenged him. Pretending to be a slightly drunk ski instructor who had been celebrating in the village, he persuaded the guard that he was genuine, but the German wanted to confirm it and invited him into the guard post. Bushell realised that he would be exposed and made a run for it. Unfortunately he ran into a cu-de-sac, with a very high wall at the end, followed by heavily armed Germans.

Returned to the Dulag Luft, he was quickly transferred to a new camp on the shores of the Baltic. Joining him were the seventeen other escapees from their previous camp. Within hours the group was hard at work planning the next escape attempt and by the end of the first year more than forty tunnels had been started. The problem was that water lay under the compound at a depth of only 4ft, and so the tunnels had to be very shallow. The Germans were well aware of this and would drive heavily laden wagons around the compound collapsing the tunnels as they passed over them.

These setbacks never once dampened the prisoners' spirits, in fact just the opposite, it spurred them on to think of other ways. However, before they could put any of their ideas into action, they were herded into railway cattle trucks and shipped off to an unknown destination somewhere in Germany. During the journey, Roger and a Czech officer serving in the RAF, Jack Zafouk, prised up some of the floorboards so that they could lower themselves down onto the tracks when the train slowed to a crawl.

One by one they dropped through the hole onto the tracks. Unfortunately one of the other men slipped and fell under the wheels of the train and died. Bushell and Zafouk got clear and jumped on a series of goods trains that were headed for the Czech border, where Zafouk's brother lived. When they arrived, he fed them, gave them some money and the address of a friend in Prague who would shelter them.

Arriving in Prague, the friend set them up in an apartment with a host family. They could not leave because Bushell could not speak Czech and Zafouk was afraid that some of his friends might recognise him. After some weeks, the Resistance was contacted and arrangements made to get them out through Turkey, but just when they were about to move, the deputy chief of the Gestapo, Obergruppenführer Reinhard Heydrich, was shot and mortally wounded by members of the Czech Resistance. All hell broke loose. Hostages were taken off the streets and members of the Resistance who were captured were tortured and then executed. The town of Lidice was levelled and all the men over 15 years of age were rounded up and placed in a barn. The following morning they were all murdered when the barn was set on fire. A further nineteen men and seven women, who were working close by, were sent to Ravensbrück concentration camp, where almost half of them died. The children were taken to another concentration camp. More than 1,300 people were murdered in retaliation for the killing of Heydrich.

The two men stayed in the apartment, until one morning the front door bell rang and, as none of the family was in, Bushell and Zafouk kept quiet. The next thing the door flew open, five German soldiers burst in and the men were arrested and taken to the Gestapo. The host family were later arrested, tortured and then executed.

Roger Bushell was held and interrogated by the Gestapo for several months before finally being sent to Stalag Luft III. It is said that Bushell only escaped the firing squad because of Major von Masse, the chief censor officer at Stalag Luft III, who knew and liked him. Von Masse's brother was Generaloberst von Masse, and he used his position to get Bushell transferred to the prison camp. Zafouk was sent to Colditz.

The Kommandant of Stalag Luft III was Oberst Friedrich-Wilhelm von Linden-Wildau. He was a professional soldier and had fought and been wounded in the First World War, winning both the Iron Cross First and Second Class. He was strict but very fair and would not tolerate any ill treatment of prisoners, being one of the few Kommandants who operated strictly within the rules of the Geneva Convention.

The camp itself covered an area of 59 acres and was surrounded by 5 miles of perimeter fencing consisting of two high barbed wire fences, 9ft high and 5ft apart. Interspaced at 150 yards apart around the perimeter were guard towers that were manned twenty-four hours a day and fitted with searchlights and heavy machine guns. After expansion, the camp held more than 10,000 prisoners of war.

Feeding such a large number of prisoners was difficult, bearing in mind that there was a war on and this came low on the list of priorities for the German government. The ration was made up in the following way: breakfast – very thin slices of bread, margarine and ersatz jam; lunch – the same again; dinner – potatoes with barley or sauerkraut and once every three weeks minced horsemeat.

It was estimated that each man needed 3,000 calories a day, but the rations only allowed for 1,300–1,500 and so the remainder was made up from Red Cross parcels. These were issued at the rate of one parcel per man per week. The German guards themselves fared little better with regard to food, which of course inevitably encouraged bartering between the guards and the prisoners, cigarettes and chocolates being the main currency.

The opening up of Stalag Luft III as a secure camp for habitual escapees only served to bring together some of the most skilled engineers, tailors, forgers and surveillance experts available. Bushell knew this the moment he walked through the gates and within days he was hatching plans to get out. Just after he arrived, the whole section of that camp was moved to the north compound, which had only recently been completed.

After settling in and surveying the surrounding area, Bushell noticed that the trees around the camp had been cut back for approximately 30 yards, which meant that any tunnels would have to extend 100ft beyond the wire. Despite this, he approached the senior British officer (SBO), Group Captain Herbert Massey, and the rest of the escape committee with a tunnelling idea that, if successful, would see 250 men escaping. This would, had it happened, have caused the German military horrendous problems and thousands of German soldiers to be taken away from the fighting front in an effort to catch the escapees.

The building of such a tunnel was to be a massive undertaking and would need complete secrecy and the co-operation of almost everyone in the camp. Among the German guards were a group of known 'ferrets'. These men would enter the compound without warning and search for anything that would lead them to a possible escape attempt. They would, on a regular basis, clear a hut of its occupants and systematically strip and search everything in there. If they discovered a tunnel, they would often allow the digging to continue until it neared completion, and then they would pounce. The reasoning behind this was to effect a demoralising situation in the hope that the prisoners would not bother again. In fact, it did quite the opposite.

Code-named Tom, the tunnel was one of three built from the north compound of the camp. The others, Dick and Harry, were started at the same time in May 1941, but it was decided to concentrate on just one. The head of the escape committee, Bushell, or 'Big X' as he was known, had started planning an escape from the moment he had been moved from the east compound in April 1943.

After a great deal of thought the committee gave the go-ahead, and in charge of the tunnelling would be a Canadian Spitfire pilot and former mining engineer, Flying Officer Wally Floody. Escape kits would be required for each man and that task was put under the control of Flight Lieutenant Johnny Travis. Among the most important items required were compasses. These were made from gramophone needles for the needle pivot, to which a piece of sewing needle was fitted by means of a soldered pivot joint. The solder came from the tins of bully beef that were in the Red Cross parcels. Slivers of broken razor blades were also used and incorporated into tiny cases made from melted down broken Bakelite records. Little circles of paper were painted with the points of the compass and fitted into the base of the tiny cases. Broken glass was cut into circular discs and pressed into the warm Bakelite to form a waterproof seal.

Travel passes and work permits had to be made complete with photographs and the master forger responsible for this department was Tim Walenn. To gain access to these passes, guards were bribed and in some case threatened with exposure for having traded with prisoners, which was against the rules. One guard was even cajoled into providing a miniature camera complete with film. The team of men who made the passes turned out to be master forgers and produced documents that were almost identical to the real thing. They even named their department 'Dean and Dawson' after a well-known London travel agent.

Rubber stamps depicting the German eagle holding a swastika were made from the rubber heels of old boots. Some of the documents needed had the eagle embossed, and this was achieved by making a mould out of soap and casting the stamp in lead. The lead was obtained from melted silver paper. A stamping machine was made with a centring device.

Faking some of the gate passes and travel permits caused a problem because they were typed. Tim Walenn and Gordon Brettell produced handwritten copies that were so good they could not be told from the typewritten originals. Brettell actually tested one of the passes by wangling his way onto a working party on a new part of the camp. He had hidden himself in one of the partially built huts, then when it was dark made his way to the railway station. He was caught when he asked for a ticket to Nuremberg. He produced a travel permit saying that he was a French worker, and although the papers fooled the Gestapo, his French did not. He was arrested and it was then that he found out that Nuremberg was closed to travellers because of a recent heavy bombing raid and there were signs up to that effect. It was this that had caused the guard to be suspicious.

Fortunately, the Gestapo never realised that the travel permit and identity card were forgeries and when Brettell was returned to the prison camp he had somehow retained possession of them. Such was the quality of the forgeries that Walenn had even managed to make the typed strike-overs appear to look like authentic, original mistakes had been made.

Forging the documents was a painstaking process. Some of the documents had backgrounds that equalled those of banknotes and so any mistake would be disastrous. Such was the need for accuracy that any minor mistake would result in the document being destroyed. In the time they were in Stalag Luft III, the forging department, working three to five hours a day, created more than 400 ID cards and work and travel permits.

Flying Officer Tommy Guest, a former tailor, made civilian and workmen's clothes in the continental style from uniforms. He even extended his skills to making German uniforms. He had workers shave the nap off the rough serge with razor blades and then dyed it with beetroot juice or a solution made from black boot polish. Paper patterns were made from German newspapers.

Bushell, with a group of his team, walked around the compound making notes of the drainage covers. Every now and then they would stop, for what appeared to be a debate about something, while one of their number – a small, wiry Welshman – lifted up a manhole cover and slipped down to take a look. The need for secrecy was highlighted one morning when lorries loaded with tree cuttings were leaving the compound. They were searched and a number of would-be-escapees were found buried inside. One escapee, Ian Cross, slipped underneath one of the lorries and clung on to the chassis while the commotion was going on. Just before the lorry moved off, the chief of the security officers, Oberfeldwebel Hermann Glemnitz, the chief of the ferrets, spoke to the driver and the next minute the lorry shot off towards a part of the compound studded with tree stumps. The whole of the camp held their breath as the lorry lurched towards the stumps, waiting to see Cross crushed to death as it ran over them, but it stopped just short.

Oberfeldwebel Glemnitz then strolled up to the lorry, leant down and with a broad grin on his face, invited Cross to come out with the words, 'Your room is ready for you in the cooler, Mr Cross.' Seconds later a downcast Cross appeared and was marched off, to the delight of the guards. He would spend the next two weeks in the prison block. Bushell turned to his team and pointed out that whatever they thought of the German guards, they were not to consider them stupid. It was quite obvious that the guards were well aware of what prisoners would do when there was a distraction and the opportunity arose.

It was decided that there were to be three tunnels. The first one was to go under the western wire from Hut 123 and was code-named Tom. The second was to go from Hut 122, was code-named Dick and would join up with Hut 123, while the third would go from Hut 104 and go under the northern wire. It would be code-named Harry. Bushell made the point that no one was to ever mention the word 'tunnel' again, but to refer to them always under their code names.

Bushell and the tunnel engineers visited the huts looking for likely places to place the trapdoors, because it was here that the ferrets detected most tunnels, so they had to be perfect. Within twenty-four hours they had selected the three places from where the tunnels would be started. Fortunately, German workmen had left some cement in the compound and this was quickly spirited away. The man assigned to making the trapdoors was Flying Officer Minskewitz, a Polish officer serving with the RAF. He measured up the size he needed and cast a concrete slab 2ft square. The slab was reinforced with bits of scrap wire that had been picked up. He also used the wire to make a couple of lugs that were recessed into the concrete, but could be levered out with a knife. Once out, wire could be passed through them to form a handle so that the whole thing could be lifted with ease.

Chipping out a 2ft square from the concrete close to a dark area by the chimney, Minskewitz slotted his trapdoor in perfectly with the delicate precision of a watchmaker. The result was perfection, and so good that Bushell took Group Captain Massey, the senior officer in the camp, to see it. After showing Massey where it was proposed to start digging Tom, Massey enquired how they were going to camouflage the trapdoor once they started. At which point a smiling Bushell pointed out that the trapdoor was already there, delighted that Minskewitz's handiwork had fooled the 'old man'.

For the second of the tunnels, Dick, Minskewitz devised one of the most cunning trapdoors ever invented. In the middle of Hut 122's washroom was an 18in square iron grating that was used to take away the overflow of water. With 'stooges' (lookout men) by the door, Minskewitz lifted the grille and mopped up the water in the well of the hole. This done, he chipped away one side of the well until it exposed the earth beyond. He then made a separate piece of concrete to replace it and filled the joint with a mixture of soap and sand. The grille was then replaced, refilling the well with water.

When digging started in earnest, it took only minutes to bale out the well, remove the slab and start digging. Later when they were digging away from the tunnel entrance, the slab and grille could be replaced and the well filled with water, while they were underneath. There was no way that any ferret would ever find that entrance.

The entrance to Harry was also an example of sheer cunning. In Room 23 of Hut 104, the stove in the centre of the room was lifted to reveal some square tiles. Carefully removing these, Minskewitz transferred them onto a wooden frame made by the carpentry section, the whole process taking ten days. Exploratory digging beneath found a layer of brick followed by concrete, before earth was finally found. The shaft down was going to have to be at least 30ft before tunnelling started because of the microphones the ferrets had planted in the ground around the compound.

The escape committee pinned up a notice inviting volunteers to form a cricket team. This was, in fact, to interview skilled tradesmen who could be used in the escape organisation. Those who had no skills that were needed became either 'stooges' or 'penguins'. Penguins were the men whose job it was to disperse the sand recovered from the tunnels. This was a particularly important job because if they were to be discovered disposing of it, it might ultimately reveal the location of the tunnel. The locations of the trapdoors were known only to a handful of people.

Almost all the camp was involved in one way or another. Some of the jobs were quite onerous and boring; one in particular was the 'duty pilot', who sat beside the main gate watching and recording every person who came in and out of the camp. While he was there, other 'stooges' watched him for any signal the ferrets were coming into the compound. More than 300 'stooges were rostered in shifts to maintain a complete watch on German activities.

In the New Year the digging started in earnest and in Tom they discovered bright yellow sand just 6in below the grey dirt of the topsoil. This immediately caused a problem because if any of the ferrets saw the yellow sand in the compound they would know that a tunnel was being dug. Lieutenant Commander Fanshawe came up with a solution that if every hut had a garden, then the appearance of yellow sand would be considered normal. If the grey topsoil from each garden was saved and mixed with the sand from the tunnels it could be dispersed around the compound.

The method of dispersing the sand around the compound was solved with the idea of cutting off the legs of long johns, tying off the tops after filling them with sand and hanging them around the neck of a penguin. The sausage-like bags would then be pushed down each trouser leg. At the bottom of the bag would be a pin attached to a piece of string that was fed up inside the trouser leg into the pocket. As the penguin walked around the compound, he would pull the pin and allow the sand to come out of the bottom of his trousers. Then as he walked he would scuff the sand over the surface, mixing it with the grey dust covering the compound.

An American, Major Jerry Sage, created one of the diversions used to cover the penguin as he walked about. He would give unarmed combat classes, which resulted in men milling about throwing each other around, and in the middle of all this were the penguins. Another was to have volleyball games with a crowd of spectators moving about and once again in the middle of these shuffling spectators were the penguins depositing their sand.

As the shaft got deeper, bed boards were stripped from beds around the camp to be used as shoring-up timbers. As the shaft progressed, every yard had to be shored up because the looseness of the sand made it unstable. This was highlighted when the shaft of Dick started to collapse when three of the tunnellers were at the bottom. The three men barely got out before the shaft was filled. This was a huge setback for the escape committee because they now had to dig out and re-shore up the shaft before work could start again. What would have happened to the men had they been inside the tunnel itself does not bear thinking about.

The other two tunnels, Tom and Harry, were progressing well and lessons had been learned from the accident in Dick. Such was the ingenuity of the men that by obtaining innocuous scraps of metal from the guards, they managed to make a couple of cold chisels, wood chisels, screwdrivers and even a drill. One German guard brought them an old gramophone spring, which they turned into a saw by filing teeth on it and fitting it on to a wooden frame. The guards were told they wanted the materials for cooking utensils.

Hiding the tools was one of the most difficult problems they had. Various methods were used, such as fitting the smaller items inside books. Then one of the carpenters realised that the buildings were constructed of double wooden walls. By moving one of the inside walls out by 9in and building a concealed trapdoor in it, they were able to hide almost all the tools inside the newly created cavity. Consequently, all the huts were altered in this way, giving the escape committee a large number of places in which to hide their equipment.

The acquisition of tools was a real problem and it was galling for the men to see the abundance of tools the Germans had lent them to build a theatre. They had the tools on parole and no one was going to break that; in any case the tools were counted in and counted out.

While some of the bigger engineering projects that created noise were going on, Jerry Sage organised choir practice outside the hut in which the work was being carried out. One of these projects was the creating of air pumps for each of the tunnels. The pumps' bellows were created out of kitbags with wooden frames inside them, giving them a concertina effect. The top of the kitbag was sealed with a round wooden disc fitted with a handle. An outlet and inlet valve was created out of leather-lined blades of wood, which worked off a coiled spring that had been acquired from a chest expander.

The fresh air was drawn through tin pipes (made from powdered milk tins from Red Cross parcels) via the airbricks in the foundations under each hut and attached to the pump's inlet valve. Connected to the pump's outlet valve were yards of piping constructed from the powdered milk tins, and when the pump man activated the bellows by pulling and then pushing the kitbags in and out, air was forced down through the milk tin pipes to where the diggers were working. This gave them a constant supply of fresh air.

With all three tunnels well under way, Bushell called a meeting to discuss future plans. One thing he wanted to know was how much sand the penguins could disperse in a day. The answer was about 6ft worth a day from each of the three tunnels. The reasoning behind this was that Bushell and the escape committee wanted a time frame estimated for when the tunnels would be completed. Then, depending on the time of the year, preparations could be made to get men out of the camp.

As the tunnels lengthened, lamps made from fat were created with string wicks and placed every few yards. There was also the increasing problem of getting diggers to the tunnel face and so an ingenious idea was devised. It consisted of making a rail track from the beading battens that were on the walls and ceiling of every hut. These were laid on the floor of the tunnel and nailed down. The wheels were made in two parts, with the inside disc being slightly larger than the outer one in order to guide the wheel on the rail.

The trolley was pulled along by means of a plaited cord at either end. The trolleys also carried two detachable wooden boxes in which the sand was placed. At the tunnel face the digger would cut away the sand in front of him and then push it behind him, where the second digger would scoop it up and place it in the boxes on the trolley. He would then signal to the man at the bottom of the shaft by tapping the rail, who in turn would pull the trolley back and empty the boxes into kitbags that were stored in the dispersal chamber that had been cut out at the bottom of the shaft. Then the procedure would be reversed and the trolley pulled back to the face.

The two men at the face would take it in turns to dig in an effort to rest their aching muscles. It was an arduous task because all three men spent most of the day below ground, conscious of the fact that they could have a cave-in at any time. In case any ferrets came sniffing around in the huts, an alarm system, consisting of a couple of pebbles in a tin with a piece of string attached, was hung in the shaft. In the event of a nosy ferret making an appearance, a tug on the piece of string would warn the tunnellers below. They would stop whatever they were doing until the tin rattled again to give them the all clear.

By early June, Tom was 60ft long, with Dick and Harry not too far behind. Then later that month a problem arose when about 100 Russian prisoners arrived and started chopping down trees on the south side. Massey found an excuse to see the Kommandant and asked him what was going on. He was told that an order from the Oberkommando (Supreme Command) office was to build another compound for the Americans. Realising that the Kommandant could do nothing about it, Massey called an urgent meeting of the escape committee.

If the compound were built before Tom was completed, it would mean that tunnel would be useless. Massey had asked the Kommandant for a date when the Americans would be moved, but he said he did not know, although he thought it would be around two months. The committee decided that it would be better if they concentrated on finishing Tom and put the others on hold. The trapdoors of Dick and Harry were sealed shut and all manpower moved to concentrate on getting Tom finished before the Russians had cleared the site.

It was decided to run three shifts and fifteen diggers were selected and split into three groups. The next day the first group moved the tunnel forward 10ft, the second day, despite a cave-in, they moved forward another 8ft. By the end of the week Tom was 105ft long and time was of the essence.

In a break from the rigours of preparing for a mass escape, the American section of the camp had been busily concocting alcohol from raisins and sugar for a Fourth of July party. This was, in effect, raisin wine but after distilling it again they produced a raw spirit. Then out of the blue, one of the Polish contingent, who had heard of the existence of the 'still', came forward with some additional ingredients that would make the raw spirit taste like rye whisky. The Polish officer had been a chemistry lecturer at Krakow University before the war and offered his 'special ingredients' in exchange for an invite to the Fourth of July party. No one ever did find out what the 'special ingredients' were, or maybe they just didn't want to know.

The party that followed was a memorable one, and for a few hours those who imbibed forgot where they were, but beneath the revellers' feet the tunnellers were still hard at work. Then one of the penguins got careless and dropped too much yellow sand close to a hut. One of the stooges watched as a ferret walked up and picked up some of the sand. He stared at it for some time, a quizzical look on his face, before marching off to the camp security offices. The stooge immediately warned a member of the escape committee that the ferrets might have cottoned on to what was going on. Tom was immediately closed down and the trapdoor sealed.

The following morning all of the ferret entered the compound and started systematically searching in and underneath the huts, beginning with Hut 106. This was followed by Huts 107 and 123. Later that afternoon, the gates swung open and three large, heavy lorries drove in and started to move randomly around the compound, going over the gardens and as close to the huts themselves as they could. But all the ferrets could find were a few nails and some pieces of wire.

It was quite obvious that the Germans knew something was going on, and also knew that in all probability it was a tunnel. All the time, the building in the new American compound continued. It was decided to open up Tom and digging re-commenced, but the penguins could only get rid of half of what had been taken out before because of the close scrutiny of the guards.

The next day one of the ferrets saw some fresh yellow sand in a flowerbed and immediately called out Oberfeldwebel Glemnitz. One hour later more than 100 fully armed troops entered the camp and ordered everyone out of Huts 106, 127 and 123. The Kommandant arrived with a civilian, who was later identified as the second-in-command of the Kriminalpolizei in Breslau. Then a second lorry arrived with German soldiers carrying shovels and picks. They started digging a trench from Hut 123 to the barbed wire. When they were down about 4ft one of the ferrets took a long probe and started pushing it down as far as it would go, all along the trench. By the time he had reached the barbed wire it was quite obvious that they had found nothing. Just before roll call, they gave up and filled in the trench, to the cheers of the prisoners.

Despite the cheers, the escape committee knew that this was serious. The guards knew that something was going on and the visit by a member of the local Kriminalpolizei could only mean one thing; the Gestapo could be the next visitors. One suggestion was that all the tunnels were closed down until the heat was off, but Bushell pointed out that the ferrets would not rest until they found something. In any case, if they stopped digging now Tom would have to be extended to go underneath the American compound and that would take another couple of months.

The disposal of the sand that would be taken out was causing the biggest headache, until someone suggested that they close down Dick and fill it up with the sand from Tom. Work started immediately filling Dick, taking the sand up to the face on the trolley, and as they came backwards taking away the shoring that could be reused in Tom.

One of the ferrets, nicknamed Rubberneck, was becoming a real problem and at one point he asked Glemnitz to put all the 'duty pilots' in the 'cooler'. Glemnitz refused, claiming that they would be replaced by others watching from windows and he preferred them in the open where he could see them. On one occasion, as he walked into the compound, Glemnitz went up to the 'duty pilot', and with a smile on his face told him to book him in. Minutes later he came back and said 'Book me out'. Then he asked to see the list of who had been in and out. Unable to refuse, the list was handed over. Glemnitz glanced down at it and handed it back. They discovered later that Glemnitz had gone to Rubberneck and two other ferrets and demanded to know why they had left the compound at 4 o'clock when they were not scheduled to leave until 5.

Rubberneck was given two weeks extra duty and confined to barracks, while the other two were given four days in the 'cooler'.

Then there was another setback. Because of the worry about a tunnel being dug, the Germans decided to move the trees where Tom was heading back another 30 yards. They had completed almost 200ft and now, because of the additional tree work, they were another 100ft short. One of the 'tame ferrets' told them that another compound was to be built. Digging continued, at a slightly faster rate, but problems about what to do with the sand started to be of some concern. Dick was now full to the bottom of the shaft and the escape committee refused to let it be filled to the top because they needed it to store equipment. Bushell came up with the idea of storing the sand in the Red Cross boxes that everyone had under their beds. This was alright for a while, but then one of the boxes was discovered and a thorough search of the huts took place again – once again they found nothing.

Tom was now 260ft long, was well under the wire and clear of the searchlights. Still some 40ft short of the trees, it was decided to close it down for the time being. In order to try to divert Glemnitz away from his tunnel fixation, Bushell got hold of one of the German-speaking prisoners. He suggested that the man should talk to Glemnitz and persuade him that there were no tunnels, and that it was all a ploy to tie the Germans up for weeks on end looking for something that didn't exist.

It partially worked, that was until one of the ferrets, who was carrying out a run-of-the-mill search of Hut 123, suddenly got his probe stuck in a crack in the concrete close to the chimney. Wiggling to get it free, he saw the outline of a trapdoor and called for Glemnitz. Fetching a sledgehammer, the Germans smashed open the trapdoor to reveal a shaft beneath. One of the ferrets crawled down with a torch and disappeared for half an hour, before reappearing with the news that the tunnel was close to the trees on the other side of the American compound.

This was a tremendous blow to the escape committee; all that work for nothing. This was the ninety-eighth tunnel that had been discovered since the camp had been built in 1941. A meeting was called in the camp theatre under the pretext of talking about a forthcoming production. It was decided to shut down the other two tunnels until such time that they thought the Germans had lost interest.

When the Americans were moved into their new compound, the Kommandant, von Lindeiner, refused to allow any form of communication between them and the British. Within an hour of this being announced, Massey placed a semaphore signaller in the end room of Hut 120. Standing well back from the window so that the guards could not see him, he started signalling in the direction of the American compound. Minutes later the Americans had spotted him and installed their own signaller. With communication established, a daily dialogue was kept up keeping each other informed of current affairs and the state of play. One of the British prisoners had managed to put together a 'cats whisker' radio by bribing one of the young guards to get him the bits and pieces required. With the radio, they were able to listen to the BBC and in turn able to signal information to the Americans on how the war was going.

The summer arrived and the ferrets were on the alert, because this was the perfect weather for escapees. Then came another setback as the trees outside the west fence were felled in readiness for a new compound to be built. This in effect ruled out using Dick as an escape tunnel, its only use now being a storeroom. This just left Harry as a viable alternative and all the work was concentrated on completing the tunnel. The escape committee realised that there was no way the tunnel could be used until the following summer, so plans were put in place for the escape to be made then.

Bushell was still the subject of suspicion for the Germans, mainly because of the number of times he had escaped and caused them problems. The Gestapo had ordered a watch on him, but Wally Valenta, who was the escape committee's intelligence officer and the eyes and ears of the camp, also had the ears of the guards. He was very slowly and surreptitiously putting the word to them that Bushell was a reformed character and was prepared to sit the war out in the camp. So convincing was he that Glemnitz reported back to the Gestapo to say that Bushell was no longer a threat.

Despite the setback with the tunnels, prisoners were still encouraged to put forward other plans for escape. Going through the wire was the most popular way and anyone putting forward a reasonable plan would be supplied with the necessary documents and wire cutters.

The cutters were a perfect example of ingenuity. Made from tie-bars taken from the walls of the huts, they were joined in the same manner as scissors by a rivet in the crossover section. Heating them until they were red hot, grains of sugar were sprinkled on to the edges. The metal was then reheated so that the carbon in the sugar was absorbed into the metal. They were then plunged into cold water and ready for use.

A number of unsuccessful attempts were made that diverted attention away from the tunnel. Some welcome additional equipment was 'acquired' when the Kommandant had some loudspeakers mounted in the compounds so that the prisoners could listen to German propaganda radio broadcasts after the fall of Italy. Two drums of cable that were being used mysteriously disappeared and were dumped down Dick. In all, there was more than 800ft of wire, and that was later to be used to provide electric light when digging started again in Harry.

At first it was thought that there might be some reprisals regarding the theft, but fortunately the workmen were so embarrassed at losing the wire that they failed to report it.

One amusing incident occurred when a pompous German general visited the camp in his shiny new Mercedes. He entered the compound to carry out an inspection and, despite warnings from the Kommandant about leaving his car in the compound with just a chauffeur to guard it, went on a walkabout. The prisoners crowded around the car and despite his protestations, the chauffeur was unable to stop items disappearing. Among them was a 'so-called' secret military handbook. The Kommandant had a private conversation with Wing Commander Harry 'Wings' Day, asking for the return of the book and guaranteeing that he would ignore the rest of the items as long as it was returned. It duly was, but with a stamp, which had been made out of a rubber heel, across the cover that said 'Passed by the British Board of Censors'.

As the year progressed and heavy snow falls and the intense cold deterred the prisoners from going outside, work still continued on making escape equipment. The stooges, who kept watch constantly, now became very apparent and the ferrets knew that something was going on. One of the ferrets, nicknamed Adolf because of his tiny moustache, was particularly alert and would constantly be on the prowl, causing the forgers and equipment makers to hurriedly put away their materials.

At Christmas the prisoners had a party, drinking wine distilled from raisins and for a while their whole world was a little happier. Prisoners stayed indoors for most of the winter and the guards who would check the huts welcomed the chance to sit down with some of them and have a brew.

With the New Year came new hope and the committee met with regard to opening up Harry again and finishing the tunnel. Two weeks into January the tunnellers were back digging at the face. The disposal of the sand had been a problem, but it was decided to dump it under the stage of the theatre. The first day the tunnel was extended a further 10ft and was illuminated by electric light. The electric lights could only be used at night; during the day the tunnellers had to work by fat lamps.

As the tunnel progressed so did the heightened anticipation of freedom. But sand slips inside the tunnel, where a couple of the tunnellers found themselves buried and had to be dug out, soon brought everyone back to reality. Unknown to anyone in the camp, an order had been issued by Field Marshal Keitel stating that any British or American officers who escaped and were recaptured were to be held in either civil or military prisons until the High Command decided what to do with them. Their recapture was to be kept secret.

The ferrets kept up their usual routine of surprise visits and searches, but they spent most of their time drinking tea and smoking prisoners' cigarettes. It was these visits by the ferrets and the 'friendships' created that kept Wally Valenta supplied with information.

Then Kommandant von Lindeiner called Massey and other senior British and American officers to a meeting and told them to put a stop to all thoughts of escape. He explained that he had been called to a meeting with members of the Gestapo, who told him that there would be harsh consequences for those who escaped and for those who were left behind. What von Lindeiner did not tell them was that SS General Müller, the Berlin Gestapo chief, had issued the 'Kugel' (Bullet) Order that stated that other than the British and Americans, any other nationalities were to be taken in chains to Mauthausen Concentration Camp and executed by either gas or shooting.

Respite came when the prisoners heard that the ferret Rubberneck was going on leave for fourteen days. This was the impetus the tunnellers needed; with him away they knew the ferrets remaining would not be so thorough and would take the opportunity to relax. In the following nine days the teams dug another 100ft, making Harry 348ft long, and by their calculations there was only another 20ft to go. It was when they reached that point that the team started to dig upwards and create another shaft. Then at the end of the shift, they noticed tree roots and realised that they were nearing the surface.

Keeping the excitement under control was difficult, and became almost impossible when on 14 March one of the tunnellers came back shaking with excitement and a huge grin on his dirty face. He had pushed a rod through to the surface and realised that there was only 6in of soil between them and freedom.

It was now that the timetable had to be created. Plans had to be drawn up as to how many were going and what civilian clothes were available. Documents and permits had to be arranged, up-to-date train timetables acquired – in short, 1,001 things had to be organised. This was not the time for mistakes of any sort. The dates set for the escapes were 23 and 24 March, depending, of course, on the weather. It was estimated that 230 prisoners would be able to make the breakout. It was now the escape committee's job to select those who were to go.

Seventy of those who had done the most work were chosen, including the German speakers, as they would have the best chance of making it. The remaining 130 places were drawn from a hat. That left twenty places and Bushell selected those most deserving that had not been drawn from the hat. For every ten escapees a 'marshal' was designated and it was his job to help them get what they needed once they were out of the camp. All the men attended a series of lectures regarding German behaviour and customs and train times for those travelling by rail. There was enough money in the kitty to supply forty escapees with train fares, the remainder of the men would have to walk.

Finally, 23 March arrived and there was an air of expectancy around the camp, but with snow still on the ground there was reluctance to move for those who were waiting. An emergency meeting of the escape committee was held the following morning and it was decided that the longer they waited the more chance there was of them being discovered. It was decided they would go that night.

The atmosphere throughout the camp was electric, and all those who were going started their meticulous preparations. The whole camp was on tenterhooks and it was a miracle the guards did not pick up on the tension. Preparations got under way for the 230 men to be transferred from hut to hut, and for them all to get out through Harry. The stooges were placed on red alert and extra ones brought in. Nothing could be allowed to go wrong at this crucial point. Extra lights were placed inside the tunnel and the trolley was fitted with a flat board for the men to lie on.

Then, at 6:55 p.m., the first of the men said his goodbye with the usual banter, walked to Hut 104 and was ticked off the list. He was told to wait until they were ready for him and he settled down. One heart-stopping moment occurred when the door of Hut 104 opened and a jack-booted German officer strode in. One of the German-speaking stooges went to head him off before he realised that the German officer was in fact a Polish officer named Tobolski, who was going out as a German. The uniform was almost perfect and would have fooled anyone seeing him.

At 8:30 p.m., the tunnel crew announced all was ready and the first of the men slipped down the shaft and onto the trolley. When the first seventeen were in position underground, John Bull, one of the tunnellers, opened up the last 6in of dirt and felt the cold, fresh air. Poking his head through the hole, he got the shock of his life – they were not in the trees, they were at least 10ft short of the tree line and just 15 yards from a guard tower in which he could clearly see the helmet of the guard. For one year 600 men had worked tirelessly in shifts to dig this tunnel, and they were now 10ft short.

The solution was that one man would crawl out, attach a rope to the top of the ladder and then make his way to the tree line. Once there he would give two tugs on the rope if it was clear and the next man would crawl out, and so on. Back in the hut the tension was almost at breaking point as the remaining men waited, not knowing what was happening.

At 10 p.m. the German guards began lock-down and all the huts were bolted from the outside. Inside Hut 104 every available bit of space was taken up by strangely attired men in suits and uniforms, etc.

Slowly but surely the men were slipping through the tunnel and out into the woods. Then, just after midnight, air-raid warnings could be heard and suddenly all the lights in the tunnel went out, plunging the area into an inky blackness. Those stuck in the tunnel at the time were suddenly hit with a wave of claustrophobia, but the fat lamps were still in place and they were quickly lit. Outside, the searchlights and boundary lights that had been playing all over the compound were also switched off, the guards peering into the blackness of the compound to look for prisoners hoping to take advantage of the raid and cut through the wires.

This gave the escapees the opportunity to speed up the exiting of the escapees, but more stoppages inside the tunnel were causing delays. Then there was a partial tunnel collapse that took almost thirty minutes to clear and it became apparent that they were not going to get everyone away as they only had two hours before dawn. At 5 a.m. the streaks of dawn started to penetrate the blackness of the sky and it was decided to call it a day. Three more men went down and the trapdoor was closed.

For a moment all was quiet, then suddenly the crack of a rifle was heard and then all hell broke loose. Roy Langlois had exited the hole and was on the rope, when a German sentry suddenly appeared out of the gloom and was walking towards the hole. As he got closer and closer to the hole, Langlois thought that at any moment he must see or step into it. The sentry's foot missed the hole by inches as he walked by, but then he stopped and looked at the trail in the snow that led from the hole into the woods. Then he saw Mick Shand lying motionless in the snow and pulled his rifle off his shoulder. Aiming it at the still figure, he was shocked when another figure suddenly appeared from behind a bush shouting at him in German not to shoot. Then another figure appeared out of the hole, followed seconds later by Langlois with his hands in the air.

Within minutes the men were surrounded by guards and then marched off to the guardroom. For them the escape was over. Back in Hut 104 they realised the game was up and started to destroy any incriminating tools and paperwork. The men still in the tunnel heard the shot and immediately knew there was no point in going on and headed back towards the entrance shaft. As the last man climbed out, the trapdoor was shut and sealed and the stove pulled over it. Although they knew the ferrets wouldn't be far behind, they decided that if they found their way in they could jolly well find their way out.

The four captured men were taken to the guardroom, where the Kommandant confronted them. To say he was furious was the understatement of the year. Not only had they caused the German High Command embarrassment, but there was no doubt that he would be arrested and court-martialled as the camp and everyone in it was his responsibility.

Within hours a column of German troops arrived on the scene and all the remaining prisoners were brought out of the huts and on to parade. They were all made to strip and were searched. Any clothes that looked like they could pass as civilian clothes were confiscated and all the time they were kept under the machine guns of heavily armed troops. A commotion in one of the huts alarmed the guards, then one of the ferrets came rushing out saying the Unteroffizier Pfelz, who had gone down the tunnel at the exit end, could not find a way out.

Two of the escape team took pity on Pfelz and lifted the stove off the trapdoor and then opened it. There, halfway up the shaft was Pfelz, blinking as the lights shone on him. He scrambled out of the hole, saluted the Kommandant and told him of his discovery. Then all the remaining prisoners were ordered outside into the snow and told to strip. Finding nothing, the Kommandant noted the grins on their faces and ordered them to the 'cooler'. It is interesting to note that the Germans had adopted the word 'cooler' from the American prisoners and always referred to the punishment cells as such.

The remaining members of the camp were left shivering in the snow for the next hour, while a roll call and a photographic identification check was carried out to find out who was missing. When completed, the guards reported to the Kommandant that seventy-six prisoners had escaped. At that von Lindeiner turned on his heel and walked back to his office.

Three hours later, the area chief of the Kriminalpolizei, Oberregierungsrat Max Wielen, ordered a *Großfahndung* (large-scale manhunt) and a nationwide search was instigated for the missing prisoners. Every branch of the military was put on alert, including the Home Guard and the Hitler Youth. All the ports and borders had increased security, as this was the biggest manhunt that Germany had ever seen.

Within hours of the escape two men had been recaptured, Wally Valenta and Johnny Marshall had been picked up by civilians while walking along the road. Taken to the local police station, they found three more of their fellow escapees already in custody.

'Wings' Day and Tobolski had arrived at the railway station to find it full of escapees. They managed to get their tickets and headed towards Berlin. Meanwhile, more and more escapees were being caught and taken into custody to be interrogated by the Gestapo.

Day and Tobolski managed to find somewhere to stay in Berlin the first night, but the following morning caught the train to Stettin, where they made contact with some Frenchmen in a labour camp who were working on the docks. The Frenchmen promised to find some Swedish sailors and help them get aboard one of their boats. They stayed at the camp overnight, but the following morning German soldiers burst in demanding to know where the Englishmen were. The game was up and the two men were taken away to be questioned by the Gestapo.

Before being questioned by the Gestapo, they had been taken before the local police chief of Stettin, who told them that a young Frenchman had sold them out for 1,000 marks. Day remarked that he would like to ring his bloody neck. The police chief smiled and told him that as they had no further use for him, they would tip off his fellow Frenchmen about his activities and that they would most likely do the job for him.

The massive search for the escaped prisoners also had the effect of picking up anyone whose ID documents were not perfect, or who had incorrect travel permits. Thousands of people were arrested and among them were hundreds of German deserters, criminals and people wanted for various crimes.

After two weeks of intensive searching for the seventy-six men who escaped, seventy-three had been recaptured. Two of the remaining three had reached England safely and the third was well on his way.

Meanwhile, in Berchtesgaden, Adolf Hitler had just received the first of the Gestapo reports regarding the escape. With him at the time were Keitel, Göring and Himmler, and the moment he read the reports he flew into one of his notorious rages, blaming everyone and everything in sight.

He ordered that all the escaped prisoners were to be shot on capture. Göring objected on the grounds that if that were done, then the German military would be accused of murder and reprisals would certainly follow against German POWs being held by the Allies. Göring's argument swayed Hitler into rethinking his proposal. He then ordered that half the prisoners should be shot and it was to be carried out by the SS. The Kriminalpolizei were ordered to hand over half of the prisoners to the Gestapo for interrogation. The Gestapo would then take them back to the original camp, but shoot them en route under the claim that they had attempted to escape.

The 'Sagan Order', as it became known, was issued by Obergruppenführer Ernst Kaltenbrunner, head of the SS and SD in Berlin. SS General Mueller, the Gestapo chief in Berlin, and the chief of the Kriminalpolizei, General Nebe, took the record cards of all the captured prisoners and selected the ones who were to be executed. In the meantime, von Lindeiner had been arrested and confined to his room in the camp.

The interrogation of prisoners was carried out in different districts according to where the escapees had been caught. Those selected for execution were placed in different cells afterwards and then taken away in trucks. The remainder were taken back to Stalag Luft III and placed in the 'cooler' for three weeks.

What continued to puzzle those who had been returned to the camp was that they knew some that had been captured, but had not been returned. Massey tried to make some enquiries regarding the men, but was unable to find out anything. Then one morning in April, Massey was summoned to the Kommandant's office. The moment he entered the office, Massey, together with his interpreter, Squadron Leader Murray, knew that something was wrong as there was a grim atmosphere. The new Kommandant, Oberst Braune, was standing behind his desk when Massey entered and gave a slight bow – not the usual handshake. Braune looked directly at Massey and said:

I have been instructed by my higher authority to communicate to you this report. The Senior British Officer is to be informed that as a result of a tunnel from which seventy-six officers escaped from Stalag Luft III, north compound, forty-one of these officers have been shot while resisting arrest or attempting further escape after arrest.

For a moment there was absolute silence in the room. 'How many were shot?' asked Massey through his interpreter. Braune, with his eyes now downcast, replied, 'Forty-one.' Again this was followed by an eerie silence. Massey looked at Murray and asked him to ask Braune how many had been wounded.

Braune listened to the question, then, still looking shame-faced and down at his feet, replied, 'My higher authority only permits me to read this report and not to answer any questions or give any further information.'

Massey asked Murray to ask him again, and again the question was asked. Braune turned his head away, not wanting to meet Massey's eyes: 'I think no one was wounded.' Again the eerie silence. Then Massey's voice trembled as he spoke, 'Do you mean that out of the forty-one men shot, not one of them was wounded?' 'I can only read you the report,' came the reply. 'I am acting under the orders of a higher authority and may only tell you what I am instructed to do.'

Massey realised that the conversation was going nowhere and asked for the names of the men that had been killed. Again no information was forthcoming, Braune saying that he did not have the names to give him.

Escorted by one of the Luftwaffe officers, Major Pieber, the two British officers left, both of them stunned into silence. When they reached their hut, the escorting officer looked at both men and told them that the Luftwaffe had not been involved in the killings and that it was the Gestapo who were responsible. Neither British officer replied, but Massey told Murray not to mention what had happened to anyone for the moment. He would call a meeting and tell everyone together. One hour later all the officers were assembled in the theatre and Massey told them what he had been told by the Kommandant. There was a stunned silence, some refusing to believe it and saying that it was propaganda put out by the Germans because they hadn't managed to catch the men. But deep down everybody felt it was true.

Security in the camp was tightened dramatically, mainly because the Kommandant was frightened that there was going to be some sort of backlash from the prisoners. Then one morning a notice was pinned to the noticeboard giving the names of those who had been killed. Looking at the list of names, it soon became apparent that there were forty-seven names on the list, not forty-one. Two days later another notice on the board gave the names of three more escapees that had been shot dead, bringing the total to fifty.

Those who had escaped and had been returned to the camp had spent three weeks in the 'cooler' before being released back into the compound. They were horrified to hear of the deaths of their friends and comrades and couldn't understand why they had been spared.

A number of the prisoners, who had been seriously injured when shot down, were later repatriated to England and among them was Massey. The Germans knew that the moment Massey reached England the murders of the fifty Allied airmen would be announced to the world. The governments of all those who died vowed to bring as many of those involved to justice and at the end of the war the RAF Special Investigation Branch set out to do just that.

Two weeks after Massey had returned to England, the Kommandant informed the new SBO, Group Captain Wilson, that fifty urns carrying the ashes of the murdered men had been sent to the camp. The Kommandant acquired some stone and allowed a working party to go to a nearby cemetery and build a vault to house them.

News came through that three of the escapees had made it back to England, but there was no news of the other thirteen.

At the end of the war the RAF immediately started an investigation into the murders of the fifty airmen. An ex-Scotland Yard detective, Wing Commander Bowes, was assigned the task. He formed six teams, each consisting of four men, all ex-policemen, and went after the criminals who had carried out the murders. After months and years of tireless investigation, the majority of those involved in the murders of the fifty Allied airmen were brought to trial and on 26 February 1948 at Hamelin Gaol, near Hamburg, thirteen of them were hanged. Others were sentenced to either life imprisonment or lengthy terms of imprisonment. Justice had been seen to be done.

So dramatic was the escape that in the 1960s a film was made about the story starring Richard Attenborough and Steve McQueen. There was a great deal of Hollywood artistic licence applied to the plot, including the now famous motorcycle chase that never happened, but the main gist of the story was reasonably accurate.

Not all escapees were Europeans; some came from the United States, Canada and other Commonwealth countries. The fact that the Americans did not enter the war until December 1941 does not detract from the part they played in causing confusion and mayhem among their captors once they were captured. The American philosophy of captured soldiers and airmen differed from that of the British inasmuch as they generally believed in infuriating the German guards by carrying out passive hostile resistance, whilst using trickery and deception to cause the enemy the biggest amount of problems they could. The British, on the other hand, reasoned that escaping quietly and with no fuss caused the Germans immeasurable problems regarding their security. In addition to this, once escapees had been missed, a desperate search ensued that tied up hundreds of troops that the Germans could ill afford, causing extensive problems for the military. It has to be remembered as well that a number of British people had a working knowledge of the French or German language, or both. This, of course, made it easier for some British escapees and evaders to move around.

Thousands of German troops were tied up in counteracting these escapes and evasions, causing the enemy considerable amount of disruption. There were, however, a number of escapes made by Americans, including one that involved taking a German Focke-Wulf Fw 190 from under the noses of the Luftwaffe.

14. STAFFELFÜHRER HANS ULRICH RUDEL, LUFTWAFFE

STAFFELFÜHRER HANS ULRICH Rudel was a German ground-attack pilot during the Second World War, flying mostly Junkers Ju 87 'Stuka' dive-bombers. He was also credited with the destruction of 519 tanks, achieved nine aerial victories and destroyed a number of ships. He claimed the destruction of more than 800 vehicles of all types and flew 2,530 ground-attack missions exclusively on the Eastern Front, and 430 missions flying fighter aircraft. Rudel was the most decorated German of the Second World War, receiving the Knight's Cross of the Iron Cross with Golden Oak Leaves, Swords and Diamonds. He surrendered to US forces on 8 May 1945.

In March 1944, following a raid on Russian tanks and ground forces, Staffelführer Hans Ulrich Rudel led his squadron in formation and headed back to base. Flying at almost tree-top level, Rudel could see Russian fighter aircraft flying at around 9,000ft, but being so close to the ground he knew he would be very difficult to see. Climbing sharply over a clump of trees close to a riverbank he spotted one of his squadron's aircraft in a field having made a forced landing. As he flew over them, the two-man crew waved wildly at him. He made another low-level pass to see if the ground was suitable for him to land and pick them up. Deciding it was, he made a low approach, throttled back and lowered his flaps, but the moment he touched down he realised that the ground was very soft. Without touching his brakes, he stopped in a very short distance. Beckoning to the two crew members, he waved them to climb aboard his aircraft. His gunner, Erwin Hentschel, opened the canopy for the two men to climb in.

In the distance he saw Russian ground troops making their way towards them and opened the throttles of his aircraft, intending to taxi ready to take off, but to his horror the aircraft did not move – the wheels were stuck in the mud.

Increasing the power, Rudel tried to ease the overladen aircraft out of the mud, but all it seemed to do was to make it sink further in. Overhead, his wingman, Leutnant Fischer, was circling and then offered to land, but Rudel waved him away. Realising it was now a hopeless situation, Rudel jumped down from the aircraft and called for the others to follow him. He had spotted the Dniester River earlier about 4 miles away and he knew that if they didn't want to end up in a Russian prisoner-of-war camp or be shot, they had to get across it.

After running for about half an hour with the Russians in pursuit, they came to the river but the high banks were almost sheer, so climbing down was almost impossible. The only way was to slide down, grabbing bushes and plants in an effort to try to break their fall. With the Russians now close behind they had no other choice but to go, and one after another they jumped. Landing on the riverbank with their clothes in tatters and bodies badly lacerated, the four men looked at the fast-flowing river with lumps of ice in it. The river temperature could be no more that 2–3 degrees and they calculated that it was about 600 yards across. Rudel watched as the three other waded into the water and then struck out, swimming as fast as they could before the cold got to them. Rudel stripped down to just shirt and trousers as he knew that his heavy flying clothes would only weigh him down.

As he waded in, the coldness took his breath away, but there was no alternative and he started swimming as fast as he could. Within minutes his body felt dead to all sensation as the cold penetrated his limbs, but he kept swimming automatically. Hentschel was struggling, but Rudel was unable to help him as he himself was finding it very difficult. On reaching the riverbank he pulled himself up and lay there trying to catch his breath. On hearing shouts he turned to see Hentschel waving his arms and saying he couldn't go on, then he slipped beneath the water and disappeared. Rudel was stunned; Hentschel had been his friend and gunner for more than two years and losing him like that was devastating.

Although saddened by the loss of his friend, Rudel prepared to move out and with the other two men. They checked what weapons they had and started walking southwards. Rudel still had his map and compass, so had a good idea of which direction to head for, although he realised that they were still behind enemy lines. Rudel started to feel hungry and remembered he had not eaten all day. The *Staffel* (squadron) had carried out eight sorties that day and they'd had no time to even grab a sandwich. They had landed, refuelled, rearmed and taken off again.

With the sun going down their damp clothes were beginning to freeze on their bodies. Then, despite the sun in their eyes, Rudel made out the shape of three figures walking towards them. He hoped they might be Romanians.

He told the other to hide their weapons as they did not want to startle them. As they approached, Rudel could see that two had rifles slung over their shoulders while the other carried a machine gun. The three men stopped in front of the German airmen, looking at them curiously. Rudel suddenly realised that they had no uniforms on so the three soldiers could not determine who they were. Rudel started to explain that they had made a forced landing and that they required help in the shape of food and dry clothing.

The next moment all three soldiers had their guns pointed at them. One of them snatched Rudel's gun from its holster and as he did so he could see the hammer and sickle badge on his fur hat – Russians! Rudel knew he had to escape because his reputation as dive-bomber pilot had gone before him and there would be a price on his head once the Russians discovered who he was. Looking desperately around to see if there were any other Russian soldiers, he made a break for it, ducking, swerving and zig-zagging. He heard bullets whistling past his head, then a sudden stinging pain in his left shoulder made him aware that he had been hit. Without missing a step, he continued to run as fast as he could, uphill and downhill, his bare feet cut and bleeding. Looking to the hilltop on his left, he saw more Russians coming towards him; they must have been watching and seen the whole thing unfold. They would try to catch him in a pincer movement so he had to go to ground quickly before they spotted him.

As he was on the far side of the field and down a hill he was out of view for the time being. Entering a ploughed field with its large furrows, Rudel stumbled and collapsed in exhaustion. Fearing the worst, he still tried to make himself as small as possible by scrabbling in the frozen earth to throw small handfuls of soil over himself as best he could. Keeping as still as possible, he watched as the Russians stopped and started to look for signs of movement. Two of the Russian soldiers had turned up with dogs, but for some unknown reason they kept them to the edge of the field.

The Russians started a systematic search of the field, then suddenly there was a roar of aircraft and a flight of Stukas from Rudel's squadron, accompanied by two Fieseler Storchs and a fighter escort, passed overhead. They were looking for Rudel, but he was now 6 miles further south, and a sense of despondency swept over him as he watched them fly away. The sun was starting to go down, making it even more difficult for the searchers as once again they walked across the field line abreast. Rudel thought that they must stumble over him, and then he held his breath as, in the fading light, one Russian, standing no more than ten paces away, stopped and appeared to be staring straight at him. The man looked left then right, but never down, and then moved away.

Minutes later they all vanished from sight, leaving Rudel lying on the frozen ground, shivering with both fear and cold.

As night fell and the stars appeared brighter in the sky, Rudel clambered slowly to his feet and, looking at his compass for a south heading and then lining it up with a star, he stumbled on his way. Avoiding all the roads, he kept to the fields and hedgerows barely able to feel his feet. For the following hours he just followed his compass heading and the stars, through marshland, fields and up and down hills. It was only the will to live that was keeping him going. The pain in his shoulder was replaced with numbness and a dull ache; his feet were bloodied and cut to ribbons. His clothes were in tatters and he no longer looked like the smart, elegant Staffelführer who had climbed into the cockpit of his aircraft a few hours ago.

The journey through the fields and marshes was torturous to say the least, and numerous times he found himself almost waist deep in mud, but somehow he found the strength and determination to pull himself free. After almost twenty-four hours he realised that he could not go on without rest, food and water, so he made the decision to find an isolated house. A distant dog barking made him aware of an inhabited area, possibly a village or a farm.

After another hour of walking he came across a farmhouse and knocked on the door, but there was no reply. A second house was close by and after knocking on the door and again receiving no reply, he decided to break in. As he was doing so, an old lady appeared in the doorway holding an oil lamp. Speaking no Russian, Hans Rudel pushed past her into a dimly lit room and sat down on a rickety old bed. He gestured to the old woman with his hands, asking for something to eat and drink. The old lady stared at him with fear in her eyes and then went and got him a jug of water and a large chunk of corn bread. The simple food tasted like a banquet to Rudel as he wolfed down the slightly stale bread and washed it down with the cool water. Feeling refreshed, he noticed that the old woman had gone into another room and so he decided to try to get some sleep. He awoke in the middle of the night and decided he had to continue moving. The pain in his shoulder had returned and the numbness in his feet had also reduced, making each step painful. Stumbling out into the night, he was met with heavy rain, which he knew would make the ground even more treacherous. As he set out, fearful he would run into Russian soldiers, he could see flashes of heavy artillery in the distance, which gave him an additional aid to his direction.

As dawn broke he was able to see some tiny villages from the top of the hill he had just climbed. Making his way down painfully, his bleeding feet making every step feel as if his feet were on fire, he saw an isolated farmhouse in the distance. He knew he had to get more food and water and rest; he was almost at the end of his endurance and his left arm, with the gunshot wound, was useless. On reaching the barn, he went inside – it was bare except for a rotting pile of maize leaves in one corner. Rudel scrabbled among them in the hope of finding a couple of corncobs, but nothing.

He was suddenly aware of a noise outside the barn and, crouching down in the corner, he watched as the door opened and a young girl stepped in. Behind her Rudel could see a farm wagon with a man sitting on it wearing a black fur hat. He recognised the man as being a Romanian peasant. He asked the girl if she had anything to eat. She replied, 'You can have this,' and handed him some stale cakes from her bag. It was then that Rudel realised that he had spoken to her in German and she had replied in the same language. Rudel asked her how she came to speak German. She told him that she had been in Dniepropetrovsk with the Germans and had learnt the language, and she was now in the care of the Romanian peasant, with whom she wanted to stay. They were both fleeing from the Russians.

Rudel pointed to a town in the distance and asked if there were any Germans there. The girl replied that there wasn't, but warned that there may still be Romanian soldiers. Rudel thanked them for their help and watched them leave. As they disappeared into the distance he cursed himself for not commandeering the wagon, but it was too late and he was in no fit state to run after them.

As he made his way down the path towards the town he joined a steady stream of refugees with handcarts carrying all the worldly good that they could carry. On entering the town he saw two soldiers in German uniform watching the refugees. The sight of the Germans was an unforgettable relief for Rudel. He shouted to one of them, 'Hey you, come here.' They stared at him and said, 'What do you mean come here, who do you think you are?'

'I am Staffelführer Hans Rudel,' he replied.

The two soldiers looked at him in his torn ragged clothes and bleeding bare feet.

'You look nothing like a Staffelführer,' they replied.

'I have no identification papers, but I do have this.' Rudel produced his Knight's Cross with Oak Leaves and Swords. The soldiers took one look and realised that he was probably who he said he was and escorted him to their headquarters. There a doctor cut away all his clothes, which were now stuck to his battered and bloodstained body. He received medical treatment to his shoulder wound and to lacerated feet, and then asked to be taken to the nearest airfield where he could catch a plane back to his squadron. Because he no longer had any clothes he was wrapped in a blanket and driven to the airfield at Balti. On arriving, he was met by his squadron engineer carrying fresh clothes.

They had been informed of his escape and had brought the squadron Ju 52 aircraft and the clothes to meet him. To Rudel it was the most welcoming sight.

Staffelführer Rudel returned to his squadron at Rauchowka to be greeted as a hero after an epic escape through Russian lines. What happened to his two comrades is not known, but most likely they were taken prisoner by the Russians.

Rudel died in Germany on 18 December 1982.

15. CAPTAIN BRUCE CARR, USAAF

IN OCTOBER 1944, as he leant his body against the wall of an abandoned and derelict farmhouse, Captain Bruce Carr thought back to the night before at St-Dizier, France, when the 353rd Fighter Squadron had one of its rare 'stand down' parties. The commanding officer had broken out a case of the 'Old Methuselah', a green, mission whiskey, and the party was just about to get into full swing when the Officer of the Day (OD) walked in with operation orders. The squadron was scheduled to fly the following day, and as the time was 3 a.m. it was decided that the party would have to be put on hold. The crews had just 'one for the road' before retiring.

Two hours later Carr was awakened. He quickly got into his flight gear and put on his leather jacket. At the briefing, he listened intently, between gulping down steaming mugs of black coffee, as the mission plan was unfolded. The squadron pilots left the briefing and headed for their P-51 North American Mustangs parked in the dispersal bays. Firing up the engines, they taxied out onto the runway and took off.

Their mission was to carry out a fighter sweep of the retreating German Army and mop up anything that they came across. They were not concerned with ground fire, as normally this never affected them, but they kept their eyes peeled for the odd fighter that could suddenly appear from nowhere. The sky around was blue and clear, and it felt like a routine training flight. However, the perfect reassuring beat of Carr's 1,720hp Packard engine was suddenly transformed into a horrendous grinding of metals as cannon shells ripped into it.

Frantically looking around for an enemy aircraft and seeing none, Carr realised that his Mustang had been hit by ground fire. His eyes immediately flashed to his instrument panel, where he registered that the engine temperature was about to go off the scale, while the oil pressure gauge showed zero. Grey smoke started to fill the cockpit, the windscreen was spattered with oil and he could see white smoke pouring out of the exhaust manifolds. Loosening his seat belt, he slid back the canopy to its fullest extent and pulled back on the control column. He was trying to get as much height as he possibly could before baling out because he realised that the only place his aircraft was going to go in a few moments was into the ground. Suddenly flames started to flicker around the manifold exhausts and Carr realised that it was only a matter of seconds before his aircraft disintegrated into a fireball. Standing on the seat, he hurled himself clear of the burning aircraft at 12,000ft, then free-fell down to 1,000ft before opening his parachute. He left it as late as he dared in an effort to minimise the chance of detection.

As the ground rushed up to meet him he braced himself for the landing. Rolling over in the grass, he struggled out of the parachute harness, rolled the parachute and webbing into a small a ball as possible and threw it into a nearby ditch. He then covered it with rocks and dirt in an effort to conceal it. He sat down to regain his breath and composure and looked around the countryside – at least he was alive. Then the realisation hit him, someone must have seen his parachute, so he looked around frantically for somewhere to hide.

He was in the heart of Nazi country – Austria – so he was certain that the locals were not likely to be friendly. For the next two hours he made his way along the sparse hedgerows until he came across a crumbling wall, where he settled down to try to work out a way to get to Switzerland. At least the weather was dry and warm, and there was plenty of fresh water in the streams. Food, however, was another matter, but he felt certain that he would be able to find a remote farmhouse and steal some.

Travelling by night and sleeping by day, Carr made his way slowly across the Austrian countryside towards the Swiss border. For three days he travelled, sometimes on the road, but mostly across fields keeping to the hedgerows. He had fought shy of going to some of the farmhouses he saw, fearful of getting caught, but the pangs of hunger were beginning to take hold and he realised that he was getting weaker by the day. He needed to get some substantial food inside him if he was to make the Swiss border.

On the third night Carr approached an isolated farmhouse determined to get some food. He watched as the farmer shepherded chickens and ducks into the downstairs barn of the two-storey house. One hour later he saw the lights in the upstairs rooms go out. He waited a further two hours before creeping towards the barn, hoping by now the occupants in the upstairs rooms were fast asleep. Slowly he opened the door of the barn, thankful that the farmer had kept the hinges well oiled. His eyes had become accustomed to the dark by now, and spotting a row of sleeping, plump chickens, he slowly grasped one around the neck. As he did so the chicken awoke, screeching and beating its wings. The next second the whole barn was in uproar as the remainder of the birds joined in. Grabbing his chicken, he ran for the door and out into the night, putting some distance between himself and the farmhouse. He had killed the bird while running and so started to pluck the feathers with the intention of eating the bird raw.

Suddenly Carr thought he heard the faint sound of an aircraft engine. It became louder and he recognised it as a single aircraft, probably a German fighter, as the engine sound was unknown to him. Then out of the darkness came an aircraft, flying low and directly overhead. He watched the flames flicker from the exhaust, the engine cut and saw it disappear over the hill in front of him. At first he thought the aircraft had crashed and he listened for an explosion, but on hearing nothing he headed toward the top of the hill. From the summit he could see a huge Luftwaffe airfield, with fighter aircraft dispersed all over the place.

Finding himself a vantage point, he scanned the airfield for guards along the fence line, but there only seemed to be a token number. He watched several figures crowded around a Focke-Wulf Fw 190 fighter and then heard the engine burst into life with a mighty roar. Carr listened as the engine roared until it was screaming. After running for a few minutes the engine was shut down and a man climbed out of the cockpit, closing the hood behind him, obviously satisfied with the full engine check that had just been carried out.

This was an opportunity Carr could not afford to turn down. If he could get to the aircraft there was a better than even chance that he could fly it out of there and back to his base. Taking a long careful look at the fence surrounding the airfield, he noticed it was surrounded by rolled barbed wire. Within that was a 10ft-high fence, with a guard patrolling behind. Carr noticed that the guard never varied his patrol and took fifteen minutes to complete it, and at one point was completely out of sight. Looking around the airfield, Carr noticed a number of hangars, behind which he could see parked aircraft. There was no runway as such, but a long area of mown grass, which he took to be the main landing strip.

Carr watched the guard complete his patrol, then as the he turned back to begin it again, Carr made his move and slipped down towards the fence. He realised that were he to be caught he would probably be shot, but this was a chance he had to take. Getting to the fence, he lay down behind a fallen tree to once again take stock of the situation. He knew that once he was over the fence there was no turning back.

He watched the guard stroll back and reach the parked aircraft. Then he suddenly stopped and leant his rifle against the fuselage of the Fw 190. Carr's first thought was that the guard was going to have a rest, then he saw the man fumble with his trousers and realised that he was just relieving himself. Carr gave a huge, silent sigh of relief as he watched the guard shoulder his rifle and resume his patrol. As the guard disappeared from sight, Carr made his move and slipped through the loosely thrown barbed wire and eased his 6ft 4in frame over the fence. He knew it wasn't electrified because he had seen the guard run his hand along it earlier.

Crouching low, he made a run for the aircraft and threw himself down beneath the wing. After catching his breath, he moved the wooden chocks away from the wheels and quietly clambered up onto the wing. Sliding back the canopy, which made a soft screeching sound as it did so, he eased himself into the cockpit and closed the hood.

Running his eyes over the maze of instruments and switches before him, he frantically tried to identify them. All the labels were in German, of course, and the gauges were in metric measurement.

Slowly but surely Carr began to recognise instruments, but try as he may he could not find the battery switch or magnetos, and without knowing where they were he was going nowhere. Suddenly he was aware of a movement outside and realised that the guard was passing on his patrol. Crouching down as low as he could, he waited, holding his breath. After a few moments he glanced out and saw the back of the guard disappearing into the darkness.

Feeling around in the cockpit, he discovered a large rectangular, hinged box under the right-hand side of the instrument panel. Opening it, he discovered a number of switches and, activating them one by one, he waited to see what would happen. Then he flicked a switch and the cockpit came alive, illuminating every dial and gauge. For a few seconds the light blinded him and he quickly switched it off, thinking that everyone on the base must have seen it. Having found the battery switch, he now needed to find the starter. Because the switch was in an inconspicuous place, he figured that the chances were that the starter would be similarly hidden and started to hunt around.

His train of thought was interrupted by the realisation that dawn was fast approaching and that within a couple of hours the whole base was going to be alive with people. Pushing his hand behind the box, he felt a T-shaped handle and to his amazement could make out the word 'STARTER' printed on the handle. The only word in English in the cockpit happened to be on the one thing he had been looking for.

Outside, Carr could now clearly see the outlines of buildings as dawn took hold. With a dry throat and his heart pounding, he put his feet on the rudder pedals and gripped the control column in his right hand. This was the moment when he knew he had to attempt to start the aircraft and then take off. He could clearly see the airfield now and there was nothing obstructing his way out onto the grass strip.

Pushing the throttle forward, then the mixture control to full open, flicking the battery switch to 'on' and pulling the starter handle resulted in no response. He tried it again and then again. Still nothing happened. Then he remembered that earlier when the aircraft was being put through its engine test he had heard the slow wind up of an inertial starter. Pushing the starter handle down fully, he heard the starter begin to wind up, then, when he felt it was at its maximum, he jerked the starter handle up and the engine roared into life. Releasing the brakes and opening the throttle, he taxied the aircraft out on to the strip, jammed the throttle full forward and felt the aircraft leap down the grass runway. Easing the control column back, the Fw 190 lifted off and into the sky.

As Carr pushed one of the buttons on the left-hand side of the instrument panel he felt the undercarriage retract. Setting a course for his base at St-Dizier, he settled back, the euphoria of his escape sending pleasant shivers through his body. Then suddenly the cockpit was lit up by a bright red light in the centre of the instrument panel. The only thing he could think was that it was a low-level fuel warning. Frantically looking around the cockpit, he spotted a lever projecting out from the panel just below the red light. Grabbing the handle, he pushed it all the way down and to his relief the red light went out.

The flight was uneventful as he sped over the French countryside, then the most welcome sight of all – his airfield suddenly came into view. As he made his approach, he dropped the nose of the Fw 190, and with the propeller almost touching the ground, hurtled down the runway. Then he pulled back on the control column, executed a sharp climbing turn and started to make his final approach. Punching the buttons that he thought were to lower the undercarriage and flaps, he lined his aircraft up with the runway. The flaps came down but the undercarriage remained in place. Try as he could, he could not lower the undercarriage, so he set the aircraft for a wheels-up landing. He also became acutely aware of the anti-aircraft gunners around the field levelling their guns at him. He held the aircraft steady as he made a long, low approach, then, as he cleared the perimeter fence, he let the aircraft settle. The moment the aircraft touched the ground, Carr cut the throttle and mixture and tuned off every switch he could see.

The aircraft slid along the grass for about 200ft, then stopped. Armed soldiers immediately surrounded it. Sliding back the canopy, Carr started to unbuckle his seat belt, but hands grabbed him and pulled him out. From outside the aircraft came a voice that he recognised, his CO, Colonel Bickel. Bickel strode up to the aircraft with a huge grin on his face and greeted Carr with the words,

'Where the hell'uv you been and what kind of landing do you call that?' The grin was becoming even wider. Carr was home, after one of the most dramatic escapes of the war.

16. THE FOREST OF FRÉTEVAL

WITH THE INVASION of Europe imminent, the Resistance organisations that were struggling to help the ever-increasing number of escaping and evading aircrews looked to MI9 for a solution. The decision was taken to hold them in hiding places until the invasion had taken place. MI9 was faced with the problem of organising the Resistance organisations and the escape lines into collecting all those aircrews that were in the pipeline, and moving them into a holding area. The area selected formed a triangle taking in the towns of Le Mans, Chartres and Vendôme.

What was needed was a co-ordinator, and MI9 persuaded a Belgian pilot, who was serving in the RAF, by the name of Lucien Boussa (code-named Cousine Lucienne), to go to France and set up and organise the holding camp. A fluent French speaker, Boussa was teamed up with a French radio operator by the name of François Toussaint. Boussa had been selected because as a serving officer in the RAF he would be fully conversant with everything to do with the force and would be able to detect any Germans that may have infiltrated the groups of escaping aircrews.

Boussa, together with his radio operator, was parachuted into France at the beginning of May 1944. Toussaint was taken under the wing of a local Resistance group, while Boussa made his way to Paris to meet up with the leader of the Comète Line, Baron Jean de Blommaert. Within hours of their meeting, a message arrived from England saying that the invasion was imminent and that the escape lines were to close down with immediate effect. They were told to hide all the airmen until after the invasion, when arrangements would be made to move them all out.

Boussa then contacted the head of the French Forces for the Interior of Eure-et-Loire, Maurice Caval (Sinclair), who in turn contacted two of the leaders of the Liberation Movement, Pierre Poitevan (Bichat) and Rene Dufour (Duvivier). They in turn contacted the head of the Resistance organisation for the Châteaudun region, Omer Jubault (Andre). Andre was a former gendarme who, together with another gendarme, Robert Hakspille (Raoul), had been running the local Resistance group for some time. An informer had compromised their involvement and both men had gone on the run and banded together a number of Resistance fighters. The men knew the region like the back of their hands and on being contacted and made aware of the situation, approached all the landowners surrounding the Forest of Fréteval looking for areas within the forest where they could hide groups of men and arms. Farmers, bakers and many other tradesmen were approached and asked to provide food and water for the men.

On 18 May, Boussa and Tourraint arrived at Châteaudun. They were met by members of the Resistance and spirited away on bicycles for 12-mile ride to the Forest of Fréteval. On arrival at a small gamekeeper's cottage behind a dense section of the forest, Boussa made it his headquarters. Jubault's two children, Ginette and her brother Jean, became the couriers for all the messages between the two sections.

All the Resistance groups in the area were put on full alert and their priorities switched from harassing the enemy to the setting up of camps within the forest for the forthcoming airmen. It is a miracle that the Germans never suspected anything, but such was the national hatred for the Germans and the expectations that the liberation of France was imminent that secrecy was top priority.

The unbelievable problems in helping these Allied airmen cannot be overemphasised. Food was rationed well below normal sustenance levels, with only just enough to keep families alive, yet somehow food was obtained to feed these extra men without complaint.

Clothing was another problem. Tokens were required to purchase any form of clothing, so when an escaping airman was placed in the hands of the Resistance the first thing that had to be got rid of was his uniform. Once this had been dispersed of, the man had to be reclothed with anything available. Some of the clothes do not bear description; torn, dirty and ill-fitting are just some of the more polite adjectives used by some escapees. Footwear was another problem, as most of the aircrew wore flying boots and these had to be got rid of immediately so as to avoid detection. This problem was alleviated in the Châteaudun area when a local tanner provided leather to a shoemaker in Amboise, who then proceeded to make basic shoes in a variety of sizes.

The first of the escaping airmen arrived at the railway station at Châteaudun at the end of May. The acting stationmasters were Jeanne Demouliere and her husband, who were both members of the local Resistance group. Boussa made his headquarters there initially so that he could monitor the groups as they came in. This was a risky decision because on the opposite side of the track in a small château was a German command post. However, as the station was quite a busy one and used by a large number of people, the escapees filtered through unnoticed.

The first group of fifteen airmen was met by local townspeople, who split them into groups and took them to various homes. After ten to fifteen days they were escorted to the forest camps by other local people, using different routes and varying methods of transport. Every so many miles the guides would be changed so as not to draw attention. The groups were monitored at all times by members of the Resistance, some of whom were waiting in the camps for their arrival. The risks these local people took were immense because had they been caught there is no doubt that they would have been either shot or sent to concentration camps. Despite the risks there was no shortage of volunteers.

Tents were constructed in camps dotted around the forest. One of the camps was concealed in dense woodland close to a natural spring, which gave the airmen an abundant supply of fresh water. It was also in close proximity to a farm owned by one of the helpers, Jean Fouchard and his family.

The farm was also used as a food warehouse for the airmen in the forest. The whole district was involved in one way or another. Some hid airmen before they were taken to the forest, others supplied food (this was undertaken mostly by the farmers) and others supplied or created clothes.

By 10 June all the airmen who had been hidden in various homes in the district had been delivered to one of the number of camps set up in the forest. Cooking food in the camp was initially the cause of some concern because of the smoke. Using charcoal, which was made by one of the helpers and delivered to the camps by his wife, solved the problem. All the furniture used was made from resources in the forest itself. Tables and chairs were constructed of tree trunks and branches, beds were made from interwoven branches and mattresses were stuffed with moss and grass. From the air the camps had to be concealed, as German spotter aircraft occasionally flew over the area, as did Allied aircraft who may have thought that the forest was being used to hide tanks and infantry and might have selected it as a target.

The tents had to be camouflaged and all activity stopped when any aircraft were heard flying over the forest. The camp organised themselves into a military routine to prevent boredom and maintain discipline. A series of lookouts were posted around the perimeter of the forest using any high ground available.

As the number of airmen increased, the rules within the camps were rigidly adhered to. Keeping noise to a minimum was of paramount importance as there were a number of German units still operating in the surrounding districts, including an ammunition dump, and one mistake could mean the downfall of the whole operation. It is to the credit and dedication to everyone concerned that the Germans never discovered the existence of the camps.

At night fishing parties were organised to go to the Loire River to help boost the food supplies. The Resistance men were in constant radio contact with London and bulletin boards were set up in the camps to keep the men informed about what was going on. Occasionally there was a notice of parachute drops of supplies but in fact only one ever took place. When this happened, a number of airmen, together with members of the Resistance, went into a designated field at night equipped with red torches and formed a triangle that indicated to the pilot the wind direction. The drop was successful, and when recovered the men set to work to 'straighten up' the field in order to remove all traces of them being there.

The Americans used the metal canisters from the parachute drop to make a bath. They even made wooden clubs and balls and had international golf tournaments, with the first prize being a bar of chocolate from an escape kit.

Access to the camp from the outside was restricted to a few local people. Only a handful were allowed in and this included the local doctor, Doctor Teyssier, and his son Louis, who visited the sick and wounded every day. New arrivals were stopped a couple of miles away and subjected to an intense interrogation by members of the Resistance.

To prevent detection, Toussaint, the radio operator, changed his position on a regular basis but kept within striking distance of Marcel Dauvilliers, an electrical engineer, who could repair the radio if it became faulty. Such was the determination to help the Allied airmen that even the local baker's young daughter, Roberte Guerieau, became another courier for the radio transmissions.

By the beginning of August 1944, the Forest of Fréteval contained more than 150 airmen. The D-Day landings had taken place two months earlier but progress was slow. The Resistance heard that the Americans were only 40 miles from the forest, so Boussa and two members of the Resistance commandeered a car and headed towards the American lines. Taken in to see the American intelligence officers, Boussa was pleasantly surprised to find one of the heads of MI9, Airey Neave, sitting at the table. After some discussion it was decided that a company of British commandos would make their way to the forest to escort the airmen out.

Back in the district, it was becoming apparent that the number of Germans in the area was decreasing rapidly as the Allied advance gathered momentum. So much so that on 12 August groups of airmen went down into the villages of Busloup and St-Jean-Froidmentel to celebrate after being told that the Germans had left. The locals were astonished to see so many young English-speaking men in their villages. They knew of their existence but such was the secrecy surrounding the forest that they never realised how many were actually being hidden. The wine cellars were opened and the celebrations went on late into the night.

The following day a company of British commandos arrived and the journey home for the British, American, New Zealanders, South Africans and Belgians began. Some of the aircrews returned to operational squadrons, others to training duties, but none ever forgot the sacrifices made by the local inhabitants who risked their lives daily to help them.

17. FLYING OFFICER STUART LESLIE, RCAF

WHEN ON 1 May 1944, 20-year-old RCAF pilot Flying Officer Stuart Leslie lifted his Halifax bomber, *'K' for King*, off the runway at Middleton St George, Co. Durham, his target was the railway marshalling yards at Mons, Belgium. This was part of General Eisenhower's plans to decimate the railway systems in France and Belgium in preparation for the D-Day landings on 6 June. With the railway system knocked out, the Germans would be unable to rush reinforcements to the Normandy beaches to prevent the Allies landing.

Leslie's squadron, No. 248 of No. 6 (RCAF) Bomber Group, had suffered some very heavy losses during the previous months and so there was an air of extreme nervousness among the crews. The mission required precision bombing because the targets were all close to towns and so it was hoped to minimise the civilian casualties that would be inevitable.

Because of a faulty compass, Leslie's aircraft had been delayed in reaching the dropping zone, and so when they arrived on station the others had dropped their bombs and were on their way back. This left *'K' for King* alone over the target. As Leslie dropped his aircraft to its bombing height and began his run in, the bomb-aimer warned him of heavy flak opening up around the area. Weaving the aircraft as best he could to prevent the searchlights and anti-aircraft gunners getting a fix on them, they approached the target and prepared to drop their bombs.

The fires on the ground were raging from the pathfinder's markers and the previous bombing attack, giving the bomb-aimer a clear view of the target. As they approached, there was a sudden loud bang and the aircraft rocked violently. The inside of the aircraft lit up in a bright blue flame as both starboard engines were hit by a shell and caught fire. The fuselage was peppered with red-hot shrapnel and the aircraft lurched towards the ground. After losing

about 1,000ft, Leslie managed to regain some semblance of control and levelled the aircraft.

Frantically trying to contact the members of his crew, Leslie received no
reply from the bomb-aimer, and the gunners in the rear told him that there
were a number of large holes in the fuselage. Realising that he could not control
the big aircraft for very much longer, Leslie ordered his crew to bale out. Then
the rear gunner's voice came over the intercom, telling him that the tail was on
fire. The aircraft went nose heavy and started dropping towards the ground.
Leslie unbuckled his seat belt, clipped on his parachute and struggled towards
the escape hatch a few feet away. The next thing he knew he was falling as
the aircraft literally came apart in the air. With burning debris whirling all about
him, he grabbed the D-ring of his parachute and gave one almighty tug. The
next thing he knew he seemed to come to a sudden halt in mid-air as his parachute opened. So violent was the abrupt halt that his flying boots were ripped
off his feet. Seconds later he saw the ground rushing up to meet him and then,
with an almighty thump, he landed in a field, face down in the mud.

He lay there for a few seconds regaining his breath and thanking all the gods
he could think of for saving his life. Seconds later he heard a roaring noise and
the burning tail section of his aircraft passed just over his head and smashed
into an adjoining field. His first thoughts were for his rear gunner, but the section was a blazing inferno and he thought that if the man had not got out earlier
there was no way he would get out now.

Realising that the Germans would soon be on the scene, Leslie gathered up
his parachute and ran towards a clump of trees. It was then that he realised that
he had no boots on as he trod on stones and twigs. Running towards the trees,
he suddenly found himself knee-deep in water as he stumbled into a ditch.

His bright yellow Mae West stood out in the dark, so he ripped it off and
plunged it into the murky waters, placing his parachute on top. He knew he
had to put some distance between him and the Germans so he started running again, the stones and twigs cutting his feet. Looking behind him, he could
see the headlights of a vehicle in the distance heading towards the crash site.
After an hour he stopped to catch his breath. Lighting a cigarette seemed to
calm his nerves, but then a pain in his leg started and his head began to throb.
The adrenaline that had kicked in when he had landed was now fast disappearing. Feeling wetness on his forehead, his fingers discovered a deep gash that
was bleeding profusely.

Leslie decided to press on and find somewhere to rest and possibly sleep.
Then in the gathering gloom he saw the spire of a church and then some
houses. He skirted the small town, deciding that there were possibly Germans

there, and found a small field just on the outskirts. Digging a shallow trench with his hands, he curled up and tried to sleep. He was wet and cold and his feet felt raw and painful. He dozed fitfully until about noon and was awakened by the sound of engines overhead. He watched as an armada of American Boeing B-17 bombers passed overhead on their way to their targets.

He examined his feet, which were cut and red raw. His leg was black and blue from hip to ankle and was extremely painful. His left eye was completely closed and covered with congealed blood from his head wound. He decided to move on and, although in great pain from his leg, covered about 5 miles. Finding a haystack, Leslie decided to rest up and burrowed his way in. Although feeling just as cold, it was considerably softer than the hard ground. He awoke some hours later, the warmth of the sun penetrating his chilled body. Getting up, he saw a farmhouse in the distance and decided to seek help.

Staggering across the field, he stumbled into the farmyard, giving the farmer and his wife a shock when they saw the bootless, blood-covered figure standing there. Gesturing with his hands, Leslie asked if he could wash and get something to drink. The shocked farmer's wife led him into the kitchen and produced a bowl of hot water and some soap.

After gingerly washing his face, he washed his feet and wrapped his tattered socks around the cuts as best he could. Brushing down his uniform, he looked reasonably presentable and then the woman placed a steaming plate of soup on the table, followed by another plate with bacon and potatoes. Inviting him to sit down, Leslie needed no second chance and quickly ate all that was put in front of him. After the meal the farmer produced a black cigar, which he offered to Leslie. Lighting up, Leslie offered the man some of his cigarettes, which they both sat down and enjoyed.

Noticing sleep overtaking his guest, the farmer indicated to Leslie to make himself comfortable in the chair and get some sleep. The farmer returned at dusk and Leslie awoke. After a bowl of hot soup, Leslie spread his escape map on the table and established where he was – in the middle of Flanders. He then asked if there were any Resistance organisations in the area, at which the old man became very nervous and indicated there were none. He also indicated that the Germans were very active in the area. Leslie realised that he had to move on as he was putting the lives of the farmer and his wife at risk. He thanked the couple for their hospitality and limped out into the darkness. He still had no shoes on because the farmer had no spare clothing.

Heading towards the river, Leslie hoped to get a ride on one of the barges that plied up and down. Reaching an area where there were a number of barges moored, he looked to see if there were any bargees about. Then out of the corner of his eye he spotted a figure and realised that it was a German sentry. The guard looked directly at Leslie and then turned away. For one moment Leslie's heart stopped but then realised that the battledress he was wearing was similar to that worn by the barge crewmen and in the dark they looked the same.

He decided to keep walking and came across another haystack in a field. By this time his feet were wet, bleeding and numb with the cold. Curling up in the straw he quickly dozed off. He awoke to the warm sun streaming in through the straw, and a feeling of despair was starting to gnaw away at him. He spent the day scanning the surrounding fields for locals, but it wasn't until the evening that he spotted a young man leading a horse down a lane close to the haystack.

Deciding it was now or never, Leslie got to his feet and staggered out into the lane. Greeting the man in his halting, schoolboy French, he asked for help, stating that he was an RAF flier. The young man looked at him very carefully, taking in the RAF uniform, and indicated for him to stay where he was. Leslie crouched down in the undergrowth and waited. About thirty minutes passed before the young man appeared again, this time accompanied by a much older man and a young woman. They talked about him excitedly in Flemish, before indicating that he should follow them.

On reaching the farmhouse, he was greeted warmly by the farmer's elderly wife and another young man, obviously the brother of the young man he had first met. They first attended to the cut on his forehead and then his raw and blistered feet, before producing a simple but wonderful hot meal. However, having experienced the previous farmer's lack of knowledge regarding Resistance organisations, he didn't hold out much hope for any help in that direction. What he did require were some clothes and shoes. He explained his predicament as best he could and produced a bundle of French francs. The farmer pushed them back at him with an angry shake of the head and Leslie felt embarrassed, feeling that he had insulted the man.

The family produced a pair of blue overalls and a selection of boots, none of which were his size. Selecting a pair that was slightly larger than his size, he eased his feet gingerly into them and stood up. As he did so, there was a knock on the door and the younger brother entered the room followed by two elegant and aristocratic-looking young women. In perfect English one of them said, 'Hello, how are you? We are friends and are here to help you.' They then produced a bottle of English gin and a first aid kit. The feeling of relief that spread over Leslie was almost indescribable.

It appeared that the younger brother was also a courier for the Resistance and had contacted another member, who in turn made the arrangements.

The two young women had brought with them some civilian clothes, but wanted everything that identified Leslie as an evading airman, including his dog tags. One of the girls looked at his cuts and his feet and then gave him the clothes to change into.

After saying goodbye to the family, Leslie followed the two young women out of the house and into the town. Following at a discreet distance, he walked nervously through the town, almost rubbing shoulders with German soldiers. The two women approached a large château on the edge of the town and went in. Leslie followed and the girls identified themselves as Elizabeth and Alice van Wassenhove. They lived in Brussels and this was the family's country home.

They showed him to their father's room, where a pair of silk pyjamas was laid out on the bed. He was then taken to the dining room, which was laid out in silver service, and he enjoyed a steak with all the trimmings. Leslie looked at the two young women and found it hard to imagine that they worked with the Resistance. After dinner he excused himself, slipped into bed and within minutes was fast asleep.

The sun streaming in through the window awoke him and this was followed shortly afterwards by a tap on the door. Elizabeth and Alice entered with a tray and while he ate breakfast they told him that their mother was arriving later in the day and they would make arrangements for him to be moved on down the line. He was told that he must not go out as there were too many Germans in the town. That evening Madame van Wassenhove arrived and explained that they would have to get him an identity card from Brussels, but under no circumstances must he go out or be seen as there were a number of collaborators in the area. She then took some photographs of him and left for Brussels.

For the next few weeks Leslie relaxed in comfort and waited for word from Brussels. In the evening he walked in the garden with either or both of the young women. Then on the morning of 25 May, almost a month since he parachuted out of his aircraft, word came to move him on. He and Elizabeth cycled all day through the picturesque countryside, arriving in Brussels late that evening. At a pre-arranged point a car arrived to pick them up and took them to the apartment of two nurses. Here Elizabeth said goodbye, then told him that none of his crew had survived and all of them had been buried in the town of Oudenaarde. Leslie said his goodbyes, which seemed totally inadequate for the help he had received.

The next day a member of the Resistance came to see him and asked him to fill out a questionnaire so that the Air Ministry in England could identify him. Once that had been verified, it was decided to move him on again and a young teenage boy and his sister called to collect him. He was taken by tram to the outskirts of Brussels, where his next contact waited for him at a busy road junction. The man identified himself as the editor of an underground newspaper, *Libre Belgique*, copies of which he carried inside another newspaper.

The two men took another tram ride to the other side of the city, where Leslie was taken to a small café. Inside, he was introduced to the owner with the words, *'Un parachutiste anglais Monsieur Leslie,'* to which she replied in almost perfect English, 'How are you Mr Leslie,' holding out her hand in greeting. Leslie was taken into a back room where he was introduced to her husband, a heavily built man who answered to the name of 'Churchill' because of his resemblance to him and his love of cigars.

The couple explained their reason for helping Allied airmen trying to get back to England was because during the First World War they had been forced to flee to that country and this was their way of repaying the kindness they were shown while there. That night two members of the 'White Army of Belgium', the activist section of the Resistance, suddenly arrived in a panic. They had been on an assignment to assassinate a Belgian collaborator and were now being hunted by the Gestapo after a third member of their team had been captured and tortured to make him talk. It was decided to move Leslie as quickly as possible, and within an hour a young woman called Madeline arrived to take him to another safe house.

That evening, the Gestapo raided the café and arrested the owners. While searching premises, the Gestapo found numerous names and addresses and a large number of arrests were made as a result, including the young teenage boy and his sister who had helped him earlier. The escape chain had in effect been broken, which left Leslie in no-man's-land. The elderly couple with whom he had been left were understandably frightened and it was obvious that he could not stay with them.

Despite the setback, the Resistance still managed to function and the following morning a man called to reassure him that they were going to move him on that day. Later a knock on the door revealed a woman, who invited him to go with her. The two of them left and walked through the centre of Brussels where, on reaching the park, Leslie waited while his companion went away. With German soldiers walking about, the tension was almost unbearable and every time one of them even glanced in his direction, his heart leapt into his mouth and he waited to be challenged.

The woman returned saying that she could find no one who could take him, so she was returning him to the elderly couple. His greeting by the couple was less than convivial, although they agreed to let him stay one more night on the condition that he must leave in the morning. No one got much sleep that night;

everyone was waiting for the knock on the door that would herald the arrival of the Gestapo.

The following morning the couple packed him some sandwiches and a bottle of beer and wished him good luck. He had agreed to meet the woman again in the park but her arrival didn't bring any good news. She had one last hope and that was with a friend of hers. The two of them made their way to a large building, which to Leslie's total shock turned out to be the headquarters of the German Commandant of Brussels. Leslie sat on a bench opposite and watched with a degree of incredulity as high-ranking German officers with large briefcases went in and out.

When his companion emerged suddenly from the building he followed her to a fashionable café that was obviously patronised by people from the Commandant's office. The women purchased a copy of the German magazine *Der Signal,* which Leslie thought was a clever touch considering the number of German officers in the café. They sat down at a table and before they could order, a tall, elegant woman approached them and exchanged greetings with his companion. She then indicated that they leave with her and they followed her to another café, where they selected a table in the far corner and ordered coffee.

As they sipped their drinks, a short, thickset man joined them and introduced himself to Leslie as Guy Schouppe. He looked at Leslie and said in a low voice and in perfect English, 'You have become something of a liability, Mr Leslie. However, my wife Louise will take you and your friend to our apartment while I find out what is to be done with you.'

Their apartment was situated opposite a Red Cross building and a church in the fashionable suburb of Ixelles. He was shown around by Louise and then taken to the bathroom. She pointed out her husband's wardrobe and told him to try to find something that might fit.

That evening as they sat down to dinner, the conversation seemed totally unreal as they all chatted in English and afterwards listened to the BBC. Leslie spent the next three days relaxing and waiting for news to come regarding his next move. Gestapo raids were still continuing so it was decided to move him into the country, where he stayed with an elderly couple in a small village. Louise had accompanied him and told everyone in the village that he was recovering from an accident and only spoke Flemish.

Two days later the door of the cottage was flung open and a slightly hysterical Louise shouted, 'It's come … the landings … the invasion … the Allies have landed in France!' Her husband Guy arrived and explained that the Resistance was up and running again and the escape line was being put back together.

The Germans were now on a full invasion alert as the Allied troops swept inland. As the Germans retreated en masse, it was decided to take him back to Brussels, as it was easier to hide him in a city rather than in a small town.

The following evening the three of them returned to Brussels by train and were met by a member of the Belgian Secret Police, who also happened to be a member of the Resistance. Leslie was taken to a safe house in the suburb of Anderlecht. On his arrival he was pleasantly surprised to find three other evaders there – an American, a Canadian and an Englishman.

In the meantime the Resistance had discussed plans for keeping the evaders in Brussels until it was liberated, but it was realised that that was not going to be imminent. And so it was decided to move them on down the chain and into France. At the end of June, Leslie was told he was being moved and a woman arrived to escort him to a rendezvous point outside the city where a small truck was waiting. The driver was dressed in a smart grey suit and told him their destination was Namur.

As they set off down the road, Leslie saw numerous people hitch-hiking and the driver stopped to pick up as many as he could. He explained to Leslie that as there were very few private vehicles on the road it would look strange if he didn't pick up people and give them a lift, and the German field police were always watching out for this. If they were stopped, because of the number of passes and identity cards the police had to look at, any discrepancies would easily be missed.

The first test came when they were carrying a full load of hitch-hikers; they were stopped at a checkpoint and ordered out of the truck by German soldiers. As the group presented their documents, Leslie noticed that they were different to the Germans he had seen in Brussels, these had darker uniforms and, although covered in dust and dirt, on their collars he saw the lightning flashes of the SS.

While they were standing outside, the truck was systematically searched, but finding nothing, the documents were returned to them and they all got back on board. As they drove down the road, Leslie noticed that the driver was sweating profusely. He explained that the reason for his concern was that the SS guards who had searched them and the truck were a detachment of the fanatical Liebstandarte Adolf Hitler, the personal bodyguard of Adolf Hitler.

On arriving in Namur, all the hitch-hikers got off and the truck proceeded on to a small house in the centre. This was just to be a stopping-off place before they were picked up again and taken into the country. Two hours later the truck returned and took him to a large château outside of town and well into the country. He was told to stay within the confines of the front garden to avoid the gardener. The family consisted of an old woman, her son and daughter and the woman's niece, whose father was a Belgian Air Force pilot serving with the RAF.

The next day the truck returned, this time with three more passengers – two Americans and an English officer. The four men settled down into the routine of the family, and for the next three weeks entertained themselves with playing cards, listening to the BBC on the radio and having conversations with the rest of the family.

Then an old wood-burning truck appeared, driven by the same driver who had brought them to the château. The four men said their goodbyes and clambered aboard. As they approached the Meuse River Bridge, where there was a German checkpoint, the four men got off and made their way downstream to where a boat was waiting for them. They got aboard and were taken across the river, joining up with the truck on the other side.

The truck continued on the open road into France and once again the driver stopped to pick up hitch-hikers. As they approached a small village, the driver suddenly slammed on the brakes because he had noticed a checkpoint.

German soldiers with guns levelled at them surrounded the truck and ordered everyone out. Documents and passes were produced and for a moment they were seemingly satisfied. Then one of the German guards, who was searching the back of the truck shouted, 'Who owns this?', holding up a small bag. One of the Americans turned and said, 'It's mine.' Then he realised that he had answered in English.

Seconds later every gun in the village seemed to be pointing at them and every German expression seemed to be one of delight. They were roughly bundled into the guardhouse and told to sit on a long wooden bench. The next moment another German soldier appeared wearing the metal badge of Feldpolizei around his neck. He searched each of them thoroughly in turn and turned up identity discs for the two Americans, at which point Leslie and the other Briton admitted that they were both RAF pilots. After two months of being on the run, it was all over.

After about thirty minutes a truck arrived bearing Luftwaffe markings, accompanied by a staff car, pulled up outside the guardroom and the four airmen were unceremoniously bundled into the back of the truck with armed guards. The truck sped back along the road they had come, through Namur and into the prison just outside the town. The four were lined up against the wall and inspected by two German civilians wearing long leather coats and slouch hats. Leslie recognised them as members of the Gestapo. They were then taken to separate cells and interrogated. All four airmen stuck to giving just their number, rank and name. For the next two days the men were questioned continuously but they remained defiant and the Germans learned nothing.

Then the cell doors were flung open and the men ordered out into the courtyard, where a Luftwaffe truck was waiting. They were taken out to an airfield, where they were placed in cells that were considerably more comfortable than the previous ones. While there a number of Luftwaffe officers dropped in for 'a chat', offering them cigarettes and coffee.

The following morning they were herded into the back of the truck again and driven away. As they passed the airfield, Leslie was looking at rows of cottages before realising that they were in fact camouflaged hangars for fighter aircraft. The two guards in the back seemed to be oblivious to their presence and at one point Leslie thought about overpowering them and making a break for it, but realised that his companions were not up for it and so abandoned his plan.

After some hours the truck arrived in Brussels and the four men were taken to a military compound in the middle of the city. They were immediately questioned by a Luftwaffe Intelligence officer who, after hearing them repeatedly give him their number, rank and name, warned them he could help them no longer and they would be handed over to the Gestapo.

Two days later three guards came and took Leslie to the Gestapo headquarters in Brussels, a bleak, grey building surrounded by a high wall. The building was bustling with both civilians and military personnel, and as he was escorted down the corridor to the cells he noted that there were a number of Belgian paramilitary men about. Entering the cell, he saw a small white card on the door with a red 'E' marked on it.

His cellmates were, for the want of a better expression, 'a dubious bunch'. Two were German and one was Austrian, and all three had been accused of crimes that broke the German military code. One of the Germans, Tony, spoke reasonably good English and explained to him the daily running of the prison. They also showed him the way the prisoners communicated with each other by tapping on the pipes that ran the length of the building.

The guard in charge of the block, who was about 50, told him that he had been a POW of the British during the First World War. He showed Leslie a photograph of his sister who lived in New Jersey and was married to an American fighter pilot. Leslie maintained a pleasant relationship with the man because he realised that he may need him at some time.

For three weeks nothing happened, then the cell door was flung open and two guards ordered him out; they were taking him to the interrogation centre. Bundled into the back of a truck, he was surprised to see the two American pilots who had been arrested with him.

On reaching the centre, the three men were taken into a comfortable room, where two young men were seated. They were apologised to for the rough treatment they had received and offered cigarettes. The soldiers told them that they were from the German security service and were obliged to ask them a series of questions. They then asked if they were being treated all right and not being abused in any way. The three men immediately complained that they were prisoners of war and should be treated as such. The two men replied that a mistake had been made on their part and it would be rectified as soon as possible. The two men then told them that they had both been undercover working with the organisation and by doing so had broken it, making numerous arrests. Leslie realised that this was a ploy on their part to undermine their confidence and to try to show them that they were in control.

They were returned to their cells but two days later Leslie was taken back to the centre, this time by himself. He was taken into a sparsely furnished room where a man in the black uniform of the SD was waiting. The gloves were off. The interrogator started his questions, to which Leslie replied as he had always done – number, rank and name. For more than an hour the man shouted questions at him until he realised that he was getting nowhere. One of the guards was called in and Leslie was taken away, only this time he was taken to the punishment block. The cells in the block were tiny, airless boxes that were so small that it was impossible for a normal man to stand upright and so narrow that it was impossible to lie down at full stretch. There were no lights or bedding and no windows. Barely edible food was brought twice a day and shoved through a hatch in the door. A bucket was provided for all his sanitary needs.

For fifteen days, Leslie wallowed in his own mess, unable to tell night from day and slowly losing the will to resist any more. Then suddenly one night the door opened and light from a bulb in the corridor flooded in, momentarily blinding him. It was the old guard from his previous cell. Placing a finger to his lips, he whispered, 'Follow me.' He unlocked the cell next to Leslie's and from it emerged the American, Bradley. They both looked at each other in shock at the haggard person who stood before them. The guard took them upstairs to a washroom, where they showered and shaved. He then gave them some cigarettes and a blanket and took them back to their cells, warning them not to say where they got them.

It was a simple humanitarian gesture, but one that made a tremendous difference to both of them. They used the blanket as a mattress on the solid concrete floor as the heat from the pipes caused the airless cell to be like a sauna. Just when he thought he could take no more, the door was flung open and a guard ordered him out into the corridor to join a line of other prisoners. The prison rang with the noise of running feet and shouts and the inmates realised that the jail was being emptied.

They were being forced out into the courtyard where a line of trucks was waiting. News filtered back through the column of prisoners that a spearhead section of the British Army was forcing its way into the city and the Germans were in full retreat. The Belgian Resistance was now out in the open, fighting the Germans from the inside and causing mayhem.

As the trucks rolled through the streets of Brussels towards the railway station, Belgians lined the roads shouting obscenities at the Germans and hurling stones. On reaching the station, the scene was one of total chaos as civilian and military prisoners fought with the guards, who were prodding them with bayonets and clubbing them with the butts of their rifles in an effort to get them onto the cattle trucks that were lined up.

The airmen, under the control of the Waffen SS, were marched to one of the trucks, where Red Cross workers handed them each a small parcel of food and other items. Once inside the truck the doors were locked and the men made themselves as comfortable as they could. Outside, the noise of screams continued as the German guards fought to try to keep some semblance of order. As the day wore on the noise continued unabated but still the train did not move, until just before dark there was a hissing sound, followed by a shrill whistle and it lurched forward.

Disappointment showed on the faces of the forty airmen in the truck as the train gathered momentum. The train proceeded for about 20 miles and then stopped; the Resistance had blown up the track. All that night the train remained stopped there. In the morning it started again, only this time it was going backwards, back to Brussels. The men found out later that when the Belgian train crew had discovered that the line had been sabotaged, they had killed the fire in the engine's boiler and disappeared. The Germans finally found them and brought them back at gunpoint in order to get the train moving.

Back in Brussels the railway station was in total chaos as the train dispatchers had gone and the remaining members of the railway were doing everything to sabotage the railway system to prevent the Germans from leaving. While in the station, Leslie could see a Red Cross train parked alongside, full of German wounded. Fleets of ambulances were bringing more and more wounded to the train and it was becoming more and more obvious that the German Army was in total disarray.

In the meantime, the Belgian Resistance was determined to stop the prison train being moved and offered to allow the Red Cross train, with the wounded aboard, to leave unmolested if they would give up the prison train. If not, they were prepared to kill everyone aboard the Red Cross train if necessary to prevent the prison train from leaving. From their vantage point the airmen watched the scene of total pandemonium as the Germans fought to get through the jammed roads that led out of Brussels; staff cars jammed with luggage, half-tracks with soldiers hanging on the sides and tanks with men clambering all over them in a desperate effort to get away. The noise of guns and small-arms fire could be heard in the distance, getting louder and louder by the minute.

Then they heard the engine getting up steam, followed by the distinctive sound of it being uncoupled and then leaving. The noise outside continued for a while longer, then suddenly silence.

Cautiously opening the door of the truck, the men peered out – Germans had gone. All the other prison trucks were empty and the only people around were not concerned with them. They discovered later that the Germans had agreed to release the prison train in exchange for safe passage for the hospital train.

As Leslie and Bradley walked in the centre of Brussels, a woman approached them and invited them into her home. There they bathed and were fed. The woman even managed to find them some clean clothes, as the ones they were wearing were indescribably filthy. Feeling refreshed, the two men headed towards the British lines to welcome their rescuers.

By September 1944 their ordeal was over, but the bravery and suffering of the Belgian people who helped them would live with them for the rest of their lives.

18. CAPTAIN JOHN TREVOR GODFREY, USAAF

JUST FIVE MONTHS after the 'Great Escape' from Stalag Luft III another determined escaper arrived – Captain John T. Godfrey, USAAF. Godfrey had been captured after his P-51 Mustang fighter had been hit by anti-aircraft fire while strafing a flight of Ju 52s on the ground at a German airfield. With more than thirty-six kills to his credit he was a major prize for the Nazis. Although badly injured from the forced landing he had to make after his engine failed, Godfrey managed to evade capture for almost a week before being cornered in a haystack by a German farmer wielding a pitchfork.

After being arrested by German soldiers, he was taken to Durchgangslager der Luftwaffe (Dulag Luft), a transit camp for captured airmen, prior to being to being moved to a POW camp. While there he was interrogated by the Gestapo for several days, before being sent to Stalag Luft III.

Within hours of being there Godfrey attempted an escape by trying to cut through the barbed wire and crawling underneath. He was spotted after he had only just cut one of the wires, and given a week in solitary confinement for his trouble.

In January 1945, with word coming that the Russian Army was rapidly approaching eastern Germany, the Nazi hierarchy decide to move all prisoners of war deeper into Germany and Stalag Luft III was to be one of the first to move. They were to be marched almost 260 miles from Sagan to Nuremberg in one of the coldest winters for years. Through freezing temperatures and driving snow, the prisoners were force-marched, accompanied by heavily armed soldiers. During the march some tried to escape by diving off the road into the bushes and trying to make a run for it. A few succeeded but most didn't and were either shot or forced to re-join the column at the rear. Some just collapsed from sheer exhaustion and the cold and were shown no mercy by the guards, their bodies being dumped beside the road as a warning to others.

During the march, food and shelter was very limited for both prisoners and guards, and on reaching Nuremberg the prisoners were put into an old POW camp with straw mattresses that were crawling with lice and body crabs. There was no heat and one bowl of watery cabbage stew per day as food.

With the Allied advance getting nearer by the day and the Rhine River having been crossed, it was becoming obvious that the Third Reich was in a state of collapse and that the German Army was in full retreat. The German military hierarchy, however, refused to accept defeat and decided to move the Allied prisoners of war deeper into Germany, with Munich being the bastion. The consensus of opinion among the prisoners was that ultimately they were to be used as bargaining chips in conditional surrender terms, or to aid the senior party members to make their good their escape.

The march to Munich was to begin on 4 March 1945, and Godfrey knew that this next 100 miles or so was going to be fraught with danger as the guards might be ordered to kill them if Allied troops closed in. While at the camp in Nuremberg, Godfrey spotted a manhole cover in the area between two compounds. During one dark night he had crept out and lifted the lid to discover a dry cistern with enough room for one person to crouch down in. The following day he approached the escape officer and told him of his plan. When the camp moved out he would stay behind, hidden in the cistern, try to make his escape and meet up with the advancing Allied troops. It was agreed and he was supplied with extra rations and a container of water. That night a fellow officer, Lieutenant Smith, offered to help him, so carrying all his escape kit, the two men made their way between the two fences to the manhole. Carefully and quietly they lifted the manhole cover and Godfrey slid into the black hole. Lieutenant Smith handed down the kit, the food and a blanket, then silently slid the cover back into place.

Now inside the cramped hole, the first thing Godfrey did was to see if he could move the cover from the inside, and putting the palms of his hands on it, he gently pushed and turned it. He now knew that when the time came he could get out. There was a gentle tap on the cover followed by a whispered 'Good luck. John.' For the next few hours there was only the faint sound of the guards moving about and then the camp started to wake up and prepare to march out.

The noise was quite loud as the guards shouted at the prisoners, but after a couple of hours the noise faded and then there was a comparative silence. Then there came shouting in German as the guards went through the camp with a fine-tooth comb making sure that no one had stayed behind. Even though he was well hidden, Godfrey held his breath as he heard boots walking across his manhole cover. The search went on for what felt like hours as the Germans methodically went through every inch of the camp. Then there was silence. Then in the distance he heard the sound of machine guns and immediately thought that the guards were shooting the prisoners.

As dusk fell the RAF carried out another bombing raid on Nuremberg. The concussion from the exploding bombs was amplified in the manhole to such an extent that Godfrey was almost deafened. He also worried about being buried alive if some of the bombs hit the camp and through the night he was haunted by a sense of oppression. The raid over, all he could detect after his hearing returned was the sound of fire engines and the crackle of burning buildings. The next day dawned to complete silence and he strained to listen for any guards that might still be in the compound, but there was nothing. Still not wanting to move, he decided to wait until the following morning to leave and so settled down as best he could for the night.

The following morning, just as dawn was breaking, Godfrey slid back the manhole cover and eased himself out. Gathering all his kit together, he looked around him. There was no sound and he couldn't see a light anywhere, and he suddenly felt a massive feeling of exuberance as the feeling of freedom swept through him. Cautiously he made his way between the fences and walked out of the camp. He had food and water, and he realised that no one was looking for him as they probably hadn't realised in all the upheaval that he wasn't there.

The camp was situated south-west of Nuremberg and close to a large wooded area. Godfrey headed straight for the dense wood and walked until the sun was starting to climb to its zenith. Finding a small clearing that was bathed in sunshine, he stopped to rest. The next thing he knew the sun had started to disappear and, feeling refreshed, he ate a tin of corned beef and started off in a westward direction. He followed a path through the forest until he came to the edge of a town.

He thought about entering the town then changed his mind as he realised that it would be far too dangerous. He headed back into the woods, intending to circle the town, and carried on down another path. This path ran parallel to the road but was concealed by thick bushes and dense trees. After walking for about an hour he heard the sound of engines and, crouching down, watched as forty German lorries passed. Minutes later another convoy passed towing artillery. Godfrey watched as the lorries slowed down to a crawl, then finally stopped. Godfrey's immediate thought was that they were heading for the front line and he watched as the drivers got out of their cabs and lit cigarettes. All the 88mm artillery was covered in canvas to protect it from the weather, so

Godfrey decided to sneak a look and see if he could hide somewhere beneath the canvas. If he could he might get himself a free ride to the front and once there hopefully join up with the Allied advance.

It was just starting to rain again as he slipped under the canvas covering the 88mms, and although it was pitch black he managed to feel and find the gunner's seat and straddled it, much like you would a bicycle. He could hear the rain getting heavier and bouncing off the canvas. It was then he heard engines burst into life and his lorry lurched forward to continue its journey. The ride was extremely uncomfortable as the trailer bounced along the road, but for every hour he endured it saved him at least a day's walking. For what seemed like an eternity the gun bounced along the road, shaking every bone in Godfrey's body, then it stopped. He slid slowly from beneath the canvas and realised that dawn was beginning to break. Crawling on all fours, he crept across the road in the darkness and into some dense bushes that lined the road.

He had no idea where he was, but he thought he must have travelled at least 30 miles through the courtesy of the German Army. The rain was becoming extremely heavy and, soaked to the skin, he knew he had to find shelter very quickly. Stumbling through the forest, he came to a clearing and saw across the road a farm with a large barn. He cautiously approached the barn and stepped inside. At the far end he could see a hayloft, and stripping off most of his wet clothes, he rolled himself in the hay and fell fast asleep. Some hours later he was awakened by a noise and, opening his eyes, found himself staring at a shocked German farmer standing less than 3ft away.

Struggling to remember the little German he had acquired, he told the farmer that he was an American and that he had escaped from a POW camp. The man looked stunned for a second then said, 'You wait here for Americans, yes?' His reply left Godfrey speechless, then he realised that word had got out about the rapid advance and figured that the farmer was hedging his bets so that when the Allies came through his land they would look upon him more favourably. Godfrey smiled and nodded his reply, and with that the farmer left. Godfrey sat wondering what to do or whether or not to trust the farmer, but then just ten minutes later the farmer returned with a hot cup of coffee and large bowl of porridge covered with cream. Then in the evening the farmer's daughter came with a plate of supper. That night he slept like a baby curled up warm and dry in the straw.

The following morning he was woken by the farmer, who told him he was going into the town and would be gone for most of the morning. Later his daughter came with another bowl of porridge and a cup of coffee. As the morning wore on, she returned and indicated that he should have a bath and produced a large wooden tub. Filling it with hot water, she then left him to bathe. He put his dirty clothes in the bath with him and afterwards shaved off his six-day growth of beard. He looked almost human now.

The farmer's daughter brought him some of her father's old clothes as his were pretty ragged. Later that afternoon the farmer returned looking worried. He told Godfrey that the town was full of SS troops and that he might have to house some of them. If Godfrey was caught there and they suspected the farmer and his family of helping him they would all be shot. Godfrey immediately said his goodbyes and thanked them for their help, then left. Dusk was falling and the stars were out. Keeping the North Star over his right shoulder, he knew he was walking in the right direction.

After walking through the night, he looked for somewhere to rest and get some sleep. On the edge of a field he saw a pine tree whose branches touched the ground, so crawling beneath and feeling quite safe he fell asleep. Then around noon he awoke feeling apprehensive; it was as if a sixth sense had made him aware of someone or something nearby. Cautiously he peered through the branches of the tree and spotted two figures slowly making their way along the edge of the field. The way they were dressed made them look familiar, then as the got nearer he realised that they were two American POWs. As they passed where he was hiding, he called out to them. The sound of his voice practically scared them to death. They dropped what they were carrying and started to run away. Godfrey called after them to stop, shouting, 'I'm a POW, too.' The two men stopped and came back, their faces showing complete relief, and after introducing themselves they grasped his hand and then crawled under the branches. It turned out that they too had been in the same camp as Godfrey but in the NCOs' compound. Godfrey asked how they escaped and about the machine guns firing. They told him that while they were marching in columns, two P-47s flew the length of the columns and the guards started firing at them. They took advantage of the confusion by diving into the bushes at the side of the road and then they kept running.

The farmer that had helped Godfrey had given him a good supply of food when he left, so he was able to share with the two sergeants. Because he was wearing the farmer's old clothes, he was less likely to be questioned, so when they set off he led the way in single file. Again they walked through the night and rested during the day, but then their luck ran out. As they walked around the edge of a field and were about to enter a wood, a voice rang, 'Halt'.

The three men looked round and saw the unmistakeable green uniform of the German Home Army. Instinctively the three men started to run. Shots rang out and one of them smacked into a tree alongside Godfrey. He realised that the game was up and stopped running, then raised his hands. The other two men did the same and watched as the Germans approached, their guns pointing directly at the Americans' chests. The expression on the Germans faces were enough to tell the three that one wrong move would result in them opening fire. Looking around, Godfrey saw foxholes all around with German soldiers looking at them – they had walked right into a German camp.

They were taken to a clearing in the camp where they saw three German officers looking at maps. The moment they saw the three Americans they put the maps away and walked up to them. One of the officers spoke a little English and asked them who they were at what they were doing there. Godfrey said they had been en route from one prison camp to another when an American fighter plane attacked their column. They had run into the woods for safety but got lost. The officer then asked what camp they were in and when told Nuremberg, laughed, and said they certainly were lost, Nuremberg was 50 miles away. The younger of the officers had been looking at one of the sergeants and asked him his name. The sergeant replied, 'Sergeant Joe Silverman, sir.' The young Leutnant's face contorted in anger and he spat in the sergeant's face, shouting, 'Jew bastard.' Before anything else was said a flight of P-47s screamed overhead and machine gun and cannon fire ripped through the trees. The Germans dived into dugouts, while the three Americans crouched in terror behind some large trees. The noise of the explosions followed by the screams of the wounded was almost deafening. Then there was a lull in the raid, but then minutes later another wave of aircraft, this time dive-bombers, arrived and the terror started all over again. Bits of trees, dirt, German equipment and human body parts showered down over the area. What was once peaceful woodland was now covered with human and mechanical wreckage, and stumps of what were once tall proud trees that had dotted the landscape.

With the raid over the Germans emerged from their dugouts and started to take stock of their situation. The cries of the wounded could be heard and Godfrey was concerned that there might be some sort of retaliation against them as a result of the raid. But there was none, in fact one of the officers offered them cigarettes and left them alone. At noon they were told they could open their bags and eat what food they might have, and it was then that the Americans took a long hard look at the Germans. What they saw were mostly boys between 15 and 17 and old men of 50 plus, all of whom looked frightened and dejected. In fact it was hard to see even one who could be described a genuine soldier.

That evening the senior of the three German officers ordered them to prepare to leave, telling them they were to be taken back to where they had come from. After writing a short note, he handed it to one of the accompanying soldiers and they were marched off. On leaving the woods they came across the shattered remains of a troop train, which was what the fighter aircraft, and dive-bombers had been after; the camp had just been on the periphery of the attack. The devastation was horrendous, with carriages lying on their sides, railway tracks twisted and uprooted and bodies lying everywhere.

After crossing the railway tracks, the group came upon the road and they headed eastward. The guard with them tried unsuccessfully to try to obtain some form of transport, but to no avail. For the next two days they trudged along the road past parked trucks and cars that could not dare move in case marauding American and British fighter aircraft spotted them. Time after time Godfrey saw P-51 Mustangs, P-47 Thunderbolts, Typhoons and Spitfires screaming along at hedge height looking for targets. It was quite obvious that the Allied advance was now well under way and that the German Army was in full retreat with only pockets of resistance remaining.

For a further three days the group trudged wearily along the road until they reached a small village, where the guard managed to persuade a truck driver to give them a lift to Nuremberg in his already overcrowded truck. On reaching the camp, which was once again a POW camp full of prisoners from every country fighting the Nazis, they were handed over. Such was the confusion that they were taken in but not registered. The guards appeared to be just going through the motions, obviously realising that the war, as far as they were concerned, was a lost cause.

Early in the morning of the following day, loud explosions rocked the camp and Godfrey awoke to see the top of his tent gone and the sides peppered in holes. One of the other occupants was lying wounded, blood seeping through his fingers as he clasped his hands to his stomach. Crawling over to him, Godfrey knew he had to get him to the sick bay where there was a French doctor. With the help of Silverman, he placed him on a blanket and dragged him across the compound to the sick bay.

More shells rained down and the inmates wondered if the Americans knew that this was a POW camp they were targeting. An American lieutenant decided to try to leave the camp and contact the advancing soldiers, so Godfrey decided to go with him and headed for the gate. A German guard stopped them and when they explained what they wanted to do, he offered them his rifle and opened the gate. Godfrey did not want to be caught with a rifle, especially a German one, and declined. They left the compound and ran down the deserted road until there, coming towards them, were American soldiers in single file either side of the road. Waving their arms, they ran towards them and told them that there was a POW camp just up the road. It turned out that the shells that were hitting the camp had come from German 88s and not from the Americans. The American officer in charge told them that he knew of the camp and it was to be his job to take charge of all the POWs inside. The war for Captain John Godfrey, USAAF, was over.

19. FLYING OFFICER
TOM WINGHAM, RAF

TOM WINGHAM, TOGETHER with the other members of the crew of their Halifax II bomber, belonging to No. 102 (Ceylon) Squadron, had just returned from a bombing mission to Germany, when they were told to report to Boscombe Down to test the latest Halifax bomber – the Halifax III prototype. They still had three more trips to do before they completed their tour but they had been selected for this job because they were the most experienced crew in the group. This was a welcome relief for the men as the losses within the squadron were mounting with each mission and the odds of survival were diminishing.

The development tests were scheduled to last for about five weeks but problems with the aircraft resulted in the five weeks turning into five months. On their return to their home base of Pocklington in Yorkshire they discovered that they had been 'screened', which meant that the three trips needed to complete their tour had been deemed to be done. The crew was then split up and Wingham chose to go to Rufforth, just outside York, as a bombing instructor with the Heavy Conversion Unit.

By March 1944, Wingham was becoming restless and although his job as an instructor was important, he wanted to get back into the war. His opportunity came when a drinking companion, Flying Officer Jim Lewis, a navigator who was part of a crew that was being re-formed, asked him if he was interested in joining them. Wingham jumped at the chance and they and two gunners, Warrant Officer John Rowe and Flight Sergeant Harry Poole, who were both instructors from Driffield, joined the crew. The other members were pilot Squadron Leader Stan Somerscales and wireless operator Flying Officer Jack Reavill.

On 20 April 1944, the crew took over a brand-new Halifax that had been delivered just two days earlier by an Air Transport Auxiliary (ATA) pilot.

She maintained that it was one of the best Halifax bombers she had flown. The crew took it on air test to ensure everything worked as it should and declared it fit for operations. On 21 April the crew carried out two raids on railway yards in France and Belgium and then stood down for another bomber crew to take the bomber on a raid to Düsseldorf. The second crew was led by the CO of No. 76 Squadron, Hank Iverson, but Group HQ ordered them to stand down as they had completed their quota of trips for that month. Somerscales and his crew were taken off 'stand down' and given the green light to take part in the raid.

At 10.36 p.m. on 22 April the big Halifax bomber once again lifted off the runway at Holme-on-Spalding-Moor, Yorkshire, together with other bombers, and headed south towards northern France. As they passed over Liége, Wingham settled himself down in the prone position to carry out checks on the bombsight. Minutes later there was a muffled thud and the aircraft shook slightly. Over the intercom came shouts of 'What was that?' Then Flight Sergeant Harry Poole in the mid-upper gun turret shouted, 'The wing's on fire!' They discovered some time later that they had been attacked by an Me 110 night-fighter flown by Oberfeldwebel Rudolph Frank, one of the Luftwaffe's top night-fighter aces with forty-five victories to his credit, using an upward-firing cannon called Schräge Musik.   ·

Within seconds, Somerscale ordered the crew to bale out as he knew there was no way of saving the aircraft. Wingham immediately jettisoned the bomb load to make it easier for the pilot to maintain control and then, clipping on his parachute, moved his seat from over the escape hatch. Being a new aircraft, the hatch was extremely tight and it took the combined efforts of himself and Jim Lewis to force it open. All the time the flames were creeping along the wing and into the fuselage. As he watched Lewis drop out, Wingham looked back along the fuselage, which by now was enveloped in smoke and flames, and saw Jack Reavill about to leave by one of the other hatches. Sitting on the edge of the hatch, Wingham dropped out and as he pulled the ripcord of his parachute he saw the burning aircraft plunging towards the ground. He discovered later that the aircraft crashed between Maastricht and Aachen.

Wingham remembered nothing after pulling the ripcord until he came to in the middle of a field. He lay there for a while trying to collect his thoughts, and then his back and legs started to become extremely painful as he struggled to his feet. Hitting the ground like a sack of potatoes while unconscious hadn't helped his situation. He glanced down at his watch and was aware that he was having great difficulty in focusing. His jaw was also swollen and tender. He realised later that he was suffering from concussion probably brought about by the heavy metal parachute clips hitting him either side of the jaw as his parachute opened. Gathering up his parachute and harness, he rolled it into as tight a bundle as possible and then struggled across the field and hid it under a hedgerow.

Looking up at the stars, Wingham managed to fix a position and headed in a south-westerly direction. He waded across a small river, then decided to settle down for the night. In the morning the sun spread a warm feeling through his aching and bruised body but his vision was still out of focus, which was causing him some concern. He decided it would be safer to travel at night and so rested beside the river until dusk. With the gathering darkness, he started off, not knowing where he was headed for or indeed what country he was in. He had, in fact, crossed the Dutch–Belgian border during the night and was now in Belgium. The walking had helped ease the pains in his back and legs and, stumbling on through the darkness, he came upon a village. Although he could hear voices he could not identify the nationality, so decide to skirt the village and continue in a south-westerly direction.

His vision was still giving him cause for worry and the only way he could work out his course was to lie flat on his back, identify the North Star and line up his body to the south-west. This, of course, was conditional on clear nights, but on the second day he was caught out in the open during a violent thunderstorm and within minutes was soaked through to the skin. He could hear the sound of engines as bombers flew overhead on their way to targets in Germany, then suddenly he heard the sound of gunfire and minutes later saw a burning Lancaster bomber hit the ground and explode just a mile or two from where he was standing.

Wingham realised that he was in dire need of help and decided to trudge back to the village he had skirted earlier and make his way to the church. He found the church deserted, so he decided to wait in the undergrowth until the dawn came. Then he saw movement and watched as a woman emerged from a cottage. She opened a pen full of sheep and proceeded to drive them towards a field close to where Wingham was hiding. Taking a chance, he stepped out and explained to the woman in a mixture of gestures and sign language that he was a member of an RAF bomber crew that had been shot down and had parachuted into a field. The communication proved to be difficult but then the woman realised what he was trying to say and she quickly ushered him into her cottage.

On entering the cottage he was confronted by three men – the woman's husband and their two sons. After managing to explain to them that he was a downed RAF airman, they helped him take off his wet clothes. Meanwhile, one of the sons went across the street to another cottage where he knew there was a Dutch policeman, Herman Ankoné, who had been visiting some friends in the village. The woman Wingham had approached for help was known as the worst gossip in the area and so the policeman, aware of this, was wary of offering his help. However, they had approached him and by doing so had compromised themselves, so he decided to check Wingham out in case he was a German 'plant'.

Entering the cottage, the policeman barked out a number of commands in German and, getting no response from Wingham, proceeded to verify that he was who he said he was. Wingham was initially shaken but after realising that the man was not German he relaxed. Again the language barrier was causing problems, so the policeman indicated using sign language and pencil and paper that an English-speaking policeman would come later that morning.

At 9 a.m. a tall policeman in uniform entered the cottage and began to interrogate Wingham until he was satisfied that he was indeed an RAF airman. Introducing himself as Sergeant Vermullen, the policeman told Wingham that he and all the other officers in the district just over the border were members of the local Dutch Resistance.

After being given fresh clothes and a meal, Wingham was taken to another house in the village, where he was instructed to wait until he was collected by other police officers that evening. At 6 p.m. three Dutch police officers, including Sergeant Vermullen and officer Ankoné, arrived to take him to the border into Holland. He was taken to a farmhouse close to the border and introduced to Richard Linkens and his wife, Cisca. The couple were members of the Resistance who helped escaping and evading Allied airmen, and had aided more than forty since the beginning of the war. In order to allay suspicions from the German border guards, the couple maintained a very friendly relationship with them and on numerous occasions entertained the guards in one room, while in another room Allied airmen were enjoying a meal. During the two days Wingham stayed there he remembers having supper with Cisca while her husband was having coffee in the next room with some of the border guards.

On the evening of the second day, the three Dutch policemen arrived to escort him to another safe house in a village called Slenaken. On the way the group ran into a patrol of German border guards and Wingham had to jump out of the vehicle and hide in an orchard until they had passed. The group resumed their journey and for the next three days and nights Wingham stayed at Sergeant Vermullen's home in the company of his wife and three children.

Again this aid and hospitality was extended willingly despite the risk that the families might pay for it with their lives if discovered. Then, after the third day, a guide turned up to take him to another safe house. After saying farewell and thanking his hosts, Wingham and the guide set off on a two-hour trek through pitch-black woodland to an isolated farmhouse over the border in Belgium. The farmer and his wife welcomed him but were nervous about him being there. They emphasised the point to the guide that it could only be for one night. The next morning he was told that another guide would come and collect him after lunch but lunchtime came and went, with the farmer and his wife becoming increasingly agitated. Then a message came to say it would be the following day before he could be collected. Despite Wingham feeling a sense of embarrassment at being foisted on the couple, he had no choice but to stay put until the following day.

Just after lunch the following day, the farmer gave Wingham an old bicycle and was taken to a lane some distance from the farm. There he was told to wait until his guide arrived to take him to his next point of contact. After about thirty minutes a woman and a young girl, Madame Coomans and her daughter Mady, suddenly appeared on bicycles and stopped beside him. Once again there was a problem with language but Madame Coomans spoke a few words of English and managed to explain to Wingham what was going to happen. The mother and daughter would cycle in front with at least a 50-yard gap between each of the bikes. In the event of the mother being stopped by a German patrol, the daughter would turn round and cycle back towards Wingham. He in turn would turn around and take the next turning off the road. Then Mady would catch up and overtake him, then lead him off to safety.

Still suffering from concussion, Wingham set off behind the two women, all the time having great difficulty in focusing. Fortunately everything went smoothly and just before dark they reached the small town of Wandre. They parked their bicycles at the rear of the house of the parish priest, before entering the Manse. Here they were warmly welcomed and the priest's housekeeper provided them with a hot meal. The priest, who spoke good English, explained to Wingham what was going to happen next. He was to go and stay the night at the home of Madame Coomans and the next day he was to travel with a guide to Brussels to join up with a group of evaders who were going down the escape line to Spain.

The following morning he was woken to be told that he was too late to join the others in Brussels due to a directive from London to the escape organisers to suspend all movement of airmen, so he was to stay with the Coomans. This created a major problem because Madame Coomans' husband had no knowledge of his wife's Resistance activities. Nevertheless, Wingham moved into the small house and lived there for the next seven weeks without Monsieur Coomans' knowledge as he went to work as a miner blissfully unaware of who was living in the spare room upstairs.

Madame Coomans' husband worked a regular 2–10 p.m. shift, so she set out her husband's timetable for Wingham:

8 a.m. – Got up and had breakfast.
10 a.m. – Went to local *estaminet* (bar) to play cards with friends.
12.30 p.m. – Returned home for dinner.
1.25 p.m. – Departed for work at the mine.
10.20 p.m. – Returned from work.
11.00 p.m. – Went to bed.

In between all these times Wingham was allowed out of his room, but never allowed to leave the house – not even to use the outside toilet. The stairs from downstairs led directly into the first bedroom, there was no landing, while the door to the second bedroom was at the foot of the bed in the main bedroom.

During the day visitors, in the shape of the local priest, a member of the escape committee from Liége and sometimes the paymaster for the Resistance, would occasionally visit to see if Wingham needed anything and to pay Madame Coomans for his food. Wingham was constantly concerned about what would happen if Monsieur Coomans ever found out that he was in the house. He was told that he would probably just tell him to leave, as he was neither for nor against the Germans and equally he was neither for nor against the English.

As the days turned into weeks the arrival of June heralded the beginning of summer and Wingham longed to be able to walk in the warm sunshine. Then, on 6 June, news came through of the D-Day landings and the retreat of the German Army. Two weeks later Wingham's world almost collapsed around him when he heard a sudden screeching of tyres and the slamming of doors and shouts in German for the doors to be opened. He had been betrayed to the Gestapo.

Wingham had been listening to the BBC on the radio at the time, so switching it off and changing the dial settings, he raced upstairs with the intention of escaping through a window at the back of the house and into the woods. As he went to open the shutter, he saw a leather-coated figure trying to force a window in the back. Now desperate, he raced downstairs and into the cellar, frantically looking for a place to hide. It took a few moments for his eyes to become accustomed to the darkness and it became obvious that there was nowhere obvious for him to go. The cellar was cluttered with old boxes and the usual items found in a cellar. Upstairs he heard the Gestapo searching the rooms. Suddenly he spied a tiny alcove behind the stairs that led to the cellar, surrounded by old crates. The alcove, which was about 4ft high and just 18in wide, was his only hope and so he somehow squeezed in and pulled the crates behind him.

He heard heavy footsteps pounding down the wooden staircase into the cellar. Barely daring to breathe, his heart was beating so loudly that he thought the Germans must have been able to hear it. The two Gestapo men stopped and struck matches to enable them to peer into the inky blackness. Fortunately for Tom they had not thought to bring torches with them and after a few minutes, including a time when they moved close to the crates behind which he was hiding, they left. Wingham remained crouched while he heard the banging around upstairs and then he heard car doors slamming shut, followed by an engine starting and the scream of tyres as they sped away.

He waited almost an hour before emerging from the cellar just to ensure that they had gone. He discovered later that the Gestapo had gone to the mine, picked up Monsieur Coomans and taken him to their headquarters in Liége for questioning. After many hours of questioning the Gestapo determined that he knew nothing of his wife's involvement with the Resistance, which of course he didn't, and released him. Monsieur Coomans returned home in the early hours of the morning, not knowing that Wingham was still in the house.

That evening Wingham had slipped out of the back door and made his way through the dense wood to the Manse at the other end of the village and explained what had happened to the priest. He was then passed on to another Resistance group, who took him to a small terraced house in the village where he stayed with an elderly widower who lived alone. Once again Wingham found himself confined to the house, not even being allowed to use the outside toilet.

The reason for this was because one of the attached houses was the home of members of the Belgian Nazis (Rexist Party), and one of their sons was away fighting with the Waffen SS. Their bedroom window overlooked the widower's outside toilet and it was too dangerous for Wingham to even consider stepping outside in case they spotted him.

After a week some members of the Resistance came and took him to a farm a couple of miles outside the town. The farmer named Monsieur Schoofs, his wife, a son called Paul and two daughters made him very welcome and he quickly became an integral part of the family. This was a complete change for Wingham, inasmuch as he could walk freely around the farm and help in the fields picking fruit. It also gave him a chance to repay their hospitality in a small way and not feel completely obliged, although this had never been suggested or hinted at by any of the people who had helped him.

One evening one of the Resistance members called and asked him if he was prepared to join up with an RAF pilot and steal a German plane from a local airfield and fly it back to England. Wingham immediately jumped at the chance but the town priest suggested that he be allowed to check on the validity of such a daring proposal. The priest returned saying that it was indeed a genuine proposal and arrangements were put into place to take Wingham to Liége to await final instructions. He was taken into the town and placed in the care of an elderly couple in their third-floor apartment.

After two days of waiting and hearing nothing, it was soon realised that the whole project was a non-starter. Increasing German patrols and searches by the Gestapo in the town made the old couple extremely nervous. The Resistance was contacted and arrangements were made to take Wingham back to the farm. Early one evening a member of the Resistance, a Belgian Intelligence agent, arrived with two bicycles and the two men set off to cycle back to the village of Wandre. They had just left the outskirts of Liége when another cyclist, a German soldier, joined them. He accompanied them almost all the way to Wandre before leaving them. Just a mile from the farm, the two men stopped and parted and Wingham walked the rest of the way, while the Belgian took the other bicycle back to Liége.

Towards the end of August there were a growing number of German soldiers retreating from the advancing Allies. Then suddenly the farm was surrounded by German troops camping out in the fields, hedgerows or anywhere else they could. The officer in charge told Madame Schoofs that he was taking over part of the farmhouse and making it his headquarters. He told her that their barns would be commandeered as billets for his men. Taking Monsieur Schoofs to one side, Wingham suggested that he should leave so as not to cause problems for the family in the event of him being discovered. But because of the situation, and the reduction in the level of danger, the couple decided that Wingham should play the part of a deaf Flemish mute, as it might arouse suspicion if he left suddenly.

That lunchtime the family, including some of the workers from the fields, sat down in the kitchen to enjoy a rather sumptuous roast lunch of veal. At one point the whole family, with the exception of Wingham, left the table to harangue a bunch of dejected, straggling soldiers as they trudged their way through the farmyard. As they did so, Wingham, still at the lunch table, looked up to see two German soldiers looking longingly at the pile of food on the table.

Wingham's chair was situated close to the door leading into what was becoming the German officer's control room and suddenly it was pushed ajar violently and he was almost thrown to the floor. The German officer's head peered around the door shouting out commands. On receiving no response he shouted even louder. At this point Madame Schoofs, on hearing the commotion, stormed into the kitchen and started to berate the officer about how she felt a German officer should behave and how she did not want dirty Boche boots soiling her Belgian kitchen floor. For a moment there was silence, then the officer muttered something, quietly shut the door and locked it.

Word started to come through that retreating bands of Waffen SS troops were killing young Belgian men indiscriminately, so it was decided that Wingham should be moved to a safer location. The problem was how to get him past the German troops now surrounding them and even camped within the farm itself. Within the hour Paul told Wingham to get ready to move and he prepared himself for one of the most nerve-racking moments since he baled out of his aircraft. Paul came in to fetch him and the two men walked out into the farmyard. Waiting in the middle of the farmyard was a fat peasant woman of around 35 years of age holding a battered pushchair. With her was a young child aged between 2 and 3 years old, who was playing with some German soldiers.

The woman glanced at Wingham and then shouted for the child to come to her or Papa wouldn't push her in the chair. Wingham was stunned for the moment as he realised that he had just been 'married off' and, dressed in ill-fitting pinstripe trousers and a black jacket, he tottered off with the woman, followed by goodbyes and laughter from the Schoofs family and the totally bemused looks from the German soldiers lounging about.

The couple made their way back to Wandre, where members of the Resistance were waiting. After saying goodbye and grateful thanks to his 'bride' of a few hours, Wingham was placed in a safe house,

Two days later an American tank column entered the village and Wingham was able to arrange passage to Paris, where he met up with his navigator. The two men returned to England on 16 September.

Wingham returned to operational flying, this time on Mosquitoes with No. 105 Squadron. He completed four more missions, including, on the night of 2 May 1945, being in one of the last four aircraft of Bomber Command to bomb Germany.

It cannot be emphasised enough the dangers that the men, women and children placed themselves in to help Allied soldiers and airmen to escape the clutches of the German Army and Gestapo. The identities of the vast majority of these people will never be known, as after the war they just went back to their normal way of life. The debt owed to these people can never be repaid but should never be forgotten, as they helped in their own way to shape the course of history.

20. FLYING OFFICER JACK GOUINLOCK, RCAF

JACK GOUINLOCK WAS an RCAF navigator when his aircraft was shot down. He evaded the Germans for some time before being captured. He then had the terrifying experience of digging his own grave before facing a firing squad.

Ten days before D-Day, the bomber offensive against Germany was increased dramatically. Bombers from RAF Bomber Command and the US Eighth Air Force pounded the gun emplacements, the railway yards, military camps and the roads in both France and Belgium in an effort to prevent the German Army rushing reinforcements to Normandy when the invasion took place.

On the night of 27 May 1944, Flying Officer Jack Gouinlock sat in the briefing room at RAF East Moor in Yorkshire listening to the information regarding their target that night. They were to bomb a large German military camp that was situated right in the middle of the Belgian town of Bourg Leopold. This was a call for very precise navigation and bomb aiming on the part of the crews of No. 432 Squadron TCAF. One hour later, Gouinlock's Halifax bomber, LK811 'N' for Natch, lifted off the runway and headed for the Belgian coast.

The crew was mixed, inasmuch as three were RAF, four were RCAF and one was American. The three RAF were Flight Sergeant John Clark (flight engineer). Sergeant Jack Rowan (wireless operator) and Flight Sergeant Tom McClay (tail gunner). The four from Canada were Warrant Officer Herb Rogers (mid-upper gunner), Flying Officer Jack Gouinlock (navigator), Flying Officer Don Rutherford (bomb aimer) and Pilot Officer Howards Menzies (pilot). The American was Sergeant Richard Hall (co-pilot).

As they approached the target they could see where the pathfinders had dropped their markers and so made their bombing run. In the nose of the Halifax, Rutherford hunched over his sights and when lined up, released the whole bomb load. The moment he heard the call 'bombs gone', Gouinlock gave the pilot the course home. With their target now in flames, the air-craft turned and headed for home. Then, just south of Eindhoven, they were 'bounced' by a Focke-Wulf Fw 190, which suddenly appeared as if from nowhere. The first anyone knew of it was when the tail-gunner shouted 'Fighter coming in' and opened up with his Browning machine guns. Seconds later the mid-upper gunner opened up with his Brownings, followed by a roar of the Halifax's engines as the pilot poured on the power in an effort to take evasive action. The next second there was a violent explosion and both port engines burst into flames.

The next second Menzie's voice came over the intercom, 'She's going down – bale out.' Gouinlock needed no second warning and, swiftly clipping on his parachute, he opened the forward escape hatch that was directly in front of his position and dived through it. He was met by a violent wind that tore the breath from his lungs and his boots from his feet. Fumbling for the D-ring that would open his parachute as he plummeted towards the ground, he gave it an almighty tug, which was followed by a jolt that jarred every bone in his body, and then he was floating gently towards the ground. Twisting round, he watched as his aircraft smashed into the ground and exploded in an almighty fireball. As he floated down to earth he wondered how many other members of the crew had managed to get out.

He landed in the middle of a ploughed field and for a moment just lay there recovering. Scrambling to his feet, he unclipped his parachute and bundled it up. Then, while moving over to the edge of the field towards a clump of trees, he realised that his feet were only protected by thin socks. On reaching the edge, he buried the parachute beneath a pile of wood and covered it with leaves. He then took off his battledress top and removed all the insignia, and at the same time recovered the tiny compass that he had sewn beneath his navigator's wings. Checking the contents of his escape kit, Gouinlock headed off in a south-westerly direction.

His thin socks were soon shredded as he stumbled across the fields. He walked through the night and as dawn was breaking he came across a number of people going to work in the fields. They stared at him suspiciously and gave him a wide berth when they saw the Air Force blue battledress jacket. Gouinlock realised that he was going to have to try to make contact with the Resistance before one of the local people turned him over to the Germans out of fear.

He continued to walk through the morning, seeing no one else until he came across a small farmhouse and a man working in a field close by. With his feet badly bruised and cut, Gouinlock knew that he could continue no longer and approached the man. Taking a phrase card from his escape kit, he managed to explain that he had been shot down and wanted help. At first the man was suspicious, but then invited Gouinlock to follow him into his house. There the farmer's wife made him a meal out of bread and meat, and then she dressed a cut on his forehead and the numerous cuts on his feet. Gouinlock asked where he was and found out that he was right on the Dutch–Belgian border. The farmer then produced an old pair of overalls and a pair of strong shoes, which were slightly too big but fitted because his feet were so swollen.

As darkness fell the farmer shrugged his shoulders and indicated that he would like to have helped more, but he had a wife and children and the penalty for helping an Allied airman was death. However, he led him to the canal that marked the border between the two countries before saying goodbye. Gouinlock thanked him for all his help and started walking along the canal path looking for a place to cross. He came across a bridge but then spotted a sentry box with a German guard. Realising that it was too risky to cross at that moment, he found a small clump of trees away from the canal that still enabled him to see the bridge.

Tiredness was now overcoming Gouinlock; it had been more that twenty-four hours since he had parachuted out of his burning aircraft and he needed to sleep. After crawling into a clump of bushes just inside the wood, he fell sound asleep. He awoke suddenly and for the moment was confused as to where he was, but quickly it all came back to him. He glanced at his watch, which showed 2 a.m., and then walked silently towards the bridge. As he crept closer he could hear a snoring sound and realised that the German guard too was catching up on his sleep. Taking off his shoes and hanging them around his neck, Gouinlock crawled on all fours silently across the bridge and into Belgium.

Determined to put as much distance as he could between himself and the border, Gouinlock strode briskly southwards. Around midday he stopped to eat some of his escape rations and take stock of his situation. His feet were still sore, but nowhere near as bad as they had been. Walking on a bit further, he came across a farmhouse and decided to take a chance on getting some help.

When he knocked on the door, it was opened by a middle-aged woman who, after he had explained who he was, welcomed him in with great enthusiasm. He was taken into the kitchen, where a large plate of bread and cheese was placed in front of him. He devoured it with great relish and the noticed the woman whispering something to two of her children, who slipped out of the door.

The woman could not help but notice his uneasiness at this stage and quickly assured him that he was among friends. Thirty minutes later the door opened and the children returned accompanied by two young women who introduced themselves in excellent English as Mary and Golly Smets. While the two women were questioning him, he realised that they were no amateurs when it came to interrogating people. Satisfied that he was who he said he was, they relaxed and told him that they would have to move him as the farmhouse was a regular place for Germans to visit when looking for food. Gouinlock also felt a sense of relief because now he knew he was in the hands of a section of the Resistance.

At sunset, the farmer took Gouinlock to a secluded wood, where he was to wait until the two women arrived and led him through the trees and into a small village called Exel. They took him to a small house, where Madame Smets, the girl's mother, was waiting. She welcomed her visitor, sat him down and interrogated him once more. Gouinlock thought the girls were thorough, but their mother was an expert. She explained, once she was satisfied, that they could not afford to be careless because the Gestapo was infiltrating the Resistance using English-speaking agents posing as downed airmen and a large number of arrests had been made because of this.

Once he had settled in, Gouinlock discovered that he was the seventh guest in as many months and arrangements were being made to take him to another safe house the following night. Their home appeared to be the 'clearing house' for escaped airmen, but because of its close proximity to the local Gestapo headquarters it was not the safest of places in which to hide them.

The next evening a man arrived to take him to a safe house some 2 miles outside the village. The family, the Vanderhoedoncks, consisted of three sisters and a brother who ran a small farm producing a variety of vegetables that they supplied to a nearby German hospital. In return the Germans allowed them an additional ration of foodstuffs. This also gave them special status as far as the Germans were concerned, which meant that they were left alone except for those who came to barter with them.

When Gouinlock arrived, he was made aware of another visitor living at the farm, an orphaned German schoolboy whose family had been killed in an Allied air raid. No one except the immediate members of the family was to know of Gouinlock's presence and so a system of schedules and signals was created so that he was never seen, even by the local labourers who worked for the family. There was one other guest at the farm and that was Freddie Ceyssens, a young nephew of the family who regarded Gouinlock's presence as a great honour, but one that was to be kept secret.

Gouinlock did not realise it at the time but this was to be his home for the next two months. Two nights after arriving word came through that the Germans were looking for an Allied airman, and so Gouinlock was hustled out into a nearby wood together with some blankets just in case the Feldpolizei paid a surprise visit. This was to be part and parcel of Gouinlock's stay at the farmhouse and one way he found to relieve the boredom was to tutor young Freddie in English while learning Dutch himself.

As well as regular visits by the Germans to buy or requisition food, there were regular visits by the Resistance, and on one of these occasions they brought a new identity for Gouinlock. He was given a forged identity and work permit in the name of Jean Victor Boland, using the photograph he had taken before he left England that was put inside his escape kit.

As the days passed into weeks, news came through that the Germans were retreating, but not as fast as had initially been anticipated. The roads were crammed with German troops being rushed to the front and refugees fleeing away from the fighting. Then suddenly the situation changed when on 24 July an American B-17 bomber returning from a raid was shot down. The entire ten-man crew managed to bale out and, of the ten, nine managed to evade capture and were picked up by the Resistance. The tenth member of the crew, the pilot, had broken his ankle on landing and was captured.

The nine men put a great deal of strain on the Resistance's resources and caused immense problems in finding enough safe houses for them. It was decided to move them all, including Gouinlock, much to the dismay of the Vanderhoedoncks because he was now regarded almost as a member of the family. It was an emotional day for the family when he left and the two Smets girls arrived on bicycles to take him to Bourg Leopold, where he was placed in another safe house. Leading the way to the town was young Freddie, cycling ahead and acting as scout. Gouinlock had certain reservations about his welcome in Bourg Leopold, as it was this town that his squadron had bombed when he was shot down. He knew the bombing had been quite accurate, but he surmised that there was bound to have been bombs that had gone astray.

He was boarded with a middle-aged couple whose house was directly opposite the German base. They were a fearless pair and insisted on taking Gouinlock with them when they went for their evening walk past the camp. They introduced him to their many friends in the café where they would stop and have a drink. Gouinlock realised that this was probably the safest move, because by acting naturally it would not draw any suspicion on them and it was much easier than having the problem of concealing him.

Two days later he and the American crew, who were staying in another part of the town, were moved again, this time to Liége. They were given instructions on where they were to board the tram and how to recognise their guide. Boarding the trolley alongside German soldiers was very unnerving for Gouinlock and sitting among them he prayed that no one would ask him a question or try to engage him in conversation.

Gouinlock had spotted his guide at the tram stop and upon reaching the town of Hasselt he got off, indicating that the airman should, too. The others also got off at this stop, where there were members of the Resistance waiting to meet them and take them on to Liége. Gouinlock's guide, Arthur, who was the leader of the Resistance in the area, indicated to him to follow him and turning a corner he saw his guide get onto a motorcycle. Climbing onto the pillion, Gouinlock clung on as the bike roared off. The fact that petrol was in short supply was an indicator that Arthur had some very good contacts. Speeding through the lanes and passing nothing but German Army lorries heading towards the front was quite worrying for Gouinlock but it did not seem to faze his guide one bit.

On arriving at Arthur's house, Gouinlock was introduced to the Resistance leader's wife, Jeanine. Inside the house was one of the American B-17 crew, the rear gunner Jetty, together with a German deserter. Over dinner that evening Arthur and his wife conversed in German with the deserter and in French with Gouinlock, who in turn translated the French into English for the American.

The following morning it was all change again. This time Gouinlock was housed in an apartment above a tobacconist's shop. The owners of the shop, Monsieur and Madame Victor Volders, also lived in the apartment with their 12-year-old son René. Gouinlock discovered later that almost the entire street was heavily involved with working with the Resistance and almost every house had an escaped airman or airmen in it. Opposite the Volders' apartment lived an old lady named Miss Julia, who, during the First World War, had worked as a spy for the Belgian government. Now deemed to be too old for active service, she helped the Resistance by offering her home as a safe house, and was harbouring two of the B-17 crew. Gouinlock carried on a correspondence with the two Americans via René, who delivered letters back and forth.

To enable the families to feed their 'guests' the Resistance had supplied them with forged ration coupons, which they had been given by Allied intelligence in London.

Time went on and then at the beginning of September news came through that the Allies had broken the German resistance and the German Army was in full retreat. To Gouinlock it appeared that it would just be a matter of days before Allied troops entered the area. Then suddenly German soldiers appeared rounding up hostages. Word filtered through that two German soldiers had disappeared completely in mysterious circumstances and the military wanted answers. A lorry appeared outside the Volders' shop and soldiers jumped out and battered down the door that led to the apartment. Gouinlock realised that he was trapped and decided to bluff it out. After all, he had identification stating that he was Jean Victor Joseph Boland, a Belgian citizen.

The Germans burst into the apartment and forced him downstairs and into the street at the point of a bayonet. They were not interested in his protestations about being a Belgian citizen; in fact they did not even ask to see his papers. He was bundled into a column with about thirty other male residents of the street. The group was then marched off out of the town and into the countryside.

At one point the column was halted and two Belgians, who Gouinlock later learned were members of the Resistance, were dragged out and subjected to a severe beating with rifle butts and boots. The two bleeding, battered men were dragged back into line by other Belgians and the march continued. As dusk came, the Germans stopped the column at a nearby farm and requisitioned a barn to be used as a lock-up. The German officer shouted at the men in German just before the door was closed and locked. Gouinlock asked one of the other prisoners what the German had said and a cold shiver went right through him when the man told him they were to be shot in the morning as a reprisal.

All through the night there were moans and weeping from the prisoners. Some prayed, others cursed the Germans and the war. At dawn the door to the barn was flung open and the men marched out. They were handed shovels and told to work in pairs to dig holes 6ft long and 6ft deep. Gouinlock chose an elderly man as his 'partner'.

As they started digging, Gouinlock watched the officer talking earnestly with two NCOs. In the distance the rumble of guns firing could be heard getting closer and closer. At noon the holes had been dug and the group waited anxiously for what was to happen next. Two of the guards then stepped forward and pulled the two men who had been beaten the previous day and placed them in front of two holes. At the command of the officer the other soldiers lined up. At a given command their rifle bolts rattled as they pushed bullets into their rifle chambers. At another command they raised their rifles to their shoulders followed by the command 'Feuer'. A volley of shots rang out in the still, cold air and the bodies of the two men fell backwards into the open graves.

Gouinlock felt sick and despite the warmth from the sun he shivered visibly and closed his eyes. The officer turned to the remaining prisoners and Gouinlock waited for his turn to stand in front of the grave that he and his companion had dug. The officer looked long and hard at them all, then said simply, 'You are free to leave.'

For a moment the only sound that could be heard was that of the distant guns, then as one they all moved and started to run back towards the town. Gouinlock glanced behind him as they went and noticed that the Germans had already climbed on board a lorry and were speeding away. He reasoned that the Germans let them go because of the Allied army that was now approaching with speed. They would treat the execution of innocent civilians as unjustified and an act of terrorism, and would exact retribution for it. But the shooting of the two Resistance men could probably be justified at the extreme end of the rules of war.

As the group reached the edge of town, Gouinlock saw René Volders at the front of the crowd waving to him. The boy led him to where the rest of the family was waiting and they all headed back to the Volders' apartment. They passed a number of German soldiers on their way back packing their equipment onto lorries but they were not interested in the family, only the need to get away from the advancing Allied army.

The streets were virtually empty as the remnants of the German Army retreated. The Volders waited in their apartment to see what was going to happen, when suddenly the unmistakable sound of a Jeep engine became music to Gouinlock's ears. Looking out of the window, he saw an American Jeep coming down the main street with four dishevelled soldiers aboard armed with machine guns and carbines. They were an advanced reconnaissance party. The streets were suddenly filled with people and British and American flags started to flutter from almost every window. Standing in the middle of the street, Gouinlock could not believe his eyes at the number of Allied airmen that emerged from houses. He had known that Liége was one on the main centres of the Belgian Resistance movement but the hundreds of Allied airmen now in the streets proved the extent of the town's involvement.

21. LIEUTENANT COLONEL TRUMAN A. SPENCER, JR, USAAF

THE B-25J MITCHELL bomber of the 42nd Bomb Group (13th Air Force) lifted off the runway at Mars Field at Cape Sansapor, West New Guinea, early in the evening of 5 October 1944 heading for an island south of Ceram Island in the Pacific. The routine flight to carry out harassment raids on the Japanese-held island of Ambon in the south-west Pacific Ocean started quietly enough. The pilot, Lieutenant Colonel Truman A. Spencer, Jr, had briefed his crew, stressing that this was just a routine mission as by now it was accepted that Japan was on the back foot, but still able to cause a few problems. The weather was quite good with a few scattered heavy rain showers, but with a full moon giving the crew a clear view of the ground below they commenced their bombing run of the Japanese airfield. There was a scattering of anti-aircraft fire as the B-25 climbed away after dropping its bomb load and set course back to Mars Field.

As the B-25 thundered for home at 10,000ft, they were 90 miles from base. The weather started to close in so Spencer decided to go on instruments and started to descend hoping for better weather at low level. Down at 3,000ft the weather was still murky so he climbed back to 5,000ft and started to check his position. The radio operator called for a QDM (a magnetic bearing to a station) from Sansapor and received a reply 'QDM 165 degrees magnetic'.

Spencer queried this as it did not seem correct, but after discussing it with his navigator, Lieutenant John Burns, he agreed to follow the new heading. As time went by there was no sign of any landfall and after forty-five minutes it was quite obvious that they were in trouble and nowhere near their base. They were lost.

They were now thirty minutes past their estimated time of arrival (ETA) when they received a QDL (a bearing that is transmitted at regular intervals).

FREEDOM TRAILS

The B-25 was flying at an altitude of 1,000ft with less than an hour's fuel supply remaining, when suddenly the airwaves were full of QDL transmissions coming from unknown radio stations. After frantically asking for only one radio station to transmit, Spencer got a new heading – '240 degrees'.

Tracking on to the new heading, the crew kept a watchful eye out for any sign of landfall, but then after almost an hour, with the engines running almost on fumes, a light was spotted to the south. Banking the aircraft round, Spencer headed for the light. In an effort to lighten the load of the aircraft, and aware that a water landing was to be the likely outcome, the crew jettisoned the waist and turret guns, and anything else that was not required.

As they approached the light, which turned out to be a burning oil storage tank, Spencer saw a landing strip and then received a flashing green light from the tower on the side of the airfield. Lowering the landing gear, he readied the aircraft for landing but then suddenly he realised it was a Japanese airfield called Boela.

Slamming the throttles forward, he banked the aircraft to the left and climbed into a blinding rainstorm. Glancing at the fuel gauges, which were hovering around empty, Spencer continued to fly until the engines quit, which was very soon after. By this time he was almost skimming the waves but before he could warn the crew, the engines spluttered to a stop and the aircraft hit the water at about 120mph. The waves were running about 3ft high. The rear section of the fuselage broke off and it was only the empty fuel tanks that gave any buoyancy to what was left of the aircraft. Spencer was thrown through the windscreen and suffered serious facial wounds. His co-pilot, Lieutenant Joe Ivy, managed to get to the escape hatch in the forward compartment, followed by the bombardier, Lieutenant Mark Ingram. The navigator was crushed on impact by part of the upper turret falling on him, killing him instantly. The radio operator, Technical Sergeant Nicholas La Presti, was catapulted through the waist gunner's window, which fortunately had been removed. Lieutenant Fiezl, the intelligence officer, was also thrown through the waist gunner's window. The engineer/gunner, Staff Sergeant Thomas Sutton, managed somehow to get out but suffered a compound fracture of his right leg. However, the tail gunner, Staff Sergeant Richard Joyce, was knocked unconscious and never got out of the rapidly sinking B-25 bomber.

With the crew now in the water, and just before the aircraft sank, La Presti somehow managed to rip open the hatch containing the raft and pull it clear. The moment it hit the water the raft inflated and slowly the survivors clambered aboard. They had lost two of the crew and now in the middle of the night they were at the mercy of the sea.

The six men took stock of their situation as the raft bobbed up and down. They had lost all their personal equipment save for their handguns and the life raft's emergency equipment. All but Spencer were violently sick from the salt water they had swallowed during the ditching. Sutton was given morphine and his wounded leg bandaged as best they could in the cramped conditions. By morning they had all recovered enough to feel better and with the warm sunshine their spirits were raised. Allied aircraft flew overhead, too high to attract their attention but it raised their hopes that they would soon be spotted and rescued. As the day progressed Sutton's condition worsened and Spencer decided to raise the sail on the dinghy and try to find a safe place to land. A strong breeze carried the raft along the coast of Boela Island, the crew keeping a wary eye out for any sign of Japanese soldiers, although at one point one of the crew said he thought he had spotted a native watching them from the edge of the jungle. A small beach came into view and the raft headed in on the surf. Once ashore, the crew opened some of the emergency rations, only to find that they had become contaminated with seawater and leaving them only three small cans of water.

Sutton was carried onto the beach and made comfortable while the crew hid the raft in the mangroves that bordered the beach. Spencer made a short reconnaissance trip and on his return posted a sentry at either end of the small beach. He then made the decision to try to set Sutton's broken leg by pulling it straight. Giving him the last of the morphine, they pulled his leg in an attempt to get the bone straight, causing him excruciating pain. It didn't work so they decided to put the leg into splints to prevent movement. As they were doing this, a cry came from one of the sentries, 'Japs!' The crew decided that they would be hopelessly outnumbered and decided that making a run for it with the injured sergeant was out of the question.

The Japanese had captured the sentry, Ingram, and had him tied up. He had tried to fire his pistol but it didn't work and he was subdued. The leader, an officer, was identified by his samurai sword and uniform, the remaining three moving along the beach toward the Americans were dressed in ragged clothes and looked scruffy and unkempt. One was left to guard Ingram, and as they approached, the Americans raised their hands in the air but still held on to their pistols. The three Japanese soldiers, accompanied by a native, advanced toward the American crew waving their weapons. Spencer realised that they had no intention of taking them prisoner as they broke into a run shouting. The Americans opened fire with their pistols. La Presti shot the officer in the head, then shot a second in the chest. He then went towards where Ivy was struggling with another of the Japanese soldiers and dispatched him with a shot to the head. Within minutes it was all over and there were three dead Japanese soldiers lying on the beach. Ingram, who after hearing the shots and commotion believed that the rest of the crew were either dead or had been captured, was being pushed at bayonet point towards the beach. The remaining Japanese soldier, who probably thought the same, was shocked when on reaching the beach, he saw the bodies of his comrades lying in the sand. Before he could react, Ivy ran forward and knocked him to the ground. La Presti then placed his pistol against the soldier's forehead and pulled the trigger, but the gun misfired. He then hit him with the butt of the pistol but not hard enough to knock him out. With that the Japanese soldier leapt to his feet and ran into the jungle at a speed that the survivors described as 'absolutely amazing'. Fiezl, who had been posted as a sentry, was last seen on the edge of the jungle. It was believed he had been shot by one of the Japanese soldiers during the fight.

Dragging the bodies into the jungle, the Americans pushed the raft back out to sea and paddled as fast as they could. About 2 miles out, they dropped a sea anchor and settled down for the night. During the night the sea became rough and the spray was continually soaking the crew. Sutton was becoming delirious and by daybreak the men were in a sorry state. Then disaster struck when it was discovered that they had lost what was left of the meagre rations, including the water. They had no equipment left and the sail had been lost. To compound their misfortune it was found that the raft was leaking and taking on water. Spencer decided that they had to try to find another beach and while two of the crew slipped into the water to lighten the load and help push the raft by swimming, the remaining members would either paddle or bale out the water. After an exhausting day they spotted a beach and despite their almost deflated raft they managed to struggle ashore.

After dragging the raft up the beach with Sutton still inside, the crew collapsed with exhaustion and fell asleep. After a couple of hours they were awakened by Spencer and moved further into the jungle. There they made a crude litter that enabled them to carry Sutton a lot more easily. Taking the opportunity to get some more rest, they slept until dawn. This was the third day they had been on the run from the Japanese, who by now would have found the bodies of their comrades.

As dawn broke, two of them went foraging for food and water and returned a couple of hours later with some coconuts and fresh water from a nearby stream. They decided to move camp closer to the stream and discovered a native trail close by. After finding a good concealed campsite, they were surprised to hear voices and then two unarmed Japanese soldiers with large backpacks walked by close to the camp. They immediately thought about attacking the two men and taking what they could, but realised that the two men were probably part of a Japanese garrison and would only bring armed Japanese back to look for them.

That night the men got their first uninterrupted night's sleep and woke in the morning feeling much refreshed. Even Sutton was feeling better as the pain had eased. However, camping beside the stream brought its own problems in the shape of mosquitoes, flies and ants, which, as one crew member put it, 'ate them alive'.

Every day two of the crew were sent to the beach to watch for any friendly aircraft flying overhead. They were to try to signal them with a mirror if they had the opportunity, while all the while keeping a wary eye open for the Japanese. The men scratched a message in the sand that read 'HELP − SPENCER − FOOD' in the hope that an aircraft flying overhead might pick up on it.

For the next few days they kept vigilance on the beach until on the fourth day a flight of twelve P-47 Thunderbolts roared overhead and the men were convinced that they had seen their message in the sand. The following morning a PBY Catalina cruised at low altitude up and down the shore, but failed to see them. Disappointed, the men did not give up hope because they realised that the Air Force knew they were there and sooner or later they would be rescued. The next day two B-25s circled the beach, spotted the two watchers and then dropped an Australian jungle kit, a flare and food. One hour later a US Navy PBY Catalina touched down just offshore and a small boat left for the beach. In less than an hour Spencer and four of his seven crew were safely aboard and airborne.

Eight days after leaving Mars Field, Sansapor, Spencer and his crew arrived at the Army hospital at Biak.

22. FLIGHT SERGEANT ERIC NOAKES, RAF

WHEN HIS FLIGHT leader asked Eric Noakes to 'fly spare' on the day after D-Day, he willingly agreed, although he had flown three missions that day and he was just about to go on leave. 'Flying spare' meant that when the flight took off, the 'spare' would go too, but would circle the airfield just in case one of the scheduled aircraft developed a problem. If this happened then the 'spare' would take its place.

After passing out from flight training school, Noakes had been posted to No. 245 Squadron, also known as the Northern Rhodesia Squadron, flying Typhoons, or 'Tiffys' as they became affectionately known. This was one of the most lethal ground attack aircraft around, and with eight rockets mounted beneath the wings, it had the firepower of a battleship. His squadron had been one of the first across the Channel on D-Day, seeking out 'targets of opportunity', and sweeping the countryside with a devastating effect on the German Army.

As the squadron got airborne on D-Day plus one, he heard one of the pilots call to the flight leader to say that he was having trouble lifting his flaps. As he circled the airfield, Noakes suddenly had the feeling that this was not going to be his day. Seconds later the flight leader confirmed that he was going to have to take the place of the other aircraft.

As they swept over the crowded, smoke-covered beaches of Normandy and into the French countryside, the squadron was on the lookout for retreating convoys of Germans. Then they spotted a large convoy of German trucks crawling up a hill going away from Normandy. The squadron leader, a former Spitfire pilot, led the attack and one by one the Typhoons streaked down and launched their rockets, blowing lorry after lorry off the road. Noakes saw his rockets strike home as he peeled away and climbed back into the sky. Suddenly he saw the flight leader line up again for another pass, something that was not normally done. Once the element of surprise had gone, the men on the ground usually started to fire back and this time was no different.

As Noakes lined up his aircraft for another pass and approached the burning convoy at a speed of 400mph, he saw the Germans ripping off camouflaged tarpaulins from some of the lorries and revealing four-barrelled, 20mm cannons on single mountings called *vierling flak*. This cannon, Noakes knew, was capable of hurling a curtain of steel in front of an aircraft and destroying it. As he closed in on the convoy he saw a twinkling coming from the muzzles of the cannons and then orange-coloured balls zipping towards him. Firing off his remaining rockets, he started to climb away at over 400mph, but then there was a loud bang, the aircraft shuddered violently and the engine stopped.

He was now too low to bale out, so was left with the alternative of crash-landing the aircraft. Trying to control the aircraft, he realised that the hydraulics had been shot away so, manually pumping the flaps partially down, he lined himself up on a field. Pulling the nose of the aircraft up as best he could, he steadied the aircraft for a wheels-up landing. He knew he had to get the nose up because beneath the Typhoon was a large air scoop and if that hit the ground first then the aircraft would cartwheel all over the place and shatter itself – and him – into a thousand pieces.

Keeping the nose up, he watched the field get larger and larger, and then the tail touched the ground first, followed moments later by the fuselage, the air scoop digging a large furrow. The aircraft bounced along at 130mph before finally tipping up on its nose and then settling back down.

For a few seconds Noakes sat stunned in the cockpit, then he quickly pulled back the canopy and clambered out. He looked at the aircraft and was surprised to see that there was only a small amount of damage to the aircraft itself. Overhead he heard the sound of one of the other Typhoons and seconds later saw it streaking towards him. He realised that his aircraft was about to be shot up and destroyed to prevent it falling into enemy hands, so he ran for a clump of trees on the edge of the field. Seconds later he heard the sound of cannon fire and then came a loud 'crump' as the fuel tanks on his aircraft exploded, turning his Typhoon into a fireball.

He watched as the other Typhoon roared up into the sky, waggling its wings as it climbed and headed back towards the coast. He realised that the Germans would now be looking for the aircraft and its pilot, and the column of black smoke emanating from the wreckage would soon lead them to it. He was not that far from the convoy that he had shot up minutes earlier and he did not want the survivors to catch him as there would not be much chance of them treating him with kid gloves if they did.

Heading on through the wood, he was determined to put as much distance between him and the wreckage of his aircraft as he could. After covering about 5 miles he stopped and took stock of his situation. As the escape officer for the squadron, it was his responsibility to ensure that every pilot was equipped with an escape kit, and as luck would have it he had four in his possession. This meant that he had four compasses and four amounts of French francs. He was also wearing the latest flying boots, which could be converted into shoes by cutting away the top parts that covered the calf. After cutting these off, he proceeded to remove all the insignia from his battledress, his wings and sergeant's stripes.

He now had a choice; he could head back towards the beaches of Normandy, he could try to find help from the French Resistance or he could find a nice comfy place to hide and wait until the Allied troops reached him. He chose the second of option. He could speak French quite well and had a good working knowledge of German; before the war started he had been working part-time as a translator in both these languages. As darkness fell he came upon a farm-house and, taking a chance, he knocked on the door. For a moment there was no sound, but then the door slowly opened and the young frightened face of a teenage boy peered at him. The door then opened fully and behind the boy was an elderly couple looking equally frightened.

Noakes explained to them that he was an RAF pilot who had been shot down and showed them his dog tags to prove it to them. Their attitude changed immediately and broad smiles appeared across their faces, accompanied by tears in the eyes of the elderly couple. They ushered him in quickly and sat him down. Bottles of wine suddenly appeared together with some bread and cheese, all of which was quickly devoured. After celebrating with the family, Noakes broached the subject of shelter and the family led him into a room in which there was a bed. Within minutes of lying down he was fast asleep.

The following morning, after a simple breakfast, the family gave him some old, ill-fitting civilian clothes. Accompanied by the young teenager, Noakes set off to the nearby village of Bonnemaison. During escape and evasion lectures, crews were always told to find the local priest or schoolteacher, as they were usually the community leaders and would probably know how to contact the Resistance. On the outskirts of the village Noakes hid himself in a barn while the young lad went in search of the local priest and schoolteacher. After about an hour, the lad returned with about fifteen villagers, among them the school-teacher. Noakes greeted them with some trepidation and when introduced to some of the men was received with nothing more than grunts. The school-teacher, on being introduced, immediately stated that he must be handed over to the Germans or they would all risked being shot if he were to be discovered.

It was then that Noakes discovered that there was a German Red Cross supplies depot in the village. There was an underlying air of hostility towards him, rapidly being fuelled by the schoolmaster's almost hysterical outbursts. All the escape and evasion lectures he had attended seemed irrelevant now, but fortunately for him, a large, swarthy-looking man forced his way to the front and glared at the schoolteacher with contempt. He told the man in no uncertain manner that they did not hand their friends over to the Nazis. Turning to Noakes, he introduced himself as Jules Rogues and told him to follow him to his farm where he would shelter him. Glaring at the remaining villagers, in particular the schoolmaster, he told them in a way that left no room for doubt or argument that the Germans would not be told of Noake's existence. It was quite obvious that this man was the local community leader of the village and was not to be argued with.

Following his newfound friend, Noakes walked to Jules' farm, where he met the rest of the Rogues family. His ability to speak French was a tremendous asset, and after he had been told that there was no Resistance organisation in the district and the chance of finding one was very remote, he decided to stay put for a while. Noakes knew that the Allies were advancing and so became a farmhand to help pay back some of the hospitality shown by the farmer and his family. For the next few days Noakes worked on the farm, watching German lorries trundle by loaded with troops going away from the advancing Allies.

Then one day the farmer was throwing the residue of butter into the pig's trough, when Noakes grabbed a pitcher and poured some of the residue into it. He swigged down the 'buttermilk', to the astonishment of the farmer, and started to take some with him whenever he went into the field to work.

A couple of days later, whilst Noakes was sitting on the side of the road, a German lorry stopped and an officer got out. When the officer saw what he was drinking he asked if he could have some too. So started a thriving little business for the farmer and a stall was quickly set up outside the farm entrance selling 'buttermilk' for francs or cigarettes. It was while doing this that Noakes spotted a German Red Cross ambulance going through carrying ammunition to the front.

He also noticed the correct way in which the Wehrmacht soldiers conducted themselves when in contact with the local citizens. That was until an SS (Schutzstaffel) column entered the village and took over the local café, eating and drinking everything they could lay their hands on without paying. Then as quickly as they came, they left, leaving behind a diminished village. The only good thing was that they were going away from the front and back towards Germany.

The increasing number of Germans now coming through the village and the surrounding countryside made Noakes realise the danger he was bringing to the farmer and his family, who would be shot immediately for harbouring him if his true identity was discovered. He decided that it was time to try to make it back to the Allied lines. A young man from a neighbouring farm, who wanted to join the Free French Forces, offered to guide him, and after a fond farewell to the Rogues family the pair set off on a horse and cart in the direction of Caen.

Their progress was slow because of the increasing amount of refugees fleeing from the fighting. They were then stopped by a German patrol and told that they and their cart had been commandeered to carry supplies to the front. Noakes now found himself in the incongruous position of being employed by the Wehrmacht. Their wagon was loaded with supplies and placed in a column consisting of a mixed jumble of old lorries and horse-drawn carts travelling towards Caen. The slow-moving convoy was suddenly 'bounced' by a flight of Typhoons, which started sending rockets into the line of lorries and carts.

Noakes saw the aircraft sweeping into attack and knew first-hand the kind of devastation they would create. He grabbed his companion and dived off the cart into a ditch on the side of the road. After the attack, Noakes realised that the Germans were more interested in themselves than anyone else, and so leaving his companion with the horse and cart, headed off toward a clump of trees. Realising it was pointless going on, he headed back across the fields towards Bonnemaison. The devastation that greeted him in the surrounding area was staggering. The once lush green fields were pockmarked with huge craters where B-17 bombers had dropped their bomb loads in an effort to destroy German gun emplacements that had been camouflaged in the area. Small villages that had been in the path of the bombing run were almost non-existent, just crumbling ruins.

Entering Bonnemaison, he was staggered to see that the entire village had been taken over by the German Army and the residents were emptying their homes onto carts and leaving. Making his way back to the Rogues farm, he saw too that they were loading their possessions onto a cart. When he asked why they were leaving, Noakes was told that the Germans were ordering all civilians out as they were intending to make a stand in the area. Jules was in tears but defiant, determined that no Germans were going to make him leave his home and animals. Noakes and the rest of the family finally persuaded him that there was no choice and after loading the cart they joined the rest of the residents on the crowded roads.

The Rogues family, together with Noakes, headed for the home of a distant relative just outside Belfonds. After travelling for two days they reached the farm of Marcel Loubier, who immediately made them all welcome. He was grateful for the additional help they would be able to give him on his farm, realising that he too could be moved out if the Germans kept retreating. The days turned into weeks and the weeks into months. Information kept coming through that the German Army was being steadily forced back into Germany and that Allied bombing raids were having a devastating effect on the German people. Then news came through that Field Marshal Rommel had been badly injured in an attack and it soon became obvious that the German front was crumbling rapidly, General Patton's armoured corps was making lightning strikes into the area close to Belfonds, and the roads were jammed with fleeing Germans, whose army was now in total disarray.

Then a German column suddenly appeared at the farm and a dust-covered officer in a stained uniform demanded to know who owned it. Marcel Loubier stepped forward. The officer told him that they were requisitioning the farm and that the family and workers would all have to leave immediately. Loubier said that no German was going to take his farm and took a pace forward towards the officer. Immediately guns were levelled at the family, but the farmer did not flinch. Noakes then stepped forward to support his host, realising that they were now in a desperate situation. For a few minutes nothing was said but then a motorcycle roared up and the officer was handed a message. He then turned to his men, barked an order and they all clambered back aboard their vehicles and roared off in a cloud of dust.

Ten minutes later another rumble of tracked vehicles filled the air, only this time they were Sherman tanks belonging to the Americans. The celebrations that followed left the village almost dry of wine and spirits. The next morning the Americans were gone, pushing on towards Germany. With the Germans gone, Noakes decided to make his way back towards the coast, hoping to pick up with a British outfit. After saying his goodbyes to the Rouges and Loubier families, he set off. After travelling for twenty-four hours he came across a Free French reconnaissance battalion. When he introduced himself, the French were very suspicious because he was wearing civilian clothes. He produced his RAF dog tags but even then they still needed some convincing that he was 'Anglais'. After a couple of hours of questioning he finally convinced them and was greeted with smiles and hugs. He was told that the British had set up headquarters at Le Mans, so with the good wishes of the French ringing in his ears and a bottle of wine in his pocket, Noakes set off.

At Le Mans he joined forces with an American Thunderbolt pilot desperate to get back to England and into the war. The whole town was crowded with refugees, soldiers moving forward and those trying to get back to their units.

In short, it was chaotic. The American pilot had somehow got word that there was an airstrip close to the town of Mont-St-Michel that was being used to ferry the wounded back to England. Acquiring some supplies, the two men walked and hitched rides until they reached it. The Americans were running the airfield, and Noakes's companion manage to persuade the dispatcher that there might be room for two more aboard one of the Dakotas.

Back in England, Noakes reported for duty to find that he had been promoted to warrant officer during his absence. He was sent to London to be interrogated by intelligence officers and then was allowed to go home on well-earned leave.

23. FIRST LIEUTENANT MELVIN J. SHADDUCK, USAF

FIRST LIEUTENANT MELVIN Shadduck, USAF, had just completed his eighty-first spotter mission of the Korean War on 23 April 1951 after laying down smoke markers pinpointing the Chinese Army from an altitude of 1,800ft and while under heavy ground fire. He had banked his North American T-6 Mosquito spotter plane to head back to base when his aircraft suffered a direct hit to the engine, upon which smoke and flames poured back into the cockpit. He immediately ordered his observer, Technical Sergeant Jack E. Gauldin, to bale out. Seconds later he followed and as his parachute opened, he saw his spiralling aircraft erupt into a ball of flame and then crash into a mountainside. He had managed to get a radio transmission out about Chinese/North Korean troop movements and now watched as US fighter-bombers struck the pin-pointed targets he had hit with his smoke rockets.

As the ground rushed up to meet him, Shadduck found himself landing in a deep canyon alongside the Imjin River. Quickly getting himself out of his parachute harness, he hid the parachute in a hole in the riverbank and quickly assessed his position. His left hand was badly burned and extremely painful, and in addition to a number of minor cuts and abrasions his leg had a deep gash and was bleeding profusely. So after patching himself up as best he could, Shadduck started to look for his observer but after searching the immediate area for more than an hour he realised that he was on his own.

He knew that the Chinese would be looking for them both as they would have seen the parachutes, so keeping as close as he dared to the Imjin River, he started to wend his way back towards the UN front line. For more than eighteen hours he slipped and slithered along the riverbank, hiding as Chinese troops searched the deep undergrowth. Then, just as he could hear the UN front line artillery firing salvo after salvo, his luck ran out. He had been crouching behind a large bush in a depression when the bush was parted by a bayoneted rifle in the hands of a Chinese soldier. He was taken to a command post and interrogated. For the next month he was continually questioned, denied food and water and medical attention and made to go on circular forced marches both day and night. Five times he was marched into a clearing well away from the command post and placed in front of a firing squad. As the order to fire was about to be given he was reprieved and taken back for more interrogation. It soon became obvious to the Chinese that they were getting nowhere, so he was thrown into a hut, where he found five more Americans, all of whom had been wounded. They had been given next to nothing to eat, were all filthy dirty and hadn't received medical attention.

Such was their weakened condition that the hut had no locks or bars and no guard outside. The men were barely able to look after themselves, let alone each other, and so Shadduck decided he had to do something. For the next two weeks Shadduck begged, foraged and stole food and bandages from the Chinese soldiers. One of the prisoners was a young man who had a badly shattered leg that was in desperate need of attention. So much so in fact that Shadduck asked the guards if he could borrow a knife so that he could amputate the boy's leg as it was becoming gangrenous. His request was refused and all he could do was to watch the man die slowly.

Shadduck realised that he had to do something otherwise they were all going to die. He decided that it would be almost impossible to lead the men on an escape as most of them could barely walk. The rumble of heavy guns was getting louder and there were large movements of Chinese troops all looking very tired and with a large number of wounded with them, making their way away from the front line. It was obvious that the Chinese were retreating in large numbers and confusion was causing major problems. It was among this confusion that Shadduck saw a chance to go for help. If there was to be a mass retreat by the Chinese then it was clear that they would not be taking their prisoners with them and they most certainly would not leave them behind alive.

Over the past few weeks he had been emptying the bedpan farther and farther away and had noticed a trail that ran down to the water's edge. If he could get down unnoticed and across a small clearing then it would be some time before the guards would notice that he was missing. They also had other things on their minds as more and more troops made their way back. He announced his plans to the others and explained his reasons for doing it. They all agreed that it was the only option and knew that he was the only one capable of doing it. He told one of the men that if the guards wanted to know where he was, he was to tell them that one of the officers took him away for questioning. It would take some time to confirm this because of the increasing ongoing confusion. Shadduck told them that when he got through he would have the air force send some fighter aircraft to circle their hut as a signal that he had made it.

With the darkness closing in, Shadduck made his move and stepped out into the night, bedpan in hand. As he moved towards the track it started to rain heavily and although it would make the ground down to the river very slippery, he also knew that the guards would keep in the dry as he had hardly ever seen either a Chinese or North Korean soldier out in the rain at night. He slid down a small hillside and then across a small field that ran alongside a road. The traffic on the road was very light because of the heavy rain but then he heard the muttering and noise of soldiers as they walked along. He decided to lie down in the field until the soldiers had passed. When it was clear, he crossed the road but the darkness made it extremely difficult in the rough terrain. As he approached the river, he stumbled a number of times but fortunately the sound of the heavy rain drowned out any noise. Shadduck stood for a moment looking at the fast-flowing river, wondering whether or not to try to cross to the south bank, but he realised that the current would sweep him away. Instead, he decided to head due south and follow the river.

After a few miles the river ran into a small canyon and through some rapids. Looking around, he saw a small trail carved out of the rock of the canyon. He had a choice of taking his chances with the river or following the narrow trail. He rested in the pouring rain, all the time debating which route to take, then he decided that the river was far too risky as he would probably be battered against the rocks as he was swept down, so the trail it had to be.

Inching his way along the trail in the pitch-blackness, he carefully placed one foot in front of the other. Then suddenly out of the darkness he saw an orange glow in the distance. As he got closer he realised that it was a fire burning on the edge of a cave and behind in the cave he could see the forms of four men huddled together. It was the last thing he wanted to see – an enemy checkpoint. This checkpoint blocked the only way out of the canyon and short of jumping into the torrent of water that was rushing through, he was stuck. As he sat in the darkness in the pouring rain he thought that his only option was to return and pray he was not caught, as he knew, if he were, he would be shot. Then suddenly the unmistakeable drone of bomber engines appeared overhead and the checkpoint guards quickly doused their fire and crouched back further into the cave. The sound of exploding bombs reverberated through the canyon and Shadduck knew that this was his only chance. He waited for a few minutes and then, crawling on all fours, inched his way along the path in the pitch black, passing within 10ft of the mouth of the cave.

He crawled for another 20ft and then got to his feet and started to run without stopping for almost a mile. As the canyon got wider and the ground started to flatten out into fields, Shadduck slowed his pace as he became aware that there were probably a lot of Communist troops in the area. Keeping to the riverbank, he followed it for a couple of miles until he came to a junction in the Imjin River where it joined a couple of other smaller rivers and flowed into the Yellow Sea. There was a sharp bend in the river that he knew well from his observation flying and he knew that if he followed the river it would lead him to friendly lines.

As dawn started to break, Shadduck knew that he would have to find a place to hide until it got dark. The riverbank was strewn with large rocks and, selecting two of the largest, he crawled between them and tried to settle down to sleep. He soon realised that this was not possible as it was extremely uncomfortable and because of the continuing heavy rain he was soaked through to his skin and feeling extremely cold. He moved higher up the bank and found a drier, sheltered spot that was well hidden from any patrolling soldiers. By now it was completely daylight and the rain seemed to be even heavier. The rain could also be his friend, as it would reduce the chances of any patrols being in the area. He decided to risk moving on and clambered down the bank, making his way along the shoreline.

After travelling for at least six hours with the terrain becoming more and more difficult to traverse, Shadduck spotted a battered old Korean skiff pulled up onto a small sandy strip. A rusty chain lay across the sand attached to an old anchor. Dragging the anchor and chain onto the boat, he pushed it back into the fast-flowing river and jumped aboard. Picking up an old rough wooden paddle from the bottom of the boat, he tried to steer along the riverbank, but the current was too strong and kept taking him out into the middle of the river. He quickly realised that he was very conspicuous and paddled the boat close to the opposite shore and jumped out, leaving it to float down the river.

The boat had served its purpose and he was now on the south bank of the Imjin River, where he knew there was less chance of encountering an enemy patrol. Shadduck walked along the south bank for the rest of the day and part of the evening, and although the canyons were steep he was still able to push his way slowly through the dense brush. At one point he had to climb up the bank because the path ran out and he discovered a barbed wire entanglement had been placed along the top. This meant that there were enemy troops in the vicinity. Making his way over the wire, he followed the path for several hundred yards and then suddenly noticed a thin wire stretched across the path. Tracing the wire he found it connected to a land mine, and then looking back he spotted two other wires that he had obviously unconsciously stepped over. He quickly walked on, now acutely aware of the danger, but suddenly there was a loud explosion and something hit him hard in the back of the neck, sending him crashing to the ground.

He lay on the ground for a couple of minutes, then felt a warm liquid running down his neck. His immediate thought was that he had been hit by a fragment of the mine and placed his hand on the back of his neck feeling for the wound. He brought his hand back expecting it to be covered in blood but instead found it covered in thick, black oozing mud. Realising that he had not been injured, he quickly got to his feet and made his way through fields, woods and paddy fields. As dusk approached he came upon a small Korean village. Hiding in the undergrowth, he watched intently for any signs of life for more than an hour. He then decided to skirt the village and continue on his way. As he made his way around, he saw three little huts away from the village and a number of people including women and children around them, but so far not a sign of enemy soldiers. After watching for some time, he decided to approach them in the hope that they were friendly. He was extremely tired, hungry and wet, and his injuries needed attention, especially his burnt hand.

As an old man approached Shadduck stepped out from behind a tree, holding up his burned hand in a sign of friendship, in his other hand, which was behind his back, he held a large rock – just in case. The old man nodded and beckoned Shadduck to follow him to a nearby hut. Opening the door, he waved Shadduck inside, but the American was wary and stayed on the porch, sheltering from the rain. A young girl had come out and the old man spoke to her. She scurried away and returned minutes later with a bowl of cold rice. Shadduck took the bowl with a nod of thanks, dug his fingers into it and pushed the rice into his mouth. Within seconds the bowl was empty, then the girl handed him a bowl of chopped onions, which he greedily demolished. A young boy turned up and Shadduck was surprised to hear that he spoke Japanese, a language of which the American had a working knowledge. The two then conversed and Shadduck told him that he was an American pilot who had been shot down about thirty days ago. He showed the boy his wounds, at which the boy smiled and showed him a wound on his own leg caused by a bullet from a UN aircraft that had been strafing the area. Shadduck questioned the boy about the presence of Chinese and North Korean troops in the immediate area, but was told that the enemy soldiers were retreating and that the front line was only a few miles away. The boy looked at Shadduck's burnt hand and then produced a small jar of Vaseline and some strips of cloth. Gently he bandaged up the American's hand and then attended to his other wounds.

The old man had been watching all the time and was obviously concerned about Shadduck being out in the open. He went into the house and returned with a bucket of hot coals and beckoned to the American to follow him. Shadduck decided that he could trust the villagers and followed him to a clump of bushes, which to his surprise concealed the entrance to a cave. Pulling the bushes aside, the old man led the way into a narrow tunnel that led into a room about 8ft by 5ft. It was dimly lit with a couple of oil lamps and the floor was covered in straw matting. The old man placed the bucket with the hot coals in the middle of the cave and indicated to Shadduck to take his soaking wet clothes off so they could be dried. Stripping off his wet clothes, he handed them to the young boy, who had followed them in, and wrapped himself in an old blanket they had given him. The young girl suddenly appeared with some bowls of steaming hot rice and after consuming them he laid down in the warm cave and fell fast asleep.

The following morning Shadduck was woken by the young boy and given another bowl of hot rice, followed by a cigarette. The boy left but returned almost immediately saying, 'Americans, Americans. Come quickly.' Shadduck got dressed as quickly as he could and crawled out through the tunnel, out of the cave and into the sunlight. He was momentarily dazzled by the bright sunshine. Then in the distance he could see a large force of UN troops moving in his direction, but then out of the corner of his eye just 100 yards away, a large group of Chinese soldiers retreating very rapidly. He immediately dropped to the ground behind a large boulder, hoping he hadn't been spotted, but it was obvious that the Chinese soldiers had other things on their mind at that moment. He inched his way back to the cave entrance and into the cave. He sat for a moment, angry with himself for not being more careful. He decided he would not move from the cave until he heard American voices. He had endured so much and come too far to lose it all by being careless.

After what seemed an eternity, the boy appeared again saying, 'Come quick Americans, Americans.' Shadduck didn't move but questioned the boy about what they were wearing, the kind of weapons they were carrying and their accents. The boy's reply convinced him that they were indeed Americans and once again he crawled through the tunnel and out of the cave. There, less than 100 yards away were a line of UN troops. He raised his hands and called out to them. A number of them dropped to the ground, pointing their automatic weapons at him, but one of them, an officer, walked slowly toward him pointing a handgun and then realised that he was an American. 'Who are you?' he asked. 'Lieutenant Melvin Shadduck, USAF,' he replied. 'I was shot down behind enemy lines on 23 April, made a POW and escaped.'

'That was thirty-four days ago,' the officer replied. 'We best get you back to Headquarters, get in the jeep.' Before he got in, Shadduck beckoned the boy over and, taking a $5 bill from his pocket, he wrote his name and serial number on it and told him to show it to the Americans, who would later come and give his family a reward for all the help they had given him. On his return to the UN soldiers' headquarters he told them about the four other POWs that were being held, and about the family that had helped him. He gave them the co-ordinates and watched nine tanks accompanied by troops head off into the woods and across fields in a 40-mile dash to rescue them. The tanks and troops managed to get to them before the Chinese decided to eliminate them, and some weeks later the whole group was reunited in an army hospital in Seoul.

APPENDIX

TYPES OF PRISON CAMP IN THE SECOND WORLD WAR

Dulag (Durchgangslager): A transit camp for prisoners prior to being sent to a designated POW camp.

Marlag (Marine-Lager): POW camp for naval personnel.

Milag (Marine-Internierunslager): Internment camp for merchant seamen.

Oflag (Offizierslager): POW camp for officers.

Stalag Luft (Luftwaffe-Stammlager): Luftwaffe POW camp for Allied aircrews.

Stalag (Stammlager): POW camp for enlisted personnel.

The German Army at the beginning of the Second World War was split into seventeen military districts and each of these was assigned Roman numerals. According to the military district in which the camp was situated, a letter was placed after the Roman numeral to identify it. For example, Stalag II-D would be the fourth Stalag in Military District II.

The following is a list of POW camps arranged by military district.

Military District I

Stalag I-A	Stablack.
Stalag I-B	Hohenstein (Poland).
Stalag I-F	Sudauen (Poland).
Stalag Luft VI	Silute (Lithuania).

Military District II

Stalag II-A	Neubrandenburg.
Stalag II-B	Hammerstein-Schlochau (Poland).
Stalag II-C	Greifswald.
Stalag II-D	Stargard.
Stalag II-E	Schwerin.
Stalag II-H	Raderitz.
Stalag Luft I	Barth.
Stalag Luft II	Litzmannstadt (Poland).
Stalag Luft IV	Tychowo (Poland).
Oflag II-A	Prenzlau.
Oflag II-B	Arnswalde.
Oflag II-C	Woldenberg.
Oflag II-D	Gross Born.
Oflag II-E	Neubrandenburg.

Military District III

Stalag III-A	Luckenwalde.
Stalag III-B	Fürstenberg/Oder.
Stalag III-C	Alt-Drewitz.
Stalag III-D	Berlin.
Oflag III-A	Luckenwalde.
Oflag III-B	Wehrmachtlager.
Oflag III-C	Lübben.

Military District IV

Stalag IV-A	Elsterhorst.
Stalag IV-B	Mühlberg.
Stalag IV-C	Wistritz bei Teplitz.
Stalag IV-D	Torgau.
Stalag IV-E	Altenburg.
Stalag IV-F	Hartmannsdorf.
Stalag IV-G	Oschatz.
Oflag IV-A	Hohnstein.
Oflag IV-B	Königstein.
Oflag IV-C	Colditz Castle.
Oflag IV-D	Elsterhorst.

Military District V

Stalag V-A	Ludwigsburg.
Stalag V-B	Villingen.
Stalag V-C	Wildberg.
Stalag V-D	Strasbourg.
Stalag Luft V	Halle/Saale.
Oflag V-A	Weinsberg.
Oflag V-B	Biberach.
Oflag V-C	Wurzach.

Military District VI

Stalag VI-A	Hermer.
Stalag VI-B	Neu-Versen.
Stalag VI-C	Oberlangen.
Stalag VI-D	Dortmund.
Stalag VI-F	Bochol
Stalag VI-G	Bonn-Duisdorf.
Stalag VI-H	Arnoldsweiler/Düren.
Stalag VI-J	Krefeld and Dorsten.
Stalag VI-K	Senne.
Oflag VI-A	Soest.
Oflag VI-B	Dössel-Warburg.
Oflag VI-C	Eversheide/Osnabrück.
Oflag VI-D	Münster.
Oflag VI-E	Dorsten.

Military District VII

Stalag VII-A	Moosburg.
Stalag VII-B	Memmingen.
Oflag VII	Laufen.
Oflag VII-A	Murnau am Staffelsee.
Oflag VII-B	Eichstaett.
Oflag VII-C	Laufen.
Oflag VII-D	Tittmoning.

Military District VIII

Stalag VIII-A	Görlitz.
Stalag VIII-B	Lamsdorf.
Stalag VIII-C	Sagan.
Stalag VIII-D	Teschen.
Stalag VIII-E	Neuhammer.
Stalag VIII-F	Lamsdorf.
Stalag Luft III	Sagan (Poland).
Stalag Luft VIII-B	Lamsdorf.
Oflag VIII-A	Kreuzburg.
Oflag VIII-B	Silberberg.
Oflag VIII-C	Juliusburg.
Oflag VIII-D	Tittmoning Castle.
Oflag VIII-E	Johannisbrunn.
Oflag VIII-F	Mährisch-Trübau.
Oflag VIII-G	Weidenau/Freiwaldau.
Oflag VIII-H	Oberlangendorf.
Oflag VIII-H/Z	Eulenberg/Roemerstadt.
Stalag Luft 7	Bankau (now Baków in Poland).

Military District IX

Stalag IX-A	Ziegenhain.
Stalag IX-B	Wegscheide.
Stalag IX-C	Bad Sulza.
Oflag IX-A/H	Burg Spangenberg.
Oflag IX-A/Z	Rotenburg/Fulda.
Oflag IX-B	Weilburg.
Oflag IX-C	Molsdorf near Erfurt.

Military District X

Stalag X-A	Schleswig.
Stalag X-B	Wegscheide.
Stalag X-C	Nienburg.
Oflag X	Hohensalza.
Oflag X-A	Itzehoe.
Oflag X-B	Nienburg/Weser.

Oflag X-C   Lübeck.
Oflag X-D   Fischbeck.

Military District XI
Stalag XI-A   Altengrabow.
Stalag XI-B   Fallingbostel.
Stalag XI-C   Bergen-Belsen.
Stalag Luft XI-B Fallingbostel.
Oflag XI-A   Osterode.

Military District XII
Stalag XII-A   Limburg an der Lahn.
Stalag XII-B   Frankenthal.
Stalag XII-C   Wiebelsheim/Rheim.
Stalag XII-D   Trier (Tréves).
Stalag XII-E   Metz.
Stalag XII-F   Forbach.
Oflag XII-A   Limburg an der Lahn.
Oflag XII-B   Mainz.

Military District XIII
Stalag XIII-A   Bad Sulzbach.
Stalag XIII-B   Weiden/Oberpfalz.
Stalag XIII-C   Hammelburg/Mainfranken.
Stalag XIII-D   Nuremburg-Langwasser.
Oflag XIII-A   Nuremburg.
Oflag XIII-B   Hammelburg.

Military District XVII
Stalag XVII-A   Kaisersteinbruch.
Stalag XVII-B   Krems-Gneixendorf.
Stalag Luft
    XVII-B   Krems-Gneixendorf.
Oflag XVII-A   Döllersheim.

Military District XVIII

Stalag XVIII-A   Wolfsberg.
Stalag XVIII-A/Z Spittal.
Stalag XVIII-B   Oberdrauburg.
Stalag XVIII-C   Markt-Pongau.
Stalag XVIII-D   Marburg.
Oflag XVIII-A   Lienz/Drau.
Oflag XVIII-B   Wolfsberg.
Oflag XVIII-C   Spittal.

Military District XX

Stalag XX-A   Torun/Thorn (Poland).
Stalag 312   Torun/Thorn (Poland).
Stalag XX-B   Malbork/Mareinburg (Poland).

Military District XXI

Stalag XXI-A   Schilberg (Poland).
Stalag XXI-B   Schubin (Poland).
Stalag XXI-B   Thure (Poland).
Stalag XXI-C/H   Wollstein (Poland).
Stalag XXI-C/Z   Graetz.
Stalag XXI-D   Posen (Poland).
Oflag XXI-A   Schokken (Poland).
Oflag XXI-B   Schokken (Poland).
Oflag XXI-C   Schubin (Poland).
Oflag XXI-C/Z   Grune bei Lissa (Poland).

There were a number of other camps that did not come under the control of the military districts:

Oflag 6   Tost.
Oflag 64   Schubin (Poland).
Oflag 79   Braunschweig (Germany).
Stalag Luft   Frankfurt am Main.
Stalag Luft S   Sudauen (Poland).
Stalag 56   Prostken (Poland).

Stalag 302	Gross Born.
Stalag 307	Biala Podalska (Poland).
Stalag 307	Deblin (Poland).
Stalag 313	Czarne (Poland).
Stalag 315	Przemyśl (Poland).
Stalag 319	Chelm (Poland).
Stalag 323	Gross Born.
Stalag 325	Zamość (Poland).
Stalag 325	Rawa Ruska (Poland).
Stalag 327	Jaroslaw (Poland).
Stalag 328	Lemberg (Poland).
Stalag 333	Ostrów-Komorowo (Poland).
Stalag 351	Berkenbrugge.
Stalag 359	Poniatowa (Poland).
Stalag 366	Siedlce (Poland).
Stalag 369	Kobierzyn (Poland).
Stalag XX-A	Brandenburg.

BIBLIOGRAPHY

Brickhill, Paul, *The Great Escape* (London: Faber & Faber, 1951)

Cosgrove, Edmund, *The Evaders* (Toronto: Clarke, Irwin & Co., 1970)

Dear, Ian, *Escape and Evasion: POW Breakouts and Other Great Escapes in World War Two* (London: Arms & Armour Press, 1997)

Eisner, Peter, *The Freedom Line: The Brave Men and Women Who Rescued Allied Airmen from the Nazis in World War II* (New York: HarperCollins, 2004)

Foot, M.R.D. and Langley, J.M., *MI9: Escape and Evasion 1939–1945* (London: The Bodley Head, 1979)

Jubault, Cecile, *The Extraordinary Adventure of the Forest of Fréteval* (self-published, printed by S. Lembeye, 1967)

Langley, James, *To Fight Another Day* (London: Collins, 1974)

Neave, Airey, *Saturday at MI9: The Classic Account of the WW2 Allied Escape Organisation* (London: Hodder & Stoughton, 1969)

Randle, Bill, *Blue Skies and Dark Nights* (Kent: Independent Books, 2002)

Sunderman, Lt Col James F. (ed.), *Air Escape and Evasion* (New York: Franklin Watts, 1963)

Williams, Eric, *The Escapers: A Chronicle of Escape in Many Wars with Eighteen First-Hand Accounts* (New York: Fontana Books, 1953)

Williams, Eric, *The Wooden Horse* (New York: Collins, 1949)

INDEX